Beyond The Eagle's Nest

Beyond The Eagle's Nest

Memoirs of a Logging High Climber

Carroll D. Ault

Published March 2005.

Order this book online at www.lulu.com.

ISBN: 1-4116-2733-4

Dedication

Unfortunately, Carroll didn't live to complete the publication of this book. But I am sure he would have dedicated it to his wife, Lillian, who worked to satisfy his wanderlust and need for diversity, and whose vivid imagination and tact carried him through many trying times.

Debby Runyan

Campbell, California

January 2005

Acknowledgements

It all started in Carmel California. Carroll had a story he wanted to tell.

This acknowledgement would not have been necessary if it were not for Noel and Debby Runyan of Personal Data Systems in Campbell California who so ably set up the computer system that made writing *Beyond The Eagle's Nest* possible. In addition, they supplied the support to get the system up and running. Without them it could not have happened.

Next came Ed Savage of Pacific Grove, a retired IBM computer expert and adult education teacher who volunteered his skills to Carroll and rescued him from many "lock ups" that at the time were frequent and scary to say the least.

After the initial shock of learning the equipment and the writing began, Carroll was soon to meet another volunteer who became a dear friend, Rex Hardy of Monterey California who spent innumerable hours reading script and making suggestions for wordage.

Maxine Shore of Carmel, who offered Creative Writing classes through the Carmel Foundation was a great supporter, encourager, and teacher. Maxine had a gift for writing that she shared willingly and was always available for a few words.

A special thanks to Peninsula Branch of the California Writer's Club that gave recognition to Carroll's writing ability and presented him with First Place Winner for Non-Fiction Book at the Jack London in March of 1998.

For all of those who assisted Carroll in whatever way, too numerous to mention, my heart and kind thoughts go out to you. All of you know who you are and I know most of you. Many thanks on behalf of Carroll.

Lillian Ault

Menlo Park, California

September 2004

Prologue

Southwest Nebraska

1922-40

Grandfather referred to me as "That boy". Friends, teachers, and neighbors seldom used my given name. Newcomers pondered my surname.

"Without a father to guide him," they whispered, "that kid'll never amount to a tinker's dam. More than once, he'll wish they'd left him for the coyotes, especially if his eyes go bad like others in that family."

*   *   *

Washington State—Big Trees, Big Men, Big Problems

1940-59

"Man on! Going up!" For fifteen years, these words sent me to the top of a 140-foot logging spar, hallmark and pinnacle of Pacific Northwest logging.

*   *   *

The Bygone Era—The VA Blind Rehab—Retirement

1959-2004

Chapter 1

Back When

Southwest Nebraska 1938

Startled by her hand on my arm, I pulled my tired eyes from the book, blinked a few times to refocus, then waited.

"The principal wants to see you in his office," the math instructor whispered.

What now? I thought. No more than ten days ago, a sophomore classmate and I had been temporarily expelled for deviltry unbecoming, so we'd been told, to young men preparing to face the world.

"He's waiting," she reminded, then marched back toward her desk, old-woman shoes clumping along the aisle.

All eyes followed me through the open doorway. Whispers and giggles spilled into the hall and trailed along the corridor.

I envisioned the principal facing the window, bony fingers and hands clasped behind a bent back.

Leaden legs carried me through the office door, where I stopped and waited. Had he heard me? Maybe he'd forgotten. I could walk out.

Suddenly, he whirled, assumed a self-righteous posture, and his eyes studied me from head to foot: roving over my home-style haircut, peach-fuzz cheeks, faded shirt, patched overalls, and worn Keds.

Momentarily, we stood face to face, authority versus defiance. Finally, the inevitable outburst.

"Young man," he railed, eyes boring into mine. "Your grades have fallen off and you have been known, so I've been told, to doze in the classroom. Rumor has it that you find it difficult to read the exam questions on the blackboard, although I see no reason why you can't read as well as other students. Your eyes look perfectly normal to me. Either apply yourself or get glasses. Otherwise, you will fail miserably."

Yes, I thought, my grades have fallen, but they're still passing. Why the fuss? His ensuing remarks not only answered my question, but they also troubled me deeply.

"You have two years to get your feet on the ground, so conduct yourself appropriately.

Mark my word, without a high school diploma, you'll go nowhere."

Should I tell him what I already suspected? Would he understand? Would he care? No, I thought, I'll tough it out. Besides, he'd blow it all over town.

My vision continued to deteriorate. Textbook print seemed more distorted, and blackboard writing appeared faded, fuzzy, and segmented. But, glasses! Nobody else in my class wore them, not even the girls. Besides, they'd call me Specs.

Only when my grades had plummeted from consistent "A's" to near failing did I secretly arrange to see an eye specialist in McCook, a small city eighteen miles west of my home town, Bartley.

"If it must be Saturday, I can get you in at ten o'clock," the receptionist said. "Don't be late, for the doctor always goes fishing Saturday afternoon."

That's fine, I thought. I could hitch a ride with a cattle truck.

His examination completed, the aging doctor seated himself, cleared his throat, and spoke with authority. "What you have is a common problem among certain families, retinitis pigmentosa. Your vision has been affected to the extent that you are now Industrially Blind."

Blind! What did he mean? I could still see, maybe not like before, but see, yes. My breath came in gasps as his hollow voice droned on.

"In addition to having narrowed peripheral vision which causes you to be night-blind, an unusual loss in the center prevents you from reading small print. More than likely, however, you'll not go totally blind for years."

Stop, stop, I pleaded inwardly, flinching each time the word "blind" was spoken, but I had no alternative except to sit and listen.

"Even though you will be able to read newspaper headlines and captions, it will be difficult, if not impossible, to read the text in the articles. Moving around or seeing large objects should present no problems, but you'll never be a railway locomotive engineer or an airplane pilot."

He paused a moment, apparently pondering a suitable recommendation, then resumed, "I strongly urge work that will carry you through life. Consider a job milking cows for a farmer. Your vision cannot be helped with glasses, an operation, or medicine. You need not see me again."

With that, he excused himself and left the room.

Pain, fear, and anger scourged my entire body and soul. I had nowhere to turn for answers to tormenting questions—questions that had plagued me for months. Growing panic soon drove me into the street where the doctor's words, definite and final, followed along. Blind! Blind! Blind!

Frantically, I sought a rationale for the injustice, fears mounting with each passing moment. Would I be like 'moon-eyed' Mel—the old guy who can't find his way home from the grocery store? Or would I be like Blind Sam—the weird looking man who has only red sockets for eyes and carries the tin cup on his violin to beg for money?

My thoughts turned back to the doctor. He couldn't mean it! Cows! Farm! A lifetime milking dumb cows? Never! I wanted to run, but run to what or where? Wanted to talk, but talk with whom? Embarrassed and ashamed. Why? Had the proclamation made me less than a whole, healthy person, forever different from others? I told no one of the trip to the eye doctor.

As time passed, inevitably, classmates, instructors, then most people in the small town knew of my irreversible sight problem. In some manner, the principal must have learned that glasses could do nothing, for I began receiving average grades, presumably to acknowledge effort and determination, rather than achievement in the classroom.

Life became a series of embarrassments, frustrations, and doubts—each requiring adjustment to a world unfamiliar with human imperfections. Most knew that blind people sold brooms, pencils, and shoestrings on the streets, but no one openly recommended this.

Several planned to attend a trade school which required extensive study and normal vision. "I'm going on to college," friends boasted. "How about you?"

Nothing, it seemed, offered hope for a person with poor eyesight. In my home town there was only menial farm work on a seasonal basis. I thought desperately, somewhere, sometime, something must change for the better, even if I, myself, must make it happen.

One evening a small group gathered outside a neighbor's house. Everyone listened intently as an aging plainsman explained, elevating the

Midwest twang, "Yep, my old dad left me the farm and the mortgage; then the goldarn bank foreclosed, so I went to sharecropping. The dust storms, the grasshoppers, the tumble weeds, and the drought forced me into town, where my kids are always in a peck of trouble. Tomorrow morning we're heading out before daybreak. I hate to leave, but there's no other way. The longer I hang around, the worse it's going to be."

I moved close to a friend and whispered, "What's wrong? Where's he going?"

"Guess he's like everyone else—broke. Heading West, I suppose."

As though he had heard the question, the ex-farmer continued, "Yep, it's off to the Northwest where they say trees grow higher than grain elevators, year around streams are chock-full of fish, and firewood is everywhere just for the taking. If you're a good shot and not too gabby about it, venison will bless your table. You can buy land for nigh onto nothing, and one acre feeds a milk cow. They tell me my boys can work in logging, where you've got to be a real man to get along.

"Sure enough," he continued, a momentary sparkle in his tired eyes, "I can sure use that kind of living." Then, as though seeking reprieve, he glanced into the cloudless heavens looking for signs of rain. Nothing.

Finally, evidently feeling that he had justified his hasty departure, the father of five turned to finish loading the timeworn car.

As the small group dispersed, I heard several villagers claim that their relatives were doing mighty fine out West, too. Impressed by the words of the departing townsman, I had watched and listened. It was then that I felt a glimmer of hope—just a thread that might guide me to a more promising future. Tall trees. Real men. Why not?

Carroll's Graduation Picture 1940

Chapter 2

The Quest

1940

That spring the daffodils, tulips, and irises, more beautiful than usual, bent in the gentle breezes as the honey bees moved from one flower to the next, gathering sweet nectar. All fourteen of my senior classmates and I made our final exit through the front door of the six-room school.

The following morning brilliant sunlight filtered through the elm and cottonwood as my two schoolmates, Red and Buck, joined me near the old brick church. Neighborhood dogs, forever vigilant, announced our presence as we huddled under the street lamp, a favorite meeting place, in daylight or dark.

Dropping tote bags stuffed with underwear, socks, and an extra shirt, we dug into worn pockets.

"Boy, it's not much," Buck said, opening his fist to reveal several coins and four dollar bills. "But I guess two dollars from Pop is better than nothing. Earned the other two planting lawns for the druggist's wife."

"Yeah," Red replied, "Mom shoved some money into my pocket and told me to be careful how I spend it. Doesn't make much of a lump, though." An open palm verified this.

The past year I had milked cows for board and room, but had only a few dollars saved while delivering newspapers and working as the school janitor's assistant. The total seemed woefully less than needed, but it might buy ten-cent hamburgers and rent a cheap hotel room each night. Regardless, we were headed for the Pacific Northwest!

Driven by young dreams, pride, and determination, we skirted the park to avoid the heavy dew, then hurried toward the main highway. With the baseball season in full swing, Red, forever testing his skills, took time to select a round rock from the gravel street, wind up, and hurl it toward the nearest telephone pole. Missed.

When he stooped for another, Buck grumbled, "Forget it, Red. Let's get going!"

From there on, the measurements of our latest movie queen, as usual, filled our conversation until the blacktop, stretching for miles in both directions, brought us up short. This time, our journey wouldn't end at the swimming hole, or even the next small town.

As though fate had decreed, an empty cattle-truck came into view. Three thumbs fanned the air. Brakes squealed and we leaped into the back. As I turned for one last look, the road narrowed and my home town became a memory.

Red, freckle-faced, chubby, and smart, always had his eye on money and girls. Towheaded Buck, a dyed-in-the-wool prankster, tormented adults and schoolmates alike. However, one redeeming trait gave victims respite. He loved to sleep and did so at every opportunity. We all looked forward excitedly to working in the land of tall timber.

"Dang!" Buck exclaimed. "I jumped into a plop of cow crap when I got in. How will I wash it off? Hope they don't have any darn cows in the forests."

Red, ignoring Buck's odorous plight, rattled on about our trip while I located an empty grain sack. Together, Buck and I cleaned the manure-covered shoe. Even so, a five-minute scrubbing failed to remove the stench.

"Wonder if the Northwest has Indians?" Red mused. "Haven't seen a real Indian since I turned twelve. Their powwows at the county fairgrounds always reminded me of the free outdoor movies shown in main street on Saturday nights. Boy! What peaches, those Indian girls."

The truck driver dropped us off in McCook at the intersection of West Third and B Streets, then we thumbed our way north. Two short rides took us into North Platte, a community steeped in frontier history. From there we headed westward along the blacktop highway that long ago had replaced the wagon tracks of the Oregon Trail.

More practiced at hitchhiking, I remained first in line while the other two moved farther down the road. Experience, a broad smile, and optimism made me an asset to our trio. My companions understood the limitations imposed by my sight problem: I could neither see in the dark nor read ordinary print. Beyond that, I matched wits and strength with others my age.

Survivors of the nineteen-thirties Great Depression, we had experienced the discomfort of empty stomachs, the uncontrollable shivering that accompanied bitter cold, the hacking coughs caused by violent dust storms, and the embarrassment of wearing patched and faded hand-me-downs.

Ours was a quiet prairie town where stoic elders protected and guided the young: Local ordinance prohibited the sale of alcoholic beverages within city limits. Devout men and women professed belief in the hereafter and optimistically raised their children to uphold tradition.

After my grandmother died from the flu, and my grandfather suffered a sunstroke while working in the harvest fields, he moved his only son and two teenage daughters into this town. Several years passed before the oldest daughter delivered me into the world. Later in life, I would learn, bit by bit, that Mother had been sent to a home for unwed mothers, that her brother and sister had welcomed us home, that Grandpa, distraught by the ordeal, had turned to the Scriptures for guidance and solace.

Hard times prevailed. Mother cooked for the family, cared for Grandpa, and raised me until poverty, village gossip, and paternal rebuff forced her to leave home and work in a distant city. My uncle, Mother's brother, worked in a grain elevator, but seasonally followed the harvests, leaving me to be fostered by an ailing grandparent and an aunt who was striving to complete high school. But for Mother's objection, I might have been adopted out. Even during the worst economic slump, she continued to write and send small amounts of money.

Although clothing, candy, and a small bag of pennies became an expected part of Mother's

infrequent visits home, it was our times together that I enjoyed most. For fleeting moments, I had a real mother—a mother who took me
for picnics in the park, who pushed me high
while I sat in the swing, who hugged me when I
hurt myself, who helped me get ready for bed,
tucked me in, and read aloud my favorite bedtime
stories until my eyelids became heavy. Then, my
wonderful mother, with tears in her eyes, closed
the book, kissed me tenderly on the cheek, and
whispered comforting words. Somehow, I kept my
promise: not to cry when it came time for her
to leave. Nevertheless, the tiny room became a
prison of sadness when my once-in-a-while mother
turned out the light, tiptoed from the room, and
closed the door.

Grandpa's health improved, and he became a
Bible-toting Christian Socialist who zealously
promoted the Townsend Plan, a program designed
to support the elderly and "save our nation", so
he claimed.

Once hooked, Grandpa, Bible in hand, took
his mission to the streets. He preached to, or
argued with, anyone he could collar in the park,
stores, and livestock sale pavilion. There were
embarrassing moments, of course, but he was sincere and persisted in his crusade.

Near my seventh birthday, our family dis-
banded. My uncle married, left his job at the

local grain elevator, and returned to the farm. My aunt also married, and Grandpa went to live with a brother. Mother continued to work in the city. Fortunately, other relatives and friends raised me until I could work and put myself through high school.

Daybreaks pushed the nights from the cloudless skies while I used to milk the butcher's cows, slop the hogs, then run from house to house delivering newspapers and hand-bills. I often took a shortcut through the park to enjoy the scent of newly mown grass, the morning greetings of song birds, the clamorous antics of bushy-tailed gray squirrels, and, yes, even the sight of gregarious black crows drift-ing lazily above the fields, buildings, and treetops.

This little town had been my world. Would I ever see it again? Would I even want to?

Thirty minutes passed before a large Chrysler slowed, came to an abrupt stop and waited as I ran to the passenger side, opened the door, then stared in disbelief. In the driver's seat sat the loveliest woman I had ever seen—even more alluring than the pin-up girl that had adorned the boys' locker-room wall for three exciting days. Slender waist, shapely legs, and inviting blue eyes combined to belie her twenty-nine or thirty years. At that moment, age meant nothing to me, for an engaging smile and subtle cologne immediately stirred fantasies of passionate romance.

"How far are you going?" she questioned softly as I slid in beside her.

"I'm going—I mean—well, my buddies and I are going to look for work in the Northwest," I stammered, stealing quick glances.

Now the woman, obviously amused or perhaps pleased by my fascination, turned to ask, "And where are your friends?"

"Oh, I almost forgot. Ahead. Can we pick them up?"

A momentary silence, then, seeing my companions, she slowed the car, examined them closely, and stopped.

As the others entered the back seat, the driver turned for a final appraisal, smiled warmly, then remarked, "We almost passed you."

"Boy! Are we glad you didn't!" they exclaimed in unison. Red continued, "We wouldn't have known what to do. We're already over ninety miles from home and have only a few dollars."

Idle scooters, abandoned hopscotch mark-
ings, empty porch swings, and kitchen lights indicated supper time as the luxurious car rolled
through a residential section of Cheyenne, Wyoming. Minutes later the driver, eyes and voice
attesting to a hard day on the road, dropped us
near the business district after offering to
meet us at the same spot the following morning.

Overwhelmed by the bustling traffic and
sea of unfamiliar faces, we stood, bags in hand,
and watched our new friend wave a reassuring
goodbye, then drive away. Doubtless, she had
gone to occupy a room in an expensive hotel. So
be it, we needed lodging that fit our pocket-
books.

Now totally on our own, Red, Buck, and I
wandered aimlessly for several blocks before
taking refuge in a hole-in-the-wall cafe, where
we gulped hamburgers and assessed our finances.
Stomachs filled, we emerged into the cool evening air and walked the littered downtown
streets, searching for a cheap rooming house.

Darkness had set in before we selected a
$1.50-and-up flophouse. Suddenly thrust into an
unknown world, we put aside comments about the
beauty of our traveling companion, entered the
street-level door, and climbed the rickety
stairs. A small bulb guided us to the second
floor where we paused, scrutinized the area,

21

wrinkled our noses at the musty odor, then ventured along the hall, keeping within arm's
length of one another.

Our apprehensions mounted as the dim light
stretched our shadows to form grotesque silhou-
ettes, and the creaking floors echoed an eerie
cadence to our advancing footsteps. Suddenly, we
stopped. The shadows stopped. The creaking
stopped. We looked and listened. Nothing. Cautiously, we shuffled forward, then stopped
again. From a distant room surged a violent and
continuous coughing—a hacking, wheezing, gag-
ging. Maybe, I thought, someone was dying? Or
being strangled?

Chapter 3

Strange, New World

Shaken but resolute, Red, Buck, and I, immobilized by the guttural outbursts, held our ground until the siege abated and became little more than heavy breathing. Nevertheless, our footsteps quickened as we neared the half-open door from which the retching had emanated, dropped into single file, hugged the opposite wall, and sprinted.

Once past, we again closed ranks and shoved on. Distance from the light had by now diffused the shadows, but the creaking continued, sounding more ominous than before. Our shoulders and arms touched. We walked as one until an open doorway guided us into a room where a bare light bulb, suspended from the ceiling by a twisted cord, revealed a smudged sign indicating "Manager".

Small-town lads that we were, each feigned courage as we scanned the shabbily furnished room. Uneasy exchanged glances, however, revealed that all of us wanted desperately to leave, but refused to admit cowardice. As we hesitated, a young woman entered who wore no clothing above her waist. A gaudy tattoo adorned each well-rounded breast; one brazenly stated "sweet" and the other "sour". Finding it difficult to divert our eyes from these spectacular statements, we remained speechless until the scantily-clothed hostess, obviously encouraged by our boyish preoccupation with her anatomy, inquired coyly, "Would you men like a room, or something even better?"

A confused jumble of "Uh, ah, mmm, yah—no," poured from our mouths. Then a harsh voice came from a back room. "Get them damn kids out of here!" the bruiser roared, stepping into full view. "You'll have every cop and church group in town looking down our throats."

Like a covey of quail evading a hunter's shots, we turned and fled toward the doorway. Once outside the room, clutching our unwieldy bags, we maneuvered for position while racing along the hall. We arrived at the stairwell shoulder to shoulder and leaped, stumbled, and slid our way to the bottom. Without looking back, we escaped to the street, ran a short distance along the sidewalk, then stopped to compare scrapes and bruises. Within minutes, however, each ignored the injuries to recount a personal version of the fiasco.

"Gosh! Did you see that?" Red asked.

"Yeah! Man, was he big!" Buck replied, wide-eyed.

"No! Not that!" Red insisted. "The girl—what she had tattooed on her!"

"He sure didn't want us around," I added. "Boy, what a getup. If Grandpa had seen that, he'd have rolled over in his grave." We laughed that one off, returned to the cafe for another hamburger, then again took to the streets.

The balmy summer evening, our fatigue, and dwindling funds caused us to doze on park benches until a police officer approached.

"Do your parents know where you are? You better go home," he said brusquely.

The moment of silence seemed an eternity. Finally realizing neither of my buddies intended to reply, I answered, "We don't live here and we're waiting until our ride leaves in the morning."

"Well," continued the officer skeptically, "stay away from this area. We've had serious problems around here. It's warm, so go out that way," he ordered, pointing his nightstick toward a well-lighted street. "It's OK there."

Somehow making it until dawn, we arrived, tired and blurry-eyed, to meet our beautiful friend at the spot where she had dropped us off the previous evening. Vivacious and smartly dressed, she asked, "Did you fellows sleep well?"

All nodded drowsily. Once in the car, we slumbered fitfully through the day, waking only to eat lunch in a wayside diner.

Tall poplars swayed in the dwindling sunlight as the car wound its way through heavy traffic near Twin Falls, Idaho. One by one, we stirred, and the driver, weary from hours behind the wheel, acknowledged our return from the dead. "You boys will never know how nice it has been having you accompany me across those dreary wastelands. I'll bet you all have nice girl-friends waiting for you back home."

No one answered directly—just with shrugs and mumbles. Regardless, if the truth were known, each of us probably wished for a girl-friend and later a wife just like our beautiful driver. I did. After a final thank you and sev-eral good-byes, we watched the car vanish down a side street.

A twenty-minute hike took us to the city limits as the sun dropped behind the western hills. To our relief, a mud-spattered milk truck gave us a lift to the next small town, where it was another hamburger supper, an uneventful night in a nameless hotel, and again on the road without breakfast. By late afternoon, we arrived in Dayton, Washington, near Walla Walla, the heartland of pea farming.

Our luck held. Before noon the following day, we found work in the local cannery. Meals and lodging provided at a sleazy boarding house in no way matched the comfort and food back home. Five or six cannery employees slept in each room on army-type cots. All workers received a mediocre morning and evening meal at the residence and carried a sack lunch.

Laboring in the extreme heat and high humidity inside the cannery, we spent entire shifts lifting heavy boxes of canned peas above our heads to form colossal pyramids.

"Gosh," said Red one evening, "this is worse than lifting alfalfa bales all day. At least we had fresh air in the fields."

"I got a cramp in my leg last night," I added, "and couldn't even get out of bed to stretch it. The first week of football practice tore me up, but this is worse."

Buck had drowsed off at the supper table. A punch on the shoulder brought him to his feet, but he merely moved to the cot in the adjoining room and resumed the slumber. As usual, he talked in his sleep, "Wasn't she pretty …. Oh, my arms …."

Aching backs and arms soon brought on cramps while we worked. Frustrated and embarrassed, we had no alternative but to admit failure. No way could we stack for a twelve-hour shift.

Easier jobs soon became available in the cannery, however, and one by one, we found less demanding positions. Others later assured us that few grown men had been able to endure the stacking.

As the harvest progressed, men with odd dialects and cash in their pockets took time to celebrate in the taverns and other infamous places near our boarding house. One night about two o'clock, a bloodcurdling shriek, followed by wild screams, brought everyone from his cot. A hefty Southerner positioned himself before the window and described the brawl to those of us who were already gawking over and around equally inquisitive workers.

Minutes later, the law arrived in a marked car. Burly officers, fully armed with guns and billy clubs, leaped to the ground, charged into the swarming bodies and viciously swung batons. Blood gushed, arms went limp, and knees buckled as the onslaught continued.

One young fellow, clad in baggy flour-sack underwear, walked toward the window, rubbed sleep from his eyes, then asked, "What is it?"

"A big fight," the narrator replied, embellishing with the gusto of a seasoned sportscaster. "And the cops are beating the devil out of those guys. Darn, look at that one trying to crawl away. Someone kicked him in the side, then jumped on him as though mounting a bucking steer. Wow! That cop just clubbed another on the head and the guy dropped like a cow heading for the butcher. Man, look at the blood! One guy's got it squirting from him like a stuck hog. The ground looks like the floor of the slaughterhouse near my home in Texas."

At that, everyone crowded toward the window, almost pushing the big fellow through the panes. Unfortunately, Red and Buck missed the excitement, for they slept soundly behind the closed door of an adjoining room.

The cops' brutality seemed extreme, but the workers brought it on themselves, and I did learn something about street fighting. Oddly enough, these unpredictable nomads, at least those who survived the night, worked side by side in the fields and canneries the following day.

Several productive weeks brought the pea harvest to an end. True migrants drifted to the next seasonal work, but we pocketed our earnings and journeyed north and west to locate the dust bowl farmer who, a few years ago, had abandoned our home town to settle in Randle, Washington.

A produce carrier took us across the Columbia River and on into Yakima. We borrowed a map of Washington state from a filling station and located Randle, a tiny village nestled in the foothills south of Mount Rainier and west of the Cascade summit.

Buck stepped into the station telephone booth, took a smudged paper from his pocket and examined the farmer's phone number his mother had given him the morning we left home. Putting the receiver to his ear, he tried his luck. Nothing.

We took turns and entered the booth at regular intervals. Finally, an operator came on.

"Lines must be down," she said. "The linemen should get it repaired soon. Try later."

We waited patiently for one hour, then two, but when the sun descended toward the mountain tops, we pursued the matter forcefully. Time and again, Buck badgered the operator to continue ringing the number. Red and I fidgeted or paced back and forth along the station drive-way.

It was with great excitement that Buck finally shouted, "Yowee! We got them!"

Running to the booth, Red and I pushed into the doorway and shoved our heads close to the receiver. A pulsing hum, periodically interrupted by indescribable static, transmitted the shouting from the other end.

"Well, I'll be goldarned! Where did you kids come from?" Without waiting for a reply, he ordered, "Tell me exactly where you are, then wait until my son comes to get you. Don't try to hitchhike over the mountains this late in the day. No one willingly travels that narrow winding road after dark, but my boy's a good driver and knows his way."

Eventually, the son arrived in Yakima, picked us up, and we exchanged hearty greetings as the 1936 V8 Ford sped through the Yakima Valley truck farms. How different from back home, I thought. On the prairie, endless pasture lands, grain fields, and feed lots extended from horizon to horizon. But here, well-managed asparagus patches, hop yards, vineyards, and orchards mapped the countryside like a patchwork quilt.

"I took the long way coming," our friend said, "but we'll try a shortcut going back."

31

The grade increased, the road narrowed, and we headed into the Cascade foothills, where mile after mile of stately pines stretched before us.

"Wow!" Red exclaimed. "I wonder how many trees are growing on these mountains? I bet more than a million. Boy are they close together."

"Yeah," Buck agreed, "and they're pretty, too—even though they have skinny leaves."

Yes, I thought, they're numerous and beautiful, but the inevitable question raced through my mind: Precisely what tasks do men perform when they "work in the woods"? We hadn't discussed that.

Our enchantment waned when the route dwindled to little more than a single-lane back road. Ominous clouds darkened the skies and raindrops freckled the dusty windshield. By the time we dropped over the mountain crest, dusk had set in, and rain was pelting the car with unbelievable force. Windshield wipers struggled.

The driver, with amazing self-assurance, maneuvered the car down the winding road. Nevertheless, Red, Buck, and I shoved an imaginary brake-pedal to the floorboard at each sharp curve.

Suddenly, the storm released its fury. Jagged streaks of lightning followed by ground-shaking booms invaded the area. What a sight! Even I, despite my poor night vision, could clearly see hundreds of feet down ravines and up stone cliffs with each volley.

The car often skidded sideways, but miraculously corrected itself before reaching the edge. To leave the road meant plunging into a chasm of unknown depth. No one spoke.

I set my jaw, braced my cold feet, and clutched the window crank with one hand and the seat with the other. Likewise, Buck and Red held onto anything within reach. Never before had I felt so vulnerable.

Within minutes, the storm, like an errant beast, rumbled into the distance, leaving small mud and rock slides where the road cut into fir-covered slopes. For the next mile or so, the son intermittently stopped the car and we ran ahead to roll the largest rocks aside. Fortunately, the hillsides had released nothing larger. The durable Ford bounced and slid crazily through each pathway.

A narrow bridge soon guided us onto an improved road where we were assured that the worst lay behind. Time to relax.

"Packwood's right up ahead," our friend announced. "Not much here," he added as we passed through. "Just a general store, a gas pump, and a cafe/card room where locals play poker and drink. Once in a while, someone gets shot, or knifed, or beaten to within an inch of his life, but nothing comes of it."

"What about the sheriff?" I asked. "Doesn't h—"

My question went unanswered, for at that moment we plunged into a sea of dense fog. Brakes squealed, tires slid, and the car slowed. Cautiously, we moved through a damp mysterious world of nothingness—no boundaries, no sense of direction, no light from the moon or stars.

Only luck kept us on the road, but the car, like a homing pigeon, pushed on and turned left at the Randle Forest Service Ranger Station, crept one half mile toward the Cowlitz River, turned left again, and pulled into the driveway about midnight.

To top off the evening, we gorged ourselves on a bountiful supper of venison, home-grown fruits, and vegetables enriched by hearty laughter, news, and gossip from back home. Red, Buck, and I ultimately crawled between heavy woolen blankets to die for several hours, relieved that the man of the house had offered us an excellent rate for meals and lodging if we found work in the area.

At five o'clock sharp, I heard the son dress and leave to work in a lumber mill that specialized in cutting railroad ties. Later, everyone rose to an ample breakfast and more chitchat.

It took only a few minutes for us to split the day's supply of stove wood while the mother and young daughter prepared to can meat from a deer killed the previous day. Chores completed, the father took time to teach us penny-ante poker, substituting match sticks for pennies. We talked of wheat and corn, cattle and pigs, good years and bad years, and what should have been.

After lunch, our host held us spellbound as he launched into vivid descriptions of life in the far west. Time and again, he emphasized the hazards of working in the woods and the virtues of living by one's own principles. Aging eyes brightened as he frequently reminded us that he owned his home outright and was also debt-free.

That evening, the son brought a reassuring report. A small lumber mill a mile or so west of Randle needed two or three men. He'd drop us off on his way to work the following morning.

A lean figure watched closely as we jumped from the car and picked our way through tree stumps, sawdust, and rough-cut lumber. Now the man, a wiry fellow nearing forty, walked toward us and asked if we were looking for work. A few short questions and our uncertain answers seemed to satisfy any concerns—greenhorns but willing to learn.

"If you guys are good workers, the pay will be three dollars a day," the owner said. "We go to work at seven o'clock. You'll need to arrive at the mill a few minutes early to grease the bearings and stay a while after work to clean up and stack lumber."

As Buck turned to watch an overloaded truck pull up to the log dump, he exclaimed, "Look at the size of those logs on that truck! The biggest one is almost as thick as I am tall! Boy, would my pop like to see that!"

Red, delighted at the prospect of actually working in a lumber mill, ignored Buck's remarks and announced lifetime ambitions. "Gee, I've never earned that much before! Three dollars a day! It won't be long until I can send money home to Mom and save for a car."

My immediate concern, however, was not whether I could earn large sums of money or buy a car, but whether, considering my poor vision, I could handle the job.

Chapter 4

Going It Alone

Several weeks of brutal mill work, torrential rains, and backwoods isolation took their toll. My friends, homesick and disappointed, made plans to pursue a less demanding vocation.

"I'm not going to hang around here and eat sawdust, pull back-breaking lumber from the head-saw, wrestle it onto dollies, and pick slivers from my hands the rest of my life," Red stated. "I've saved enough to start college and I can get a job washing dishes in a restaurant to pay for meals. There's nothing to do in this darn place except drink and fight. Besides, the girls are no better looking than those we left back home."

Buck had vacillated a few days, weighing and measuring college against a craft. "There's no future here. My clothes are always wet and smeared with sticky pitch. Just the other day I snagged my overalls on a splintered board and ripped the leg up past the knee. There went my day's wages.

"I'm not the best with books, so I'll learn to be an electrician," he decided. "They say you can get an apprenticeship in the cities. Someone told me the best looking girls are moving there to become secretaries, or nurses, or something like that."

I might have gone with them, but poor vision ruled out both college and the trades.

During those weeks, I had become a top-notch mill hand, and I knew that a willing worker could earn a living in this remote valley.

"You guys go ahead," I urged. "I'm going to stay for a while. Besides, you have family back home."

With both friends gone, I set out to learn more about my adopted homeland.

Along the Cowlitz River: Packwood and Randle

Known for its steep grade and treacherous curves, the valley road broke over the west ridge and wound its way downward toward the alpine village of Randle. Each unexpected turn revealed another of many breathtaking panoramas or a different view of one just passed. This bucolic scene, tucked into the end of nowhere, stood primitive and inviting—a no-man's-land reserved for only the hardiest.

First to catch the eye, the aging lumber mill, located in a dale near the main road, sawed logs trucked from the mountain slopes. Day after day, the boiler sent fluffy clouds of steam upward into the willowy saplings growing alongside the creek—the spring-fed stream that had supplied water to the mill power plant for years. Newly-sawed lumber, stacked randomly in the yard, indicated a prosperous operation. A cone-shaped sawdust/slab burner smoldered throughout the day while gentle breezes scattered smoke, soot, and the aroma of green lumber downwind toward Randle.

From seven to four o'clock, huge saws maintained a soothing whir until their teeth ripped into the soft Douglas fir, sending a wailing screech along the hillside.

Said to be a refugee from the old country, a weathered old Swede with the traditional Copenhagen snuff in his lip, managed the likewise aging power plant. Periodically, he glanced at the water glass to ensure the boiler maintained a full head of steam.

Throughout the year, glacial waters supplied the Cowlitz River which wound its way through the flat valley where rich soil supported grain and alfalfa. Dairy cows grazed in the logged-off pasture lands while Mallard ducks searched the ponds and grain fields for morsels.

Most huge Douglas firs had been logged from the valley floor, leaving only small clusters standing in the green fields and around unpainted farm buildings. Beyond the cleared land, virgin timber ascended into the towering snow-capped peaks, leaving clouds drifting aimlessly through and around the shadowy ravines.

Each evening, deer and their fawns left the protective woodlands to forage in the open fields, and although the animals and the game warden maintained a constant vigil, no valley resident lacked for venison. Unwelcome visitors, such as State and Federal law-enforcement officials, seldom frequented the area, nor did they become involved in the affairs of this tight-knit community. Historically, over-zealous intruders soon wore out their welcome and, for unknown reasons, left the area without explanation. Dairy farmers, loggers, mill workers, and businessmen lived by one law—their own.

The river, guided by rugged peaks, entered and left the valley through narrow gorges, leaving behind the customs, dogmas, and principles understood only by longtime friends and kinsmen.

Near the edge of town, a block-letter sign, DRIVE CAREFULLY WE LOVE OUR CHILDREN, cautioned newcomers and old-timers alike. Said to have been constructed and maintained by village mothers, the black-on-white warning stood resolute in its frame of scotch broom shrubs and wild blackberry vines.

Beyond the sign, a tiny cove sheltered the restaurant, general store, garage, post office, barber shop, a second restaurant, cheese factory, Grange hall, small church, well-constructed school, and a notorious tavern—all crunched into the equivalent of one large, square city block. A mountain creek wound its way down from the hills, danced alongside the cheese factory, passed under the street near the post office, then rushed between the dwellings to cascade into the river below.

Beyond the tavern, a U. S. Forest Service Station with manicured lawn and neatly painted buildings stood regally in a cluster of tall firs—a sharp contrast to the weathered hodge-podge of homes, garages, woodsheds, and natural yards in the tiny community.

Several spacious and well-constructed houses mingled with a dozen or more rustic, but comfortable homes. Also, unpainted one or two-room board and batten buildings, little more than shacks, stood beyond the town's official limits and generally housed the less fortunate.

Regardless of the occupants' wealth or position, all buildings, homes, barns, and other outbuildings were protected by a hand-split shake roof of the finest cedar. Shingle siding, painted, stained, or otherwise, served as low-cost building material as well as insulation from the damp cold winter storms.

Many families took pride in a brick or stone fireplace, while others had nothing more than a metal chimney protruding through the roof above the kitchen stove. Wood-smoke escaped into the clear mountain air as family and friends gathered to share old times during long winter evenings. Locals, including dairy ranchers scattered around and about the valley, recounted how their parents and grandparents had discovered this haven from the outside.

They talked proudly of the struggles and deprivation before the first road had been blasted through the west rim. The men and women, generally hardworking and fiercely independent, relished their isolation and freedom to make community decisions without statutory intervention.

These pioneers ironically called the small valley "The Big Bottom", and jokingly referred

to the young women as "big bottom girls". Even
so, woe be unto the outlander who dared question, challenge or ridicule lineage, life-style,
or morals. Able men and boys, born sportsmen,
cherished their 30-30 carbines or 30-06 Savage
rifles as strongly as they did their families
and livestock. The elusive salmon, migrating upstream from the Columbia River provided seasonal
fishing competition. Only the hardiest partici-
pated in the annual elk-hunting treks—events
that were discussed and re-discussed around the
fireplace or living room stove until the next
expedition.

Subservient only to the forces of nature,
brave men displayed hands with mangled or missing fingers, empty eye sockets, or artificial
limbs. The lumbering and logging industry showed
no favorites when claiming a misplaced append-
age; mill workers and timbermen shared alike in
the losses and accepted them with no resentment.
When a man went to work each morning, nothing
guaranteed that he would return home that night
intact, if at all.

Many claimed Irish or Scottish ancestry
with a "Mac", "Mc", or "O" before the main stem
of the family name. Proud of their heritage,
they seldom passed a chance to deride outsiders.

Displaced coal miners had settled in and
around Packwood about fifteen miles up the

river. According to locals, they had little in common with the valley residents. Hearing me mention the hillbillies in the area, an old-timer took me aside to explain the difference between hillbillies and valley folks.

The senior settled himself on the trunk of a rotting blow-down, motioned me to join him, then reached into a raveled shirt pocket and withdrew a round box containing Copenhagen snuff. As the old fellow inserted a pinch between his lower lip and gum, a satisfied smile radiated over the grizzled face. Now he was ready.

"Hillbillies aren't like us," he explained. "They came from back east somewhere and settled up the river beyond the valley. They're rowdies and suspicious as all get out. The majority are meaner than hell and they'd kill their own grandma for a slug of moonshine." His speech, sprinkled with grammatical shortcuts, portrayed a man of conviction, a barroom philosopher who willingly stated a position and accepted the consequences. "I've had a few run-ins with them, and so far I've been lucky," he continued, chuckling nostalgically. "Don't ever let a bunch get you cornered. They'll pull a knife at the drop of a hat, and they're clannish as hell."

"Now there's a few renegades who live round and about the valley. They like their booze and shy away from work. A few will steal the shirt off your back. Sooner or later, they'll return what they've taken, then stand around guzzling and laughing as though you should treat the matter as a neighborly joke. Most are not mean but the young bucks will try to take over your old lady when you're not looking." Without elaborating, he moved on to those warranting respect.

"Then there's the real men of the valley. They like a lot of fun. They're always laughing and love to pull jokes on everyone, something like the renegades, except they won't bother your old lady. They'll work hard and drink just as hard. Their biggest thing is to outwit the law. I saw one of them take the gun right off a patrolman's hip, and he wouldn't give it back until the cop agreed to let him go. They're sort of friendly enemies."

He grew silent, as though pondering whether or not to continue. Shortly, still engrossed in deep thought, he rose from the log and meandered off to relieve himself in the bushes. I wondered if everyone in the valley shared the old pioneer's characterizations.

Religious activities were confined to the small church and centered primarily around funeral services for the old and those killed while logging. A few couples married in the one-room structure, but weddings usually occurred in the homes or the Grange hall, where drinking and raising hell evoked minimal chastisement from the spiritually inclined.

Ranch hands and mill workers, to the chagrin of a few believers, spent their Saturdays overdosing in the local tavern and fighting in the town's only street.

At ten o'clock sharp, the bartender opened the doors to admit several thirsty customers waiting impatiently on the steps. Once inside, each patron occupied a customary seat and proceeded to boast of his capabilities as mill worker or rancher. A few drinks into the morning, a mill hand, at an opportune moment, might look into the mirror behind the bar, angle his vision to focus on a rancher, then comment, "Well, what do you know? How are you manure-stompers doing this morning?"

"Don't you damn sliver-pickers get smart with me," the rancher would retort, "or you'll be running down the road holding the seat of your pants and hollering, 'the rancher did it!'"

"You damn tit-squeezers can't whip your way out of a wet paper bag," came the immediate reply. "Just get your hind end outside, and I'll show you the difference between men and boys."

Chug-a-lugging the last drops from the huge beer mug, the rancher called over his shoulder as he walked out the door toward the arena, "Bartender, draw me another one now; this won't take long. One good lick and old Sawdust-for-Brains will be on his back, hollering, 'uncle'." The brew had miraculously transformed these jovial valley residents into pugnacious adversaries.

Outside in the street, cursing violently, the two men invariably squared off inside a circle of jeering and rooting tavern customers, each onlooker bolstering a favorite.

"Go get him!" "Drive his damn teeth through the top of his head!" "When you're through with him, I'll give him something to remember," rumbled through the onlookers. Suddenly, at an opportune moment, one combatant would throw a punch to the jaw, sending his opponent reeling into the crowd. But when he rushed to end it, the fellow had recovered enough to defend himself. Round and round they circled, throwing more curses than punches. Soon, as though needing to end it before the next meal, they stood toe to toe, slugging, grunting, and cursing, droplets of blood spraying into the crowd with each blow. If one dropped his arms, went down, or stepped from the ring, a bystander usually took a turn at the victor.

Within minutes, spectators joined in, slugging anyone within arm's reach, friend or foe. Quick to tire, contenders, their weekend fulfilled, wandered back into the tavern, nursing bloody faces and skinned knuckles as they finished the day drinking and bragging.

In spite of the many hardships for the women, the hazardous work and heavy drinking by the men, and the fluctuating economy within the valley, most marriages lasted throughout life. Could I be satisfied with as much? Not really, but what to replace it?

The eye doctor's words, "You'll not go totally blind for years," seemed comforting at the time, but now their implications haunted me with disturbing regularity. How many years? Then what?

Chapter 5

On My Way

Without public transportation in the valley, I relied on the kindliness of others to
take me from place to place. Even the towering
peaks, beautiful and intriguing, now seemed confining, and the mill-work became tediously routine. A growing concern for my future prompted
me to make friends with anyone who knew about
the outside world.

One crisp night an ominous fog flooded the
valley and surrounding ravines, permeating the
smallest crevice and hollow log. Even the smoke
from the early morning fires seemed confused as
it departed the chimneys and groped its way skyward.

"What a time to be on the road," I said to
a fellow millhand as he drove the battered car
along the two-lane road.

Its fenders rattled; its headlights
bounced; its chassis shimmied and swerved as the
driver squinted through the mud-spattered glass
and whipped the steering wheel first left then
right to avoid bottomless chuckholes.

"Can you see OK?" I asked.

"Hell," he exclaimed, "I've got hawk eyes. It doesn't bother—Christ! You crazy fool! Get that damn truck on your side of the roa—"

At that moment, metal crunched against metal and a cloudburst of shattered glass ended our trip. The impact had thrown me from the car onto the road. Blood streamed from my forehead. None too soon, others stopped and rushed to assist. Together, we pried, pulled, and jerked on bent steel to free the driver.

"What the hell happened?" one stubble-faced logger asked as we both jerked viciously on the bent steering wheel.

"We were rounding that rock point when this darn truck cut into our lane as he came from the other direction," I replied, adding, "What a crash! Every window shattered and sprayed glass, like buckshot coming from a twelve gauge shotgun. Can we put my partner in one of your pickups when he's free?"

"Sure," came the immediate reply. "Mine's the blue Ford over by that tree. We'll give you a hand. But how about you? You're bleeding like a buck with a 30.30 rifle slug in him."

"I'm OK," I replied. "Doesn't hurt. Just a lot of blood. Besides, it's almost stopped."

Several familiar faces stepped forward and we gently removed the unconscious millhand, placed him on a makeshift stretcher fashioned from coats and clasped hands, then lifted him into the pickup bed. I climbed in beside him and urged, "Let's go!"

With us in the back and the pickup owner and one other man in front, we began a wild race against time. Fortunately, the fog had lifted. We eased onto the road, increased speed, then the driver jammed the gas pedal to the floorboards, and the truck careened along the winding road, rounding each curve on two wheels, or so it seemed.

By now, each chuckhole brought plaintive moans from the mangled body. At least, I thought, he's reacting to something. Maybe he'll come around.

After several futile attempts to hold my companion in place by lying next to him, I turned with my back against his body and braced my legs against the truck bed. How much farther? I wondered, the blood now crusted on my face. Can't go much longer or he won't make it.

Shortly, we pulled up to the Morton medical facility, where white-clothed attendants loaded the injured man on a stretcher and whisked him inside. Within minutes, they returned and ushered me into the receiving room, and assured me that the doctor would be in soon.

What seemed like hours passed before a white-capped nurse entered, nodded gravely, and bustled me into a cubical reeking with antiseptics.

"You're certainly a mess," she began, perching me on a tall stool. "How did this happen?"

I narrated the accident as she patted and scrubbed away the dried blood, repositioned a loose skin flap, and covered the wound with a sterile bandage.

"That looks better," she remarked, proudly examining her handiwork. "Now, young fellow, I must tell you—I mean—Well, it's this way. Your wound seems superficial, but your partner wasn't so lucky … his chest and head. Sorry." With that, she gathered scissors and unused bandages, then hurried from the room.

The antiquated truck, which belonged to the mill, required extensive repairs. Even if replacement parts could be located, delivery time remained uncertain. No truck meant no logs to saw and no work for the crew. The small mill was forced to shut down.

Like so many my age, I soon received and responded to a military draft-board summons. October 1942, the induction staff, discovering my inability to read the eye chart, ordered acceptance with limited service until glasses could be prescribed. Once in the Army Air Corps as a potential airplane mechanic, further medical examinations verified the diagnosis made at age fifteen.

According to the Air Corps physician, I suffered a hereditary eye condition which defied improvement.

"That your vision should remain stable for years, alters nothing," the Major insisted. "Legal blindness makes you unfit for military service." Again, the damning words, like angry bees, attacked at will. Blind! Unfit! Unfit! Unfit!

With an honorable discharge, mustering out pay and four months in the Army Air Corps behind, I left Hobbs, New Mexico, and headed back to the Pacific Northwest.

What would friends think? Would other than lumber mill employers hire a man with poor vision? There must be something besides mill work.

After two days and nights attempting to rest or sleep sitting bolt upright in the aging railway coach, I finally arrived at the Chehalis, Washington, train depot—the same small station and brick platform from which several friends and I had departed to serve our country.

To ease the torment, I wandered the streets searching for a familiar face, or at least, someone near my age—no luck. Everyone seemed to have grown older. Middle aged men and women hurried by, airing opinions on patriotism, rationing, and paint-on stockings. The war had narrowed my lot.

Again, as during my childhood, I felt like an outsider which, in a way, freed me to consider alternative methods for earning a living. Employment that required a vision test, or reading ordinary print, or driving a vehicle, limited my opportunities, but others seemed possible.

Inquiries often encouraged speculation regarding my duty to our nation. "What's a young man like you doing looking for non-essential work? All the young guys are off to the war."

But the payoff came when the search required an applicant to complete a questionnaire and sign it in the presence of a personnel manager. With nose almost touching the printed page, I struggled, only to receive disparaging remarks. "You've taken enough time. Most applicants finish in a few minutes. You've been more

than twenty. Let me see what you've completed."
A quick glance invariably led to remarks imply-
ing below normal intelligence. "This job requires brains. How far did you go in school?
You've got to think fast when you're working for
us. I'm not sure you can fill the job. Better
look for something less demanding."

Numerous inquiries yielded nothing, but
for sure, return to the prairie to spend a life
milking cows equaled self-destruction. To heck
with city life, I thought. It's back to the valley, the land of big trees, big equipment, self-
reliant men and women, but no reading.

Luckily, a job opened at a logging camp
near Kosmos about fifteen miles down the Cowlitz
River from Randle. What a break! Now to learn
more about the timber business. The outfit
served as a winter haven for tramp loggers moving inland to escape the violent coastal storms.
Known to be excellent workers, these bruisers,
usually unmarried, heavy drinkers, and pugnacious, initiated and supported the union movement. Bringing diverse accents, strange person-
alities, and dogged curiosity to the camps,
their sharp minds possessed the wit and wisdom
of logging generations.

Each man's belongings included shaving
gear, white woolen socks, black woolen underwear, Hickory work shirt, sweatshirt, and "Black

Bear" overalls supported by wide suspenders—all topped off with a comical red felt hunting hat.

Calk boots, the woodsman's most valued possession, remained on the tramp logger's feet during most waking hours. More often called "corks" than calk boots, the heavy leather footwear held short steel spikes pointing downward from the soles. The calks prevented slipping while working in the woods and served as weapons of defense or aggression during weekends in town.

Despite an infamous reputation, the tramps' excellent work performance and ability to tolerate inclement weather drew admiration and respect from both fellow workers and employers. Generally, these rovers were intolerant of laziness or pretense but understood illiteracy, for many excellent loggers had no formal education. Know-how, rather than the ability to read or write, identified productive workers.

I hired on as a choker-setter, placing steel cables around logs to be pulled to the central landing, where they would be loaded onto trucks or railway cars. The first day turned out to be awesome, confusing, and demeaning. Giant caterpillar tractors, their motors bellowing, trailed high arches that lifted the forward end of logs from the ground and dragged them midst a cloud of dust toward the loading area, where men shouted unintelligible distortions of the language. Most disconcerting, every machine and its operator carried a nickname or ridiculous title. Caterpillar tractors became cats, the operators, skinners; stationary log-loading machines, affectionately or not, became donkeys, the operators, punchers; and on and on until every man and piece of equipment had a strange label. A foreman became a side-rod; a logging supervisor, a hook-tender; a superintendent, a supe.

The first day caught me slickshod, for I failed to purchase calk boots before going onto the job. I ran like a frightened rabbit as laughing men squalled, "This way," or "No, damn it, that way," or "What the hell are you doing over there?"

Yes, they intended to help, but I thought the pleasure they experienced from watching me flounder seemed excessive. Without calks, each step became an adventure, for my feet slipped and skidded on the slick bark and foliage, but more often than not, they pointed skyward as my backside received another bruise. A living hell, I thought, my mind and body aching for a word of encouragement. All day, like a hog on ice, I sprinted, slipped, fell, crawled, leaped, and rolled to safety after pulling and tugging until I had placed a choker around each of several logs.

Finally, the quitting whistle called everyone to the tiny speeder which carried us back to camp. I dragged myself from the motorized rail car, staggered to the company store, and purchased calk boots—the best the company sold. From there, I hurried to the bunkhouse, flopped on the bed and snored away the hour or so before the supper bell rang.

Rushing footsteps and boisterous voices made their way toward the delightful odors and soon everyone, including me, had greedily consumed a bountiful meal. I returned to the bunkhouse, stripped off down to my overalls and raced to the washroom, where I dropped the sweaty pants to the floor, stepped cautiously into the makeshift shower, and drenched cramping legs, a sore back, and scrapes and bruises too numerous to count. Never before had I seen such nasty black and blue blotches on one person.

As the corroded shower-head intermittently surged, sputtered, and belched discolored water over my body, I relived the day's work, wondering how a man could so drastically misguide his life. Given a few more hours on the job, I might have folded from sheer exhaustion, but there I stood, waging a battle of will between leaving or toughing it out. Also, the calk boots—they had cost a lot of money, and I had charged them against my first paycheck.

Only then did I fully understand the importance of the job and the expensive footwear. If I quit, I'd have no place to sleep or eat, and I had already tried to get a job in town. With the rainy season threatening more each day, I'd need the full range of foul weather gear—to say nothing of the camp meals that would be subtracted from my pay each month. Ironically, I had become indentured.

Perhaps the boots and more experience will prevent me from making a regrettable decision, I reasoned. Hang on for a few more days.

Again, the quandary. Even though I can hack it, could I ever become accustomed to working with these profane and arrogant men, who willingly sacrificed the good life for this? Without warning, the water turned icy, forcing me to jump from the cubicle, so I dried, scooped the overalls from the floor, slipped battered legs into the garment, and walked through the fresh evening air. Darkness crept in as silvery clouds floated lazily over the camp, while night birds and animals announced the end of another day.

Within weeks, the reputation had been earned: "Fast on his feet and quick to learn."

Always the youngest and smallest worker on the job, I found that old-timers delighted in assigning ridiculous tasks that provided humor for the crew. Serious-faced elders sent me for striped paint or a sky hook, neither of which, naturally, was available at the suggested pick-up point. My willingness to work and ability to tolerate the pranks soon earned a respectable position in the ruffian crew.

Even so, I adhered to my grandfather's doctrine of no smoking or drinking. Using chewing tobacco or snuff was completely out of the question. Doubtless, the old patriarch's religious dogmas also caused me to disdain customs, rituals, great causes, and hypocrisy.

The relaxed mood after the quitting whistle gave new employees the opportunity to become acquainted and foremen time to plan for the next day's work. Stomachs filled with a bountiful supper, friends discussed past experiences as they ambled back to the bunkhouse. Once inside, several weary men lounged on steel-frame cots, reading or chatting with a neighbor while others sat on powder boxes whittling, greasing their boots, or playing cards.

One evening as I watched a card game, a timber faller, perched on the edge of his bunk, read aloud to himself while the rigging-slinger, a mid-level boss, studied a dog-eared pocket dictionary. Each snuff user kept a gallon can nearby for a spittoon. The saw-filer, an accomplished carver, brushed aside the shavings, closed his knife, then turned to me. "Where did you come from?"

Before I could reply, the arrogant rigging-slinger, a born fabricator, interrupted. "Hellfire," he bellowed, "he didn't come from nowhere. You see, an old eagle laid a perfectly round egg. She couldn't make the darn thing lay still, and it kept rolling out from under her. Man, how she hated that blasted egg! Finally, she kicked it from the nest, and the darn thing landed in a nice soft bed of moss." The card players, exchanging knowing glances, discontinued their game and devoted full attention to the yarn-spinner. Readers put aside books and magazines while others cocked an ear, anticipating a bit of humor. In spite of the ludicrous narrative, the tall tales usually contained a philosophical slant which caused others to marvel at his insight. Assured he had everyone's attention, the slinger continued, "Well, the sun came out for seven days and shined on that damn egg. On the seventh day, out pops this kid, all decked out in cork boots, black underwear, overalls, and everything else, ready for the woods. So, here he is, a bit small but the cook's grub, a few cans of snuff, and a weekend in town with the ladies will grow him up."

Eyes gleaming, the storyteller paused and stared into the bare rafters as though seeking guidance from above. Moments later, the request evidently granted, he resumed the anecdote.

"Now there's only one problem with all of this. The constant rolling back and forth across that old eagle's nest caused the kid to become a tramp, like the rest of us damn timber beasts, moving from place to place, never satisfied. So we'll spend the rest of our lives, forever restless, looking for just the right camp, the right job, the right woman—of course, never finding any of them."

The slinger, intentionally or not, had diverted interest from my past life. We became close friends.

Logging Area

Chapter 6

The Arena

The more time I spent with the renegade tramps, the stronger my desire to learn the trade. Each evening I badgered seasoned woodsmen for answers to nagging questions. Their replies, often derisive but generally sincere and informative, brought forth the better side of the nomads, and I prospered.

For several months, astute loggers directed and monitored a beginner's progress, carefully guiding him through hazardous situations. Even so, the shortcomings of man and the unpredictable forces of nature could steal a life in seconds—a fact imprinted in my mind each day.

One morning I overheard the side-rod call the supervising hook-tender aside and ask, "We need another man on the landing. Can the kid handle second-loading until we get someone with experience?"

"Yeah," came the immediate reply, "but that old head-loader's a tough guy to work for. Mark my words, he'll give the kid a bad time."

"They'll have to get along for a few days. We can't shut down the loading," the side-rod growled, ignoring the hook-tender's warning. "Send him to the spar."

Delighted with the promotion, I ran to the loading area, where men placed huge tongs on logs so they could be loaded onto railway cars. Here I learned the hard way that each man has a responsibility to both himself and those with whom he works.

As the hook-tender had predicted, the old loader, furious about having an inexperienced youth working with him, continuously cursed and growled at me. "Damn it, get those tongs on the log right. What the hell are you doing here any-how? You've only been in the woods a few days, and you think you can handle loading."

Sympathetic to my plight, others assisted when possible, but few men, seasoned or not, could work for the cantankerous fellow more than a week or two without a serious confrontation.

"Don't let him buffalo you," one man cautioned. "He's a big bag of wind and only a fair head-loader, but the company keeps him because there's no one better in the area. He tries to lay blame on everyone else for his mistakes. Be careful, or he'll try it on you."

The loader had lost one eye in a barroom fight; consequently, he cocked his head to the side and seemed never to be looking directly at anything. A whiskey voice, little more than a gravelly mumble, and a crooked right forefinger further complicated his ability to convey instructions to assistants. Seasoned loggers could usually comprehend the ambiguous gestures and mumbles, but unfamiliar with log loading, I remained the target for the loader's criticisms.

Two large tongs hung from the loading boom. One placed at each end of a log usually handled average sized timber, but extra large logs required steel cable slings, called straps, to carry them from the ground to the railway cars. That morning one log, so large it required straps, lay almost touching another length of timber equal in size.

Realizing the tongs were too small, but uncertain what to do, I watched the old loader at the far end. Another onslaught. "Get a strap on your end. What the hell do you think you're supposed to do, just stand there and look?"

A fellow worker, trying to prevent further assault, shoved a strap into my hand and gave instructions as we ran toward my end. Unfortunately, we arrived to find that the sling could not be completed without one of us getting between the six foot giants; so, I leaped down between them and knelt to push the strap under.

The loader already had his strap placed, and for some unknown reason, he must have signaled the donkey-puncher, for the motor roared and the lines tightened causing the log to move. Perhaps noticing that my strap had not been hooked to complete the sling, the puncher, as any efficient operator would do, stopped the motor but to no avail. The disturbance had rolled the logs together with a thud.

Although the log I was kneeling beside shifted slightly, it was the other that rolled. I had heard the thud but gave it little thought, for most important at that moment was to push the strap under and complete the sling.

Now I heard wild shouting. "For Christ sakes!" One man screamed. "The kid's between those logs!" His words, both wild and threatening, prodded everyone into action.

"Get the cats in here!" another bellowed. "We've got to separate those logs."

"Damn it, puncher, what's the matter with you?" the loader squalled. "No one told you to move that log. We're supposed to get twenty loads out of here today. Now look what you've done. Blow the whistle!"

Only then did I understand the situation—trapped like a wild animal. Scooting backward toward the end resolved nothing, for branches and rocks blocked the way. A frantic lunge forward seemed to curb mounting panic. "Got to make them hear me," I muttered through clenched teeth, but when I drew in deeply to shout, fir needles and pieces of bark rushed in with the dust-filled air and only a croaking wheeze escaped.

"Hey, in there, can you hear …" another asked, but his inquiry, now muted by blasts from the donkey whistle, became garbled and segmented. The alarm, overwhelming and sinister, echoed through the timber and ravines: man injured!

Luckily, I had been on hands and knees when the movement occurred. However, a large bulge on one log kept them from rolling completely together, leaving just enough room to squirm forward or back but not enough to squeeze up through the opening, so it seemed.

With no alternative, I again scanned the gap between the logs, mentally measuring my body, then the space. But now I could hear the cats coming. No! I thought, don't disturb either of those logs. That bulge is the only thing keeping them from rolling completely together. Got to get out before the cats get here.

Frantically, I crouched on my knees and raised my upper body. Even though my head might have gone up through, my shoulders, now crosswise to the opening, held me down. I turned, but lacked the strength to push from the crouched position. If I could get one, or both arms up through and brace them, maybe I'd be able to lift and shove myself out.

Optimistically, I thrust one arm up through the opening. Then I felt them. Two huge hands grabbed my wrist and pulled, but my head and shoulders refused to cooperate.

"He's here but I need another hand or two," the voice shouted. "Just hold tight, kid, and we'll have you out of there in no time."

Three men leaped onto the logs and gathered around the opening. First, one fellow fished out my other wrist, then the other two, an inch at a time, worked my head, shoulders, hips, and legs upward. A few tense moments, then shouts and laughter announced victory.

They looked me over from head to foot as I raised to hands and knees, then stood, wobble-legged, and sucked in cool fresh air. Evidently unscathed, but still uncertain about details of the ordeal, I turned and peered warily back into the dark hole which, only moments before, had imprisoned me.

"By Gawd!" one of my rescuers drawled. "We thought you were a goner. It's a good thing you're a little fellow. If you'd been much bigger, or the space smaller, we'd never been able to drag you out of there. If you decide to do that again, better take off a few pounds. Us old guys can't stand all that tugging and sweating."

The loader, mouth gaping in disbelief, held his tongue, but not for long. "What the hell were you doing down in there anyhow? You damn kids are more bother than you're worth."

Ignoring the loader, the other men, no strangers to close calls, ribbed me further to show their relief, then headed back to work. However, as we took our positions, my supervisor, the hook-tender, walked onto the landing. Someone had already told him.

Acquaintances knew the fellow to be a jovial Scotsman who thrived on humor; yet, it was best not to cross him, for he could send a much larger man to the hospital and had done so on several occasions.

Eyes narrowed in anger and muscles tensed for action, he lengthened his stride and crossed the landing, stopped head-on before the loader and bellowed, "That was your doing! Now, pay attention to this, you miserable son-of-a-bitch! If anything happens to that kid, you'll answer to me. And mind you, it won't be nice. You won't be loading logs again."

So persuasive was the attack that the loader, like a child being chastised, retreated one faltering step at a time, babbling denials and excuses.

His threat completed, the hook-tender turned and directed a warning scowl toward the puncher who, knowing that he shared responsibility, stared at the ground.

Now my supervisor, his intent fully understood, turned and passed by others who had witnessed the tongue lashing, all grateful for his stand on the matter. Each man offered an approving nod and a smile of gratitude as my champion left the area.

For me, the past hour had been a jumble of disconcerting events—nothing made sense. My resentment toward the loader had increased by the minute. True, the logs had rolled together with me in between. Everyone seemed upset except me. Was I too inexperienced or dumb to realize the consequences of my error, or that of the loader, or the puncher? But beyond that loomed a more disturbing question: Why hadn't I stood up to the fellow as the hook-tender had done? Was it some inner fear that I couldn't understand or even identify? Or was this obnoxious behavior

merely a part of the job, one to be expected,
but not questioned? Even so, my time would come.

Chapter 7

The Mentor

That evening the hook-tender took me aside to explain the consequences of unsafe work practices.

"I guess you know you're lucky to be alive," he began. Without waiting for a response, he continued, "That's probably as close to dying as you'll come without getting a scratch. Now, I'm going to tell you this just once. Never, never get between two logs without everyone knowing what you're doing, especially the head-loader and the donkey puncher."

Then, eyes boring into mine, he elaborated, using me as the example. "You're caught between the logs. The pressure forces the blood to your upper body and head. You scream in pain, but the pain remains until the logs are separated, which could take from several minutes to more than half an hour, depending on the situation. You're shrieking wildly all this time. Others stand by helplessly, for there's nothing they can do until equipment can be placed to move the logs.

"When they're finally separated, the blood rushes from your head, your screeching stops, your limp dead body drops to the ground."

He paused while two men passed on their way to the washroom, then added, "They tell me that in the old days the men carried the body off to one side and resumed work. Later, the train crew placed it on a loaded flatcar and when it and the logs arrived in camp, a coroner, sooner or later, came to claim the corpse."

By now, sweat soaked my clothing and oozed down into my boots. Evidently, I had committed the unpardonable sin—foolishly acting before thinking. But more than that, I suffered from having embarrassed my mentor.

"These days," he continued, "the crew will probably carry you out on a stretcher, take the day off, and be back the next morning. Another man will be working in your place. You'll soon be forgotten.

"If anyone does remember you, it won't be for the good things. A careless worker earns no praise in the woods. The thinking is that you should never have been in logging, or that you're better off dead than being paralyzed in bed for life, or crazier than a pet coon because you got your head done in."

Feeling irresponsible, I wondered if the company would permit me to continue working on the landing—or even with the man who now stood before me.

"When you're working in the woods," the sage resumed, "you can't afford to relax one split second from the time you arrive on the job in the morning until you leave at night. A broken branch, no larger than four inches thick and two feet long, falling from a tree, can pulverize your head beyond recognition. A worn steel cable can break. If you're in its deadly path, you'll be sliced to ribbons. Many hazards are unpredictable, but most can be avoided if you're on your toes."

At that moment, my thoughts flashed back to the loader and I blurted, "I'd like to bash his darn face in."

"If you're talking about the loader, he wasn't deliberately trying to kill you," the hook-tender explained patiently. "The man is just careless and he'll get his sooner or later. He dislikes working with inexperienced young men. I know it's difficult, taking all that guff, but if you get into a fight with him while you're on the job, the company will blackball you, and you'll never work here again. Just ignore his rotten comments and do your part the best you know how. You won't be working on the landing forever."

Maybe not, but I still resented the man. I couldn't figure out why I stood for his insults. I'd never been a coward. When I was in school and someone made fun of my name, I punched him in the nose. What had changed? Was it my eyes, the work, or was it that I had been raised not to question my elders? Whatever it was, I'd had enough.

If I exchange insults with him, will others resent my obnoxious behavior, or will they admire me for standing up to the man?

If the interchanges involve my poor vision, will the company have any alternative but to fire me?

Should I meet him in town and have it out in a dark alley, chancing a beating because of poor night vision?

For several days I tolerated the loader's remarks, but finally realized my work, regardless of sight loss or age, matched that of the more experienced. Time to defend my character. To insure there would be no down-in-the-dirt fight causing me to be fired, I'd challenge him from a distance.

At the next harangue, I cut him off with, "That's enough of your nonsense. Close your filthy trap and forget all the trash!"

"You bastard," he retorted, "No son-of-a-bitch talks to me like that!"

Immediately, the reference to my lineage incited uncontrollable anger and hate. I charged. To hell with the job!

The loader, completely surprised, squared off to meet the challenge but became tangled in his own feet and fell full length to the ground. Knowing he could never regain an upright position before I arrived, the old warrior rolled to his back, arms extended and legs cocked.

Careful, I thought, watch those legs. He's a seasoned street fighter. I had seen it before. From that position, even the smallest person could kick like a mule.

As I neared, the legs shot out with the speed of a rattler's strike. Fortunately, they only grazed my pants. One step to his side placed me in position to command the situation. "One move old man, and I'll kick that good eye from your head. If you throw that arm up to protect it, I'll break every rib in your filthy body."

Looking down, I was startled at the clarity with which I could see details on the salt and pepper stubble, the snagged yellow teeth, the battered nose, the good eye staring upward with its white grossly exaggerated, but most disturbing, that empty red eye socket. Visions of blind Sam, the beggar, flashed through my mind. He had two empty red eye sockets, not just one. Was I willing to make it two for the loader? Not really.

For some reason, the man now seemed in a daze, for his head shifted from side to side without that good eye focusing. Mercilessly, the sun shined directly into the weathered face, compromising his only defense. Do's and don'ts now caused second thoughts about hasty threats. Grandpa's contradictory quotes from the Bible: "Thou shalt not …, An eye for an eye …, Do unto others …," or the plainsman's code, "Never hit a man when he's down," but "… turn the other cheek," never again.

Now the loader, completely subdued, mumbled, and grunted incoherently while others watched and listened gleefully. "Get him kid!" one bystander urged. But the most vicious came from a person who had also felt the sting of the loader's foul mouth. "Give him a boot that will drive him into the next county."

Ignoring the audience, I stood over the groveling bully for a moment, then turned and took my usual position at the opposite end of the logs. No one mentioned the incident to the side-rod, not even the loader.

Now old-timers went out of their way to become better acquainted, offering words of wisdom and caution during difficult times. No more confrontations or close calls occurred while I worked on the landing.

Clearing a Douglas Fir for Rigging

Spar Trees and Rigging

Spar Tree and Rigging

Spar Trees and Rigging

84

Chapter 8

Timber Beasts

Each weekend, unattached loggers migrated into town where they drank, fought, and spent time with "the girls". Why women, many my age or younger, sold their bodies to these uncultured rogues, puzzled me. Even more perplexing, why did these rovers show no interest in marriage or even possessing women? It was share and share alike. The gregarious females were convenient to drink with, to laugh with, to love with—all without commitment: no demands, no promises, no regrets—only the moment. The maligned women stroked and nourished the men's precarious existence, stabilizing the heartbeat and backbone of the logging industry.

Their minds and bodies rested and re-charged, the renegade loggers retreated to so-bricty, celibacy, and life-threatening work for a week or more. When they trickled back into camp Sunday evening, usually broke and hung over, a few hours sleep and fresh air soon revived the weekend warriors. The hardier drinkers who held a large nest egg returned later in the week. Others moved on to the next camp. Many avoided cat logging and sought outfits that conducted high-lead logging (pronounced high-leed, not high-led).

Curious about the tramps' tendency to favor one method over the other, I asked an old-timer to explain.

"Well," he began, "as I understand, years before the great depression and even the First World War, accessible tracts of timber had been removed by logging companies. Realizing the dollar value of virgin forests on the steeper slopes and marshlands where horse, oxen, or tractor logging proved unprofitable, the industry sought a method for logging all terrains: level, steep, or swamp.

"As you know, timber fallers felled the trees and buckers cut the downed timber into log lengths as they continue to do. But long before your time, skilled teamsters used oxen or horses to drag the logs from outlying areas to a central landing, where they were laboriously rolled into flumes, rivers, or millponds."

"Did you ever use oxen or horses?" I inquired.

"You bet," he boasted, then resumed. "Over time, bridges, dams, distance, and other impediments, often for political reasons, limited the use of waterways for moving logs to the mills.

Consequently, timber was then transported by rail or trucks, making the business less profitable. But that was only part of the problem; getting the felled timber from the outlying areas to the landing for loading remained slow and costly. The tremendous size and weight of the logs caused them to dig into the ground or lodge behind tree stumps, generating costly delays and frayed tempers."

He paused for a pinch of snuff, examined a scratch on one boot and carried on. "Greased skid roads became popular but the procedures remained cumbersome. Later, when steam donkeys, called yarders, came on the scene, the operation yielded only modest profits.

"Years of trial and error finally developed the high-lead system," my friend continued. "Initially, innovative men hung a lead block (guide pulley) from a high stump, threaded the donkey mainline through it and pulled the heavy steel cable out with a horse where it was attached to a log. This lead-block guided the cable evenly onto the donkey drum as it dragged the log toward the landing. Raised only ten to fifteen feet off the ground, the lead block lifted the forward end of the logs enough to warrant going higher. They say that adventuresome fallers, balanced on two by eight-inch by five-foot springboards inserted into chopped notches, ascended to heights of sixty feet, where they cut the top from a tree designated to be a high-lead spar."

"Really? That high?" I questioned.

Rolling large brown eyes, he flashed a devilish smile, and replied, "Who knows? You can take it or leave it." With that, he carried on. "Rather than using a horse to drag the mainline, a drum holding medium-sized cable, the haulback, and a small utility strawline drum were added to the donkey. This three-eighth-inch strawline pulled the haulback up through a block hung high in the spar, out to the far edge of the felled timber, through a small block, then through another farther along the perimeter, and back to the spar, forming a triangle which encompassed the area to be logged. The haulback and mainline were connected by the butt rigging, a series of heavy-duty steel barrel swivels and links with two or three short cable chokers dangling from the swivels. The haulback pulled the butt rigging, chokers, and mainline out into the felled timber, where one choker was placed around each log.

"Chokers in place and everyone in the clear, a 'go ahead' signal relayed to the yarder puncher by the whistle-punk sent the logs skidding, bouncing, and rolling, destroying small saplings and forest vegetation as the mainline cracked and popped like high-powered rifle shots."

Little did I realize that his next words would change my life forever.

"Over time," he rambled on, "experienced loggers, known as high-climbers or high-riggers, developed the skill of climbing, topping, and rigging high-lead spars. Instead of standing on springboards, they used belt, spurs, and a special climbing rope to scale the trees. Thus, the high-lead spar averaging 150 feet high, rigged with two sets of guylines, lead-blocks, and a log-loading boom, similar to a mast and boom on a sailing ship, made clear-cut logging extremely lucrative, destructive, and dangerous.

"Now," he added, eyes gleaming, "you've only worked around the cats and helped load at a short spar tree rigged with a loading boom where things are rather predictable and safe. But until a man has helped rig a high-lead tree, worked around the powerful and speedy yarders, escaped the maze of moving cables, run from saplings flying in unpredictable directions, dodged airborne chunks of wood flung skyward by errant lines, or scrambled to avoid a rolling log, he can't imagine the excitement. Unlike working behind the lumbering cats, every day is crammed with new experiences. When a logger gets hooked on the high-lead, he'll never be content with less. Yes, even the narrow escapes from death own a spot in the addictive lifestyle."

With my imagination and blood racing wildly, I momentarily longed to become a part of this reckless and chaotic life—simultaneously captive and conqueror. Was I ready? Did I have a choice?

Within weeks I became acquainted with the high-climber, the man who held the most demanding and dangerous job in the logging industry. Respected by other workers and bosses alike, he knew the business inside and out. While hanging rigging in a spar tree, the high-climber became the total boss. When he spoke, everyone hurried to do his bidding. This top dog of the loggers was never required nor asked to participate in work on the ground, for he needed to be available at a minute's notice when and if trouble arose at any one of several high-lead spar trees.

About forty years old and dyed-in-the-wool Irish, this man had bushy eyebrows that dominated a leathery face, a muscular body that seemed completely at home in the woods, and a sharp mind that prepared him for emergencies. After we became friends, he often loaned me his belt and spurs to practice climbing the smaller trees during the lunch break.

When the starting whistle caught me up a tree at work-time, the side-rod filled in, for this old Irishman habitually overstayed the weekends, leaving the outfit without a climber Monday morning. With experience, I could take over until he returned.

One Saturday night I found the climber standing alone outside a tavern door, soused to the hilt. Confident the liquor had loosened his tongue, I seized the opportunity to garner a few secrets about climbing.

No such luck. He ignored my inquiries, assumed an inebriated dignity, and stared through and beyond me as though questioning my existence. Finally, he blurted, "Just remember this, kid. There's no such thing as a brave man in the woods." With that, he wheeled, staggered, fell against the door frame, regained his balance, then followed his protruding eyebrows back into the barroom.

Beyond a doubt, he had no wife and home to return to each night after a hard, cold, and wet day in the woods. The climber's home, which seemed true for most tramp loggers, was either a hotel room in a small town near the logging or a camp bunkhouse shared with ten or twelve other men.

Over time, I missed the companionship of others my age. That strange urge to move on, the one which had plagued me as I drifted from family to family during my school years, clouded my thinking at unpredictable intervals. Time to get going. Each week the impulse became stronger until the nomadic tendency prevailed.

Friday after work, I packed and hitched a ride into the lowlands, which extended from the Cascade foothills to the coastal range. Older tramp loggers had mentioned the many small gyppos and large logging firms in the area. Consequently, moving from one job to another became a simple matter.

"Hell," one fellow proclaimed, "I've had two jobs in one day. I went to work for one outfit in the morning, quit before noon, then walked over the hill and finished the day for more money. They're always looking for good men."

Selecting Chehalis-Centralia, twin cities in central Washington, I found lumber mills running full blast and a Boeing Aircraft division which employed young military rejects, older men and women technicians, and several academically-minded supervisors.

Needless to say, madams, along with their "girls" and pimps, inhabited the downtown areas. Taverns and dance halls flourished, and gas, although rationed, could be obtained with proper connections. Life, an exciting and expensive fantasia, engrossed the waking hours of those who could survive the tempo.

Hellbent on becoming a high-climber as good as the old Irishman, I strapped on the belt and spurs at every opportunity and scrambled up the nearest tree. Foremen liked my guts, enthusiasm, and agility. In the back of my mind, I knew that my chance would come. Then, rather than being the kid, I'd be the climber.

Loggers on Spring Boards
Felling Cedar Tree 20' from ground in Washington
image# 10114(b)   D. Kinsey Collection
Whatcom Museum of History and Art
Bellingham, Washington

Chapter 9

New Friend

Content to spend an occasional weekend in either Centralia or Chehalis and work in the lowland or the upland camps, I accepted any job which moved me closer to the revered title of "high-climber."

One windless October morning, the side-rod hailed me as I jumped from the speeder. "There's a new hook-tender on the other side. We need a good man to work with him, so how about you going over there to set chokers for a few days?"

"OK," I replied, hastily adding, "Who is he? What's he like?" How vividly I remembered the close call when I first went to work on the landing with the cantankerous one-eyed loader.

"I don't know. I've never seen him before. You'll only be over there a few days," the foreman assured.

Determined to make a favorable impression on my new boss, I arrived breathless at the work-place to find a weathered old Swede working with an intensity that might alarm the average employee. When he failed to acknowledge my arrival, I announced myself. Tall and lean, the veteran turned with an appraising glance, then spoke with a soft but firm Scandinavian accent. "Put these chokers on the two logs over there and then help me hook them up."

Perhaps checking my worth, the aging woodsman watched closely for a short time, then turned and went about his work. Minutes later, six logs, each encircled with a choker, lay randomly on the ground. The caterpillar tractor backed into place and we gathered the choker eyes, placed them on the cat bullhook, then ran a safe distance from the moving logs.

The cat roared as the skinner winched the forward end of the Douglas firs from the ground, then maneuvered the powerful machine, its arch, and the trailing timber along the winding road toward the landing.

For the next few minutes, the hook-tender and I dug like badgers to get holes under the logs that lay flat on the ground, making it easier and faster to encircle each length of timber with a choker when the cat returned. Our preparatory work completed, we stood, wiped sweat-soaked brows, then faced each other with respectful smiles—two loggers, one experienced, one not, but cut from the same cloth.

Shortly my partner seated himself on a rotting windfall, then withdrew a round can of Copenhagen snuff from a worn shirt pocket. The tell-tale ring on the fabric indicated that the snuff can had been a constant companion. Unlike the red felt hunting hats worn by most loggers, his hat, a faded blue, was shaped like that of an Alpine herder's and sat comically atop a distinctive head.

Never before had I seen such huge, rough hands. Well-greased boots failed to hide the clean tops of the white 100 percent wool socks. Bibless overalls, cut off just above boot tops for safety in the brush, hung loosely from worn suspenders. Indulging himself from the round can, he then held it out to me, but I refused the generous offer with a polite, "No, thank you."

Back for another turn, the cat, arriving in a cloud of dust, dropped the chokers, then turned while we again threw ourselves into the work. Once more, the cat and logs departed for the landing. With a few minutes to spare, our conversation involved only work—no probing questions as to home, family, or friends.

By this time, I had become accustomed to the pleasant odor of freshly cut timber, the sawdust, shavings, and chips left by the razor-sharp saws and axes, and the crushed fir, hemlock and cedar needles, all as yet free from the dust or mud created by the cats, but not for long. For five days, we devoted our minds and bodies to supplying the landing with logs, leaving nothing but brush, uprooted or broken saplings, and a maze of cat roads leading to the spar.

That Friday evening the hook-tender and I rode to the base camp with other workers. Unlike the wildest ruffians, my partner quietly made his way through the crowd and disappeared.

Sunday night the train crew hooked the locomotive onto the railway caboose. With its years of commercial use long past, the archaic car, justifiably identified as a "crummy", creaked and swayed along the tracks as it transported the motley crew back to the upper camp.

Air inside the conveyance, reeking with snuff, cigarette smoke and freshly greased boots, became even more contaminated as the red-hot potbellied stove belched smoke each time a man opened its door to add wood.

Muted concerns regarding a pending strike now replaced the boisterous joking of the previous Friday. I hadn't seen the hook-tender enter the crummy. What would the coming week hold?

Shortly before dawn, the speeder waited near the upper camp bunkhouses, and we methodically squeezed into the small conveyance for the short ride to work. Still no hook-tender. At the landing, everyone disembarked to begin another trying week. I finally spotted the old Swede as he leaped from the top step to the ground several feet below. What a relief. Unlike a few other men who returned bleary-eyed and hung over, he seemed fresh and alert.

We hurried to the work place, secured lunch bags in a safe dry location, then took up where we had left off Friday afternoon. As the day progressed, bits of personal information passed between us.

"How long have you been working here?" the hook-tender questioned, adding, "Everyone seems to know you."

"Just long enough to become acquainted," I replied, then asked, "Do you like working in this area?"

"I'm not used to working with these cats; I'm more of a high-lead man. We usually work closer to the coast where the ground is chopped up and steep."

"I want to be a climber," slipped out, before considering how presumptuous it must have sounded to the seasoned logger. Yet, I had finally given voice to a burning aspiration—one about which I knew very little.

Doubtless, troublesome thoughts and questions filtered through the wise old mind. What has brought this young man to the woods? How long would it be before he was injured or killed? What options did he have? Should he be encouraged?

The cat came and went, once, twice and three times without a word spoken. After the fourth turn, the hook-tender motioned me to sit on a nearby log.

"Why do you want to be a climber?" His voice reflected both interest and concern.

"It pays a lot. Other loggers respect you. And, well, I guess, you're the boss when rigging a tree. You can make things happen as you want."

Taking a pinch of snuff from the trusty can, then carefully choosing his words, the old-timer launched into an analysis of my ambition.

"Is it because you don't see so well that you'd like to be a climber?" With that, as though giving me a chance to think through a reply, he looked into the distance.

Taken by surprise, yet knowing deep inside that my poor vision must be more obvious than I imagined, a suitable reply was long in coming. Finally, a mumbled question. "How did you know?"

My new friend, more observant than expected, began with an uncharacteristic kindness in his voice, "You don't follow the flight of the smaller birds. There have been times when you don't notice the signals I give to the cat skinner when I want him to do something like turning around and backing into a certain place. Unless you are looking directly at them, you often miss seeing moving objects. It came to me when we got on the crummy. You passed by and didn't recognize me in the dark."

Now the returning cat interrupted, so we worked in silence until the machine again dragged its load toward the landing.

"I've thought the matter over," the hook-tender said, getting right to the point. "If you continue in the woods, you should probably become a climber. You'd be more in control in that position than you are working on the ground. And, as you said, you'd be the boss while the tree is being rigged."

"Yes, I thought of that," I replied jubilantly, "and I'd never be more than an arm's length away from my work." He understood my situation.

"Now comes the problem," the Swede went on. "Around here, you're thought of as an excellent worker, but still a boy, not an experienced logger who knows how to rig a high-lead tree. In many ways your youth is against you. Because others your age have gone to war, most loggers are at least ten years older. A few may be reluctant to give you a chance. This is a tough business but hang in there."

"I've heard as much," I replied, knowing he was correct for my twenty-first birthday had just slipped by, and many still called me kid. "Although the climber who is here now likes me, he'll never let me go into the tree with him while he's hanging rigging. I've never ridden to the top of a rigged spar to see how it's done."

The cat returned, and we finished the day without further discussion of the matter.

During after-supper raps in the bunkhouse, other men called my partner Swede, Ole, Highball, or whatever, his actual name seemed unimportant, but on the job it was the title "hook-tender" that commanded respect.

Several days later, the cat failed to return on time, so the hook-tender jumped onto a large log and scanned the area. No cat. With that, he turned to me and said, "I'd better go in and see what's up. Why don't you stay here and dig a few choker-holes?"

Fifteen minutes later the hook-tender called me to the landing. Anxious to be involved in resolving the problem, I arrived at the spar, where nothing about the rigging seemed unusual.

Yet, the loading crew was nowhere in sight. Curiosity aroused, I again appraised the situation and noticed that the small cable passline used to pull rigging and the high-climber up the spar had been hooked to the donkey strawline drum.

The hook-tender, amused by my inquisitive nature and eagerness to assist, pointed to the six-foot chain attached to the loose end of the passline. Baffled by the gesture, I glanced first to the waiting chain, then back to my friend.

Having had his fun, my supervisor announced, "The locomotive and a bunch of loaded cars jumped the track a few miles down the hill. They took the cats down to put them back and then repair the tracks. Now's the time for you to see what it looks like up in the tree. Sit in the passchain, and I'll give signals to the puncher."

Beaming from ear to ear, I looped the single strand of chain around my legs, and bobbed my head, indicating readiness.

"Going up," the hook-tender signaled. The puncher turned the friction lever on the drum that held the passline. With pounding heart I felt the chain tighten around my legs. Up, up, slowly at first and then faster.

"When you come to the guy wires and other lines, kick out from the tree so you won't get caught under them," ordered the hook-tender as I passed the boom. A few feet below the haulback block, another order, "Kick out now."

Kicking out with all my strength, I swung out from the tree much farther than necessary. By the time I had passed the block, my body had turned, placing my back toward the spar. With a loud thud and a simultaneous grunt, I absorbed the shock and became momentarily breathless. The hook-tender, eyes riveted on me, signaled the puncher to stop.

"Are you all right? Do you want to come down?"

"No," I gasped, "I mean yes, I'm OK. Don't let me down now. I want to go on to the top as soon as I get my breath and get this darn chain back down where it belongs." The chain had slipped up my legs a few inches.

Eighty feet above the ground, my back to the tree, I ferociously gripped the small passline and attempted to lift my body so the chain would slide down my legs. No such luck. Imbedded in the folds of my clothing, it stubbornly maintained its position. Finally, moving one leg backward, I touched the tree and shoved. To my surprise, my body turned and again faced the tree. However, the chain had slipped a few inches higher.

Dangerously close to moving up over my hips, the unwieldy loop, at least for the moment, continued to support me. Beyond this point, I could lose my grip, slide from the chain and plummet eighty feet to the ground. Little by little, the strength left my hands and arms. Several deep breaths helped but for only a moment. Glancing down to the haulback block a few feet below, a possible solution flashed through my mind.

On the ground, the hook-tender mumbled concern. Then, simultaneously we both voiced the solution.

"I'm just above the haulback block and—," I shouted, but the hook-tender's booming voice interrupted.

"We'll let you down slowly until you can stand on the block. Now, when you get your feet located so they won't slip, we'll give you a few inches of slack on the passline, and you can move the chain down where it belongs. Now I'll tell the puncher what we're doing. Hold tight a few seconds."

Clutching the passline with one hand, feet planted on the block and my head touching the tree, I managed to balance myself while removing the chain from the folds in my clothing and wriggle back where I could again sit comfortably in the loop.

"Pick up the slack!" I shouted, my voice echoing relief and joy. The chain tightened, and I again became airborne. That hair-raising experience caused me to carefully regulate kicks away from the spar. The acrobatics, as frightening as they had been for the first few moments, now gave me an indescribable thrill.

Stopping above the top guy wires, more than 110 feet above the ground, I looked downward. The cable web, the huge blocks, the loading boom, the loading donkey, and the loaded railway cars, so strange from above. I had heard that if a spar had not grown in an area suitable for a level landing, one had to be dragged into place and raised. What an exciting time that might be.

"You'd better come down now," the hooktender shouted. "I hear the cats coming back."

One last look at the configuration to fix it in my mind, then, kicking out so as to miss the various lines and blocks, I arrived safely on the ground. Rubber-legged and reeking with sweat, I forgot to thank the old-timer for making the experience possible; nevertheless, we glanced at each other with a shared secret and a mutual understanding.

Within minutes, we had returned the passline to its original position, then hurried back to the logging area. A cat waited and as we approached, the skinner announced, "The side-rod saw what you guys were doing, and he's madder than a wet hen."

"He'll get over it," the hook-tender retorted. "If he doesn't, he'll be mad a hell for a long time." His statement, delivered with finality, ended the conversation.

Time and again, we sent the cat to the landing and prepared for the return trip. A few minutes before quitting time, the old Swede retrieved his sweatshirt from under a dry log and came to sit near me.

Thoughtfully, he began, "You know, I couldn't have done what you did today, but you'll need to top and rig a few trees before you can claim the title of climber. Even before that, learn all the ins and outs of high-lead logging. Until then, you'll have to live with the way others feel about your age. It won't be easy. Most men have worked in the woods several years before they even try; few make it. Just remember the old saying, 'You never get so old or so wise that you can't learn from even the lowliest man'."

I nodded understanding. Then we gathered our jackets and walked to the landing in silence—a man-to-man silence tolerated only by the best of friends.

Sunday evening, the hook-tender failed to show up for the long ride back to the upper camp. Nor did he return Monday morning. I didn't even know his name.

Chapter 10

Learning The Trade

"The cat-skinner didn't show up, so you'll have to go over to the other side and help them today," the side-rod ordered. "They're rigging a spar over there. You've never been around where they've really been highballing it, so keep your eyes open."

"OK. But what happened to the hook-tender?" I asked.

"I don't know for sure. Probably just needed to move on. He's a good man. But you know how it is, these guys come and go. The best high-lead loggers move from time to time. They learn a lot that way."

"Did you ever move around like that?"

"Um, well, some, but packing my bedroll and eating in those cook houses got damn tiresome. If they had good cooks and women flunkies, you know what I mean, real waitresses, a man could survive, but some of them couldn't boil water without burning it. Watch your step over there today. They're waiting for you."

Turning, I sprinted toward a huge log, leaped and dug my calks into the bark and momentum carried me to the top where I dashed along the fallen giant. A long jump onto the stump from which the tree had fallen; one, two, three steps and a bound to a smaller log, and another, and another. Minutes later I arrived at the new landing to find men rushing from one task to another.

Immediately, the rigup hook-tender shouted to me. "Get a hammer and spikes out to that stump and then grab that strawline and give us a hand." Without pausing, he turned and bellowed to several other men, "Get hold of that guyline as it comes down and coil it over there." Cocking his arm in a strange position signaled the puncher to go ahead on the strawline, which had been attached to a large guyline coiled beneath the spar.

Immediately, the puncher tightened the friction lever, opened the throttle and the cables slithered through underbrush and over logs with unbelievable speed. The loose end whipped up and down, side to side, sometimes in circles, flinging chunks of wood into the air and uprooting seedlings. For the next two hours, small cables pulled larger ones out from the landing, around notched stumps, then back to the spar, ready to be hung at the top.

Only one guyline remained when, caught up in the frenzy and determined to make a good showing, I took a shortcut across the forty-foot coils—forbidden territory.

The steel cable seemed harmless, but as I neared the center, the top loop moved, gathered speed and bore down—a giant snare. Somehow I managed to leap over it, and the next, but the third bounced crazily across the uneven ground, making it impossible to judge its erratic approach. What to do?

Reversing direction resolved nothing, for the noose, now only a fraction its original size, came on without conscience. Rabbit-like reflexes, rather than reason, controlled my retreat. Run! Faster! This way! No! That way! Jump high! The glistening cable nipped at my heels as I sprang.

For certain, I desperately wished the heavy calk boots never to touch the ground, but they did and momentum propelled me forward, landing on knees and elbows as though repenting past sins. Now the cable definitely had the advantage.

Never before had I regained my feet so rapidly, but what had happened as I knelt for that split second? The entire episode seemed like a warped dream, for the cable now lay motionless, leaving me standing in an eight-foot circle, perplexed but grateful. Reality returned as I braced for the inevitable reprimand.

First, I heard the hook-tender's sarcastic chuckle. A derisive outburst intended to mortify. Then, the blistering question, "What's the matter kid? Are you afraid to die? You sure do a cute dance in those loops." His point made, humor turned to concern. "Don't worry, I had one eye on you. But you've got to be wary of all cables lying on the ground. If that last loop had caught you, it would have rolled you up into a ball then spit you out in shreds like a meat grinder making hamburger. Now get over here with me while this line goes out to the stump."

All morning, we scurried here and there, responding to the hook-tender's orders until a loud toot from the donkey whistle signaled lunch time. Everything stopped: tools dropped, lunch bags appeared, and lighthearted chatter replaced serious logging jargon—even the highball hook-tender joined in the revelry. Those who knew him were proud to be working with this wily old veteran, for his reputation stood unequaled.

Soft velvety mist drifted onto our sweat-soaked backs as we wolfed down monstrous steak sandwiches, gluttonous helpings of delicious cookies, and fresh fruit—all swilled down with steaming coffee. The food, the camaraderie, and the warm fire put us in a good mood. A few adventurous souls placed sandwiches on forked sticks and toasted them over the fire; however, during rigging up, noonday fires were infrequent—no time for luxury.

A few minutes prior to the invasive shriek of the donkey whistle announcing time for action, the old hook-tender moved away from the circle to meet the high-climber who had just arrived on the scene. They conferred for a time, talking, pointing and nodding as the conversation dictated. When rigging a spar, precise communication between the climber in the tree and the hook-tender on the ground became paramount. Their conversation completed, the hook-tender turned and goaded each man into action.

Pointing at one idle worker, he barked, "Get the passrope and passblock." The fellow, as though ignited by a flame, left the lunch-time circle, returning moments later with the items in hand. Before long, every man had an assignment which he completed with dispatch.

Now the climber, passrope tied to his belt and throwing wide loops in the climbing rope, dug the spurs into the thick bark and scaled the spar. He pulled up the passblock and looped the strap over the top, then used the rope to pull the 3/8-inch cable passline up through the block and back down. With one end of the passline attached to the donkey strawline drum and a pass-chain secured to the loose end, the climber and crew went to work. All rigging was raised or lowered by this pencil-sized steel cable.

First, the climber spiked four 2" x 6" x 40" steel plates near the top of the 150-foot spar. Next the guylines. "How much end do you want?" asked the hook-tender, now shouting up to the climber.

"About nine feet," the climber replied.

The hook-tender wrapped the chain around the guyline at nine feet, which left enough loose end to encircle the tree and plates, then attach it with a shackle. Outstretched arms measured approximately six feet and both hands spread, one foot. Although the climber seemed rather casual about the measurement, everyone knew that nine feet meant nine feet—not eight or ten. While he was in the tree, the climber became the boss.

Thirty-five minutes later, six guylines had been hung, and the climber, again sitting in the passchain, shouted, "Man on. Take up the slack." The chain gently tightened around his legs. A solitary "Yo" stopped all movement. Rope untied and dangling free, he kicked away from the spar bellowing, "Cut'er loose!" Without res-ervation, the puncher released the brake.

All eyes shot upward as the plummeting body emitted a primordial shriek and gyrated crazily through the 130-foot free-fall, culminating with the climber, as gently as a drifting feather, landing without his knees bending from the impact. New men stood wide-eyed, mouth gaping; old-timers seemed never to tire of the acrobatics.

Dedicated to their trade, these two tramp loggers, climber and puncher, traveled together from camp to camp, priding themselves in a job well done, adding the hair-raising descent for a momentary thrill. Besides, they both knew the flourish gave other crewmen something to talk about in the bunkhouses, taverns, and cathouses; their reputation had spread throughout the industry.

"Get the passline from the climber and tie it in the clear!" the hook-tender shouted to me before turning to give orders to other crew members.

"OK," I responded with pride. What an honor to assist the climber and be responsible for the sacred passline. As I took the chain, something about it seemed different. There it was—the secret to riding up and down the tree. This passchain, unlike the single chain I had used earlier, was double. One strand placed around each leg prevented the occupant from sliding through when kicking out from the tree.

Having completed the assigned task, I hastened back to be available for other duties. Ordered to the stump where the guylines were being secured, I found the men taking turns driving railroad spikes into the stump on either side of the cable, preventing the fiddle-string tight guy wire from slipping during the logging process.

One man, having completed his turn, handed the eight-pound sledge to me. "Have a turn at this," he gasped, breathless from the strenuous work.

"OK," I replied, eager to try my hand at something new. Confidently, I held a railroad spike next to the line and set it into the wood with a few taps. However, when I took the handle by the end and swung with all my strength, the heavy maul struck a glancing blow, sending the spike sailing midst others waiting their turn.

"Watch it!" one man exclaimed. "What the hell are you doing? Trying to kill one of us? Give me the damn hammer."

Embarrassed and disappointed with my performance, I watched and assisted in placing the next two wraps of the cable around the stump. Ignoring me, the other men made sure they handed the sledge to an experienced person. They talked and kidded among themselves but never included me. Later I learned that many men had lost eyes to wayward railroad spikes.

After the guywires had been tightened, the hook-tender called me to the tree, where I helped send rigging up to the climber. Shortly, several shrill blasts from a donkey whistle echoed in the distance.

"Did you hear that?" the hook-tender asked. Without waiting for a reply, he continued, "How many?"

"I'm not sure, but it sounded like five or six. It could have been more but I thought six," came my uncertain reply.

"You'd better go over to the high-lead side and see if something's wrong," the hook-tender ordered.

Always quick to respond and needing a break, I abandoned the work and ran toward the spar about one-half mile over the ridge.

Why run? Most men would have walked briskly, but run, no. To me running free compensated for the torturous hours pulling and tugging on stubborn tongs and cables under the direction of log-hungry supervisors. Beyond that, it seemed to curb a lifelong desire to move on.

Within minutes, I trotted down the slope to find men carrying a stretcher toward the speeder. One fellow who had witnessed the accident from a distance, now hurried toward me and shared a few fragmented details, then moved on.

The bad news ran cold through my veins as I stood rooted in disbelief. Only then did I realize that the man on the stretcher and I had become as brothers, meeting each night after supper to toss the bull and plan for our next weekend in town. Having similar pasts, we laughed and joked about our youthful dreams and disappointments.

Before I could reach the landing, the crew had placed him into the speeder, then climbed in and sat two or three on either side. Now the conveyance moved slowly along the rails. No need to hurry. As it passed, my hand raised for a final goodbye. Then, for a split second, I wondered why they hadn't told him that I stood nearby so he could wave back.

The speeder jerked and creaked its way from sight before I turned and stood for several minutes, my eyes fixed on the mindless log that had so brutally snatched his life—rage and grief churned in my guts.

In time, I trudged back toward the spar where the rigup crew continued at breakneck speed. Catching sight of me, the hook-tender demanded, "What's wrong over there?"

"The rigging-slinger got killed," I replied sullenly. "Darn! It was a chunk no longer than twelve feet and sixteen inches through. He had been helping a chokerman before the haulback knocked the chunk loose from the cold-deck pile, and it fell on him. He only lasted a few minutes, they said."

"You two were friends, weren't you?" he asked.

"Yeah," I croaked, adding nothing more.

"Go down to the creek and get a drink. You can wait there for a few minutes until the climber gets down and the speeder comes to take us in. We'll finish rigging this tree tomorrow."

As we climbed into the speeder, the others discussed the accident at length. "The slinger was a good man," commented a chokerman who worked with him. "He just got a little careless."

"He'd have been the first guy to give one of his chokermen hell for turning his back on a cold-deck pile while the lines were moving," suggested another.

"Christ," the punk added, "the damn haulback only moved five or six feet. The whiskers from the splice caught in the splintered end

119

and rolled it right on him. They needed about one foot of slack to get the damn choker hooked. I tried to warn him, but too late. The whole thing happened in about two seconds. We were going into town this weekend. Hell, he'd been holed up in camp for over a month, and he had a real wad to get rid of."

Spotting a doe and her fawn beside the tracks, a chokerman shouted, "Look at that beauty out there with that old doe. I'll have my sights on him next year."

"He'll be a spike, so you'd better be careful. If the game warden catches you, you'll land in the can for a while," cautioned the puncher.

Shouting and whooping, several tried to frighten the doe, so they could get a better look at the spotted fawn. Their minds diverted for a few moments, friends fell to discussions of drinking and other rowdy activities during weekend trips into town; thus, the death was put to rest.

The world told me that my friend was gone forever, but my mind refused to accept. No more than two days ago, he had discussed a personal matter with me. "I know you have no choice but to work in the woods right now, but don't hang around until logging gets into your blood. Sooner or later, your time will come, one way or the other. I've tried to get out several times, but it's too late. I last a week or so on some tiddlywinks job in town and finally have to leave. My mind and body refuse to accept city life. I'm sure as hell not going to be come a damn farmer, pitching hay, shoveling dung, and pulling teats the rest of my life."

The message came through loud and clear, for I had also decided against farming. We had shared a belly laugh over the prospect of sitting on a stool beside an old cow with her manure-covered tail switching us in the face as we cursed the day we were born.

"Someone's waiting for us down the track," the speeder driver announced, concern registering in his voice. "It sure looks like the Forest Service."

Stepping off the tracks as we neared, the ranger delivered an unwanted message. "We've got a bad fire up the spur about five miles. It's across the Cispus river, so if you go about one-half mile beyond the fire, there's a windfall you can cross on. I'll throw the switch and you can head on up there. The main camp is sending cats and other tools. Sack lunches and coffee will arrive before dark. You'll meet up with about forty men from the outfit across the valley. The superintendent and head-ranger are already there. Take your jackets. You'll be there all night, and we'll mop-up tomorrow if we get her under control."

"That area is steeper than a cow's face. I don't relish digging trails along that hillside in the dark," commented an old timer. "The cats won't do much good until the skinners loosen the fan belts and ford them across the river; even then, they'll have to work on steep ground and that can be dangerous as hell in the dark."

Falling into quiet discussions regarding the turn of events, we steeled ourselves for a tiresome and dangerous encounter with one of loggers' worst enemies—fire. Contrary to our hopes, the midday mist had dissipated.

Like a tethered balloon, the orange colored sun, its perimeter perfectly outlined as it descended into the highest plumes of ominous smoke, was soon completely obliterated by the raging inferno. Sparkling embers and burning chunks sucked into the updraft caused by the licking flames were propelled high above the scorched ground, to be cast like a fisherman's fly into the surrounding trees. Spot fires sprang up everywhere.

"If we can keep it on the ground and con-tain it with hand-tools until the cats get here, we've got a chance," the head-ranger assured. "There's already a small crew working along the ridge. You take your men and head up the right edge and I'll take the rest and work up the left," he suggested to the superintendent. "There's a creek beyond the first ridge, so take a pump, five hundred feet of hose, several five-gallon squirt cans, shovels, axes, and hoe-digs. Oh yeah, I forgot, there's a box canyon near the top. If you get caught in there, you'll never make it out."

"OK," the superintendent agreed. "We'll get a trail up the hill and then help those men at the top."

Chapter 11

The Demon—Fire!!

Already weary from the day's work, we selected tools and, without complaint, hurried to the windfall that was to serve as a footbridge. One by one, we balanced ourselves on the rotting tree and moved out over the glacial waters. Several yards from the bank, an upright limb blocked the path. Holding onto the branch with the free hand, we stepped around the obstruction, then continued across the river.

Those using axes, shovels, and hoe-digs moved slowly up the hill, chopping, digging, and clearing the debris to create the narrow fire trail. Over the ridge, we unrolled 100-foot fire hoses, connected them, then hooked the snake-like assembly to the pumps. Soon all men and equipment had been organized and functioned as a well-oiled machine. Even the superintendent grabbed a shovel and bent his back. Watery eyes and running noses, combined with soot-covered faces and squawking voices, brought an occasional chuckle from everyone.

A team dedicated to saving its livelihood, each man still found time for humorous small talk. "Christ," one young chokerman exclaimed, "this damn fire's sure going to screw up my trip into town this weekend! I had it all set up to be first with Sweetness. She's sure hot after my body and, boy she ain't bad, I'm here to tell the world."

"Hell, she tells me I'm the best she ever had," retorted the older man working next to the bragging youngster. "She just lets you guys go first so she can get with us older guys who can really give her a good time."

On up the line, a muffled shout came back to the two braggarts, announcing its owner's prowess. Several other ridiculous statements brought roaring laughter from the entire crew. Rising from bent positions to rest aching backs, everyone shared a canvas bag filled with cool creek water.

Refreshed, they all took up their tools and again prodded weary bodies, digging and chopping as fervently as before. The fire trail slowly wound its way up the steep hillside.

Assigned to be the runner, I ran from crew to crew, passing messages to and from the superintendent and the ranger. Later, I met the bull-buck and several fallers laden with saws, axes, sledgehammers and wedges, as they picked their way up the hillside. Arms, shoulders, legs and

126

backs resisting further demands, they took a short break, then puffed their way through the smoke and sparks.

The bullbuck stopped to ask about the two standing dead trees which needed to be felled. I led the way as we passed the fallers and finally stopped near a steep slope along the trail. Inside the fire line two tall snags, about four feet at the base, spouted flames and showered sparks from high above. Sizing up the situation, the bullbuck asked me to return and bring two springboards. "Be sure they both have a cupped round metal piece on one end," he said, then turned back to the fallers. "It looks as though the bark's loose on the farthest one. They're both on fire at the top. Be sure and have someone watch for you while you're working."

"Yeah," the head-faller agreed. "We'll need springboards on those two, for sure. The ground's steeper than it looks. One notch high should put my partner and me level enough to chop and saw."

Each second-faller, using his razor-sharp, four-pound axe, chopped a notch on the lower side of the snag where he would be working. When the springboards arrived, each man placed a board into the notch with the cupped metal disk upward. Next, he stuck his axe high into the tree above the narrow platform and, holding onto the axe handle for balance, leaped to his work place, jumping up and down to test the board and the notch. Everything in place, they began work. The two second-fallers, each level with his partner, began chopping an undercut. The second-faller on the springboard chopped right-handed and the head-faller, standing on the ground on the opposite side, chopped left handed.

Turning to me, one head-faller ordered, "Watch the top for us."

Afraid they might think me stupid if I asked just what to watch for, I stood nearby with eyes glued to the towering snags, now showering brilliant displays into the heavens like Fourth of July fireworks. Bleary-eyed, I watched, my mind wandering back to my friend the slinger.

A loud shout interrupted those vagrant thoughts.

"What the hell are you doing over there?" roared one head-faller. "You're supposed to be watching. Didn't you see that burning bark fall from the snag? You damn kids ain't worth the powder it takes to blow you up."

"Yes, I mean no, ah," I sputtered, "I thought you just wanted me to tell you when the snag began to fall."

"Listen to me, kid," the faller retorted. "In the woods, you know or you don't know; you don't just think you know. Men get killed by guys like you who won't ask when you don't know. You're supposed to watch for falling bark while we're working. Now, wake up and let us know if anything shakes loose."

The stinging lecture made its point. The man was right. Someone could have been seriously injured. Perhaps I should have told them about my eyesight, but at this time everyone had problems seeing clearly. No, I thought, anyone could have missed seeing the falling bark.

Tear-filled eyes and drifting smoke continued to cloud my vision; I hoped for a miracle to save me from another reproach. But if need be, I decided, I'd confront the faller just as I had the old loader. Never again would I permit another man to continuously bully me.

Within the hour, the fallers completed the undercuts, drank from the water bags, then prepared to saw on the backsides.

Sinking his axe into the tree above, each second-faller, without leaving his high work station, again holding onto the axe handle for balance, placed his right toe under the springboard and, with a hopping motion, moved the narrow platform toward the backside. The cupped metal end had pivoted in the notch while the free end swung into a position that permitted the agile woodsman to maneuver the nine-foot saw.

Once at work, the sharp teeth sliced through the bark then cut into solid wood as the two fallers moved the blade back and forth in the cut, one pulling the saw toward himself and the other retrieving it, as though having a tug of war. Within minutes, they stripped to the waist, drank again from the canvas water bags, then renewed their efforts.

When the blade became fully imbedded into the snag, a long metal wedge inserted and pounded into the cut with an eight-pound sledge insured that the saw ran free. But dark smoke and burning foliage swirled around the fallers while roaring flames, rather than mere sparks, now shot skyward from the snag tops.

Ominously, the sound of metal against metal rang along the hillside as they beat the wedges deeper and deeper. Returning to the saw, both men continued their back and forth motion, taking time only for hasty gulps of water. Again to the wedges which, increment by increment, lifted the backside of the snag, thus forcing the entire dead tree forward in the desired direction.

Changing from sledge and wedge to the saw gave a degree of respite, but now was no time for a long break. Again the blade emitted a contented purr as large shavings curled from the cut to roll and bounce this way and that.

Voraciously, the teeth sliced their way deeper and deeper, and the agile second-faller hopped his way to a more advantageous position. Without complaint, the men labored and slugged down water, sweat pouring from their sinewy bodies while they joked about their most recent run-in with the cops, their toughest fight, or their favorite girl in the houses. Soon, the tapered wedges would force the burning snags to fall within the fire trails. Failing this, the demon could spread by leaps and bounds, mandating new fire trails.

As ordered, I watched nervously, throat parched, nose running, eyes burning. A familiar voice called from behind.

"How are they doing?" the bullbuck asked, looking past me.

"Fine," I replied in relief. "It's getting hard to see and I'm not—"

"Jump! Jump!" the bullbuck bellowed.

Without knowing the exact reason for jumping, the four fallers heeded the warning and leaped, landing first on their feet, then tumbling and rolling away. Tons of cascading bark, jarred loose from one dead snag, plummeted to the ground. It bent the saw and sheared the springboard at the exact spot where the second-faller had been standing.

The men, emerging with smudged faces and grimy clothes that gave them an unworldly appearance, extolled the bullbuck and drank greedily from the canvas bags. Within minutes they returned to work, alternately using the remaining tools to finish the job—all in the day's work.

"Why don't you go fill the water bags?" the bullbuck suggested. "I'll watch here. More men and tools are coming."

Delighted, I grabbed two empty bags and headed over the ridge. Away from the fire, the cool fresh air rejuvenated my optimism, but beyond a doubt, I had been fully indoctrinated into the world of treacherous fire and unyielding nature. Life could be rough at times, I thought, but, as the old saying goes, nothing is so bad that it can't get worse. Yet, so far, fate had been kind.

Temporarily free from responsibility, I relaxed and crouched by the stream, whistling a favorite tune. Most wildlife had fled the area, but the small creek remained steady as it replenished the pool from which the fire-pumps extracted precious water.

Dried sweat and smoke-laden clothing brought me back to reality; I had been sent to fill the bags. While kneeling in the cool, damp moss along the bank, I removed the cork stopper from one metal spout, held onto the rope bail with my left hand, and tossed the canvas bag into a small eddy with the right. For a moment, it floated, then sipped, gulped, and finally sank below the surface.

Both bags filled and corked, I rose to find the puncher beckoning from upstream. I hurried along the bank, shouting, "How are you doing? Boy, it's getting hot over the ridge. I heard the cats couldn't make it where we crossed on the windfall, so they went downstream to find shallow water. Now the ranger says we'll be here another day or two."

The puncher, because he wore no calks, had been assigned to the fire pumps, a confining and responsible job.

"Did you get a lunch?" I asked, moving nearer.

"Yeah," replied the weary fellow, eyes bloodshot. "But I only have one gallon of gas left for these pumps. It should last two hours, but I'll need more after that. Will you take this empty can back with you and bring or send a few gallons? There's a petcock on the speeder gas tank."

"Sure," I replied and headed back over the ridge as dusk faded toward darkness.

The two snags had been felled without further incident, so I distributed the water bags and hurried down the hill with the empty gas can. Near the bottom, it became apparent that darkness was indeed setting in. It wasn't just imagination nor the smoke-filled skies. My concerns increased. Never able to see at night without a powerful flashlight, I eased my way along the river bank, grumbling, "Where's that darn tree across the river? It has to be up this way." A stick flipped between my legs. Down I went, turning one ankle.

Swearing, I grabbed the stick to throw it from the path when it dawned on me that this pesky intruder could be a valuable ally. Continuing on, stick in hand, my doubts increased. Would returning up the hill make more sense?

By this time, the evening skies had slipped into total darkness. To go farther meant walking without sight! "Can I do it?" Reminded of the eye doctor's prediction, both eyes searched. Nothing.

"Perhaps someone will— "

I had walked point-blank into the windfall, a painful but welcome surprise. Again casting a worried glance into the skies and seeing only darkness, nothing remained but to scramble atop the fallen tree.

With the empty gas can in one hand and the stick in the other, I moved several feet before stopping to ponder my dilemma. It was absolutely necessary to walk in the middle, for to stray meant certain drowning. But the treacheries of this cold mountain river came to mind. Hunters and fishermen had warned that the currents would drag a man under the instant he touched the surface. Several unfortunate souls had never been found.

To go back and wait solved nothing, for others couldn't help me across even if they did come along. Out farther, turning around would surely be impossible. Time to put aside speculation.

Although the ominous silence urged caution, instinct took me over the water's edge where the swirling eddies and cool channel breezes muffled other sounds and cleared my mind.

The stick, Yes, I thought. Put it down beside the log for a gauge and a guide. One more moment to consider alternatives, nothing new.

Beyond the point of no return, the can, the stick, and I moved farther out over the glacial river. The dead limb flashed into mind. Don't remember just where. We held onto it as we had crossed going to the fire. Would I be able to pass with this can in my hand? I didn't drop the can—why, I never knew.

Again I inched forward. Nothing. My concern about colliding with the limb and losing balance rose with each passing minute. Now the stick became even more valuable, for it could be used as a probe. Searching ahead identified an obstruction.

"What the devil's that?" I gasped. Another quandary. Maybe it was this, but it must be that, but why? Nothing made sense.

Indecision began taking its toll. Settle down, I thought. I returned the stick to the side and shuffled forward. A knee-high protrusion blocked the way, but no dead branch.

Was this the right tree? I didn't remember that bulge. Does the tree go completely across the river? Should I try to return? No, it had sounded as if I was near the other side. Besides, the windfall hadn't been shaking when I stepped, so it must be on something solid at both ends. I now talked to the can and the stick as though they were my lifetime partners.

At this point, the old windfall, now only about eighteen inches in diameter and covered with scaly, loose bark, tested my temperament to the utmost.

Now about the bump. The shock of recognition set me back. Sure, why hadn't I thought of it before? The limb was an extension of an abnormal growth on the trunk. Earlier, as we had crossed the windfall to reach the fire, each of us had held onto the limb and swung around it, missing the projection. But it made sense that a faller had chopped off the limb with his axe as he crossed an hour or so later. Careful now, I cautioned myself, don't get excited and do something stupid.

One step to the top, another cautious step down on the other side, a few feet farther and I could no longer hear the treacherous water below. The stick touched the soft river silt beside the windfall.

High on the hill, encouraging shouts. The cats had arrived. Down the tracks, A speeder headlight signaled reinforcements.

Once more I permitted my mind to drift. My buddy, the rigging-slinger, now lying alone on a cold slab in the morgue, wouldn't be happily perched beside me on a worn bar stool this weekend. Then, as if they might know, I questioned the can, the stick, and the Universe. "I wonder what his real name was?"

No reply.

Chapter 12

The Tramp

Several predawn hoots from a distant owl foretold the end of darkness. The night hunter shook the rain from its feathers, preened, then flew deep into the forest. Within the hour, camp garbage dump scavengers would resume their bickering over tidbits left by the nocturnal foragers. The bullcook quietly entered each bunkhouse to build the morning fire; light sleepers ignored him while others snored through the intrusion. Inside the dining hall, the cook and flunkies busied themselves preparing breakfast and lunches. At five o'clock sharp, the metal triangle spurred the entire camp into action.

I rolled from bed earlier than usual, packed my few belongings, and left the bunkhouse before the others returned from the washroom. This move, unlike so many others, would be a new experience involving mixed feelings. Just thinking about life as a tramp logger bolstered my confidence and raised expectations.

Although I would be without mentors, it was now or never. Three weeks of continuous rain, the warnings against becoming married to a job, and a burning desire to become a high-climber compelled me to leave friends and once again venture into the unknown.

I stepped from the plank walk, turned my back to the driving rain and buttoned the woolen jacket. Now sloshing through the mud with several weeks pay in a dry pocket, I arrived at the tracks, where the locomotive stood idly hissing and puffing billows of white steam from worn valves and dark smoke from the towering stack. Partially blinded by the black giant's headlight, I skidded and stumbled to the engineer's side and inquired, "Are you going to the lower camp?"

"After we pick up a string of loaded flats down on the siding," replied the bill-capped engineer, who wore a red bandanna around his neck.

"Mind if I ride down with you?"

"OK, but we won't get down till we take those loads to the interchange. Several need to be reloaded before the Milwaukee will move them on to the mill. That new loader isn't the best. He'll be counting ties if he doesn't improve."

I tossed my bag to the high platform, climbed up the steps, then passed from the rain into the warm area behind the boiler. As the brakeman signaled for the main-line, the engineer settled deeper in his seat, eyes glued to the rails. Clear liquid fidgeted in the water-glass as the old locomotive swayed back and forth along the worn tracks.

The fireman, alternately shifting his eyes from the water-glass to me, periodically operated the injector to maintain boiler pressure. The fireman's job, although a comfortable position, sometimes became lonely and lacked excitement. The engineer, known to be a private person who took his job seriously, refused to engage in logging small-talk; little conversation passed between the two trainmen.

Several minutes passed before the fireman, with a strong Appalachian accent, inquired, "What have you been doing at the upper camp?"

"Oh, a little bit of everything," I replied. "Mainly working behind the cats and rigging up the new sides. Some day I want to be a climber."

"Until I lost my leg while working on a cold-deck of logs," said the fireman, "I could do almost everything except climbing. I really never wanted to be a climber. Never been one for heights and, besides, it's damn hard work. Not everyone can do it, even if they want to. But I liked working on the high-lead logging crews. The men are different—wild, full of hell, and always ready to take on the world. We had a lot of fun together, especially when we went into town on the weekends. One of my buddies got himself killed last year working up in Alaska. That's rough country, they tell me."

"How long had you been working in the woods before you lost your leg?" I asked, trying to show a proper level of compassion.

"Oh, nigh onto twenty years, I guess. I started as a whistle-punk relaying signals from the logging crew to the donkey-puncher when I turned fifteen. If you looked old enough and big enough to do the work, they hired you. I went to the high-lead rigging as a choker-setter on my eighteenth birthday. It was damn tough in those days." He paused, as though uncertain how to proceed, then continued with a sparkle in his eyes, "I worked at one camp where they had put a sign in front of the office stating, 'If you can't fly, don't light here—we kill a man a day,' and they came damn close to it. We never knew whether the company or the men put up the sign.

"In another camp, the guy who cut wood for the boiler on the steam-donkey placed a smoldering corncob pipe in his hip pocket before unhooking a choker. Two logs rolled together on him and squashed his body; they dragged him off the landing and went on working. The side-rod, obviously annoyed by the delay in production, noticed the dead man as he arrived on the scene. Curious about the smoke coming from the man's hip pocket, he rolled the body over with the toe of his boot, then shouted to the landing crew, 'Why the hell did you kill this man? He still has fire in his ass.' Although it wasn't easy to watch these things, we soon got used to them, and they became a part of the day's work." Without explanation, he made an adjustment to the harness that supported his artificial leg.

What a life, I thought, to live with something like that.

"Yeah, it was sure rough in those days," he continued, "but we had good times, too. It all balanced out somehow."

Then he turned to a more serious subject. "You know, there are no books to teach men how to be good loggers; they learn from doing. If you're serious about becoming a climber, you'll need to move from one camp to another, learning something at each outfit. A good man can soon go anywhere and get a job. If I were you, I'd head for the coast. They have some darn good high-lead loggers down there. It's strong union, though, so you have to be careful about what you say and who you're seen with. Don't get too involved with any radical groups or company men; either one can get you into a hell of a lot of trouble."

The fireman turned in his seat to watch the brakeman, who stood on the locomotive's front step.

Now the nimble trainman, brake stick in hand, threw switches to guide the one hundred-ton locomotive onto the siding, where they connected it to the loaded railway cars.

Slipping drive-wheels indicated a heavy load. Even so, dry sand applied to the tracks provided traction to start the cars moving, and soon the locomotive roared along the valley floor, bellowing warnings from its steam whistle at each crossing.

"How will you get to your next job?" the fireman asked when the crew was again settled for the ride to the lower camp.

"I don't know," I admitted, then added confidently, "I'll make it some way."

"Better come home with me tonight," suggested the fireman. "Tomorrow morning I can get you a ride toward the coast with a tie-hauler who lives next door to me. We can toss the bull this evening, and Mama will probably enjoy having someone besides me to talk with. We don't have another bed, but we have plenty of blankets. We'll soften it up some way; besides, the floors are soft pine."

Chuckling at his last remark, he added, "We'll drop you off just this side of the lower camp, and you can walk to my car. They don't like us to haul men out of the upper camp in the locomotive. My jalopy is the old blue Model B Ford. Take your bag and wait there for me. I'll be about an hour."

Bright rays of warm sunlight broke through the morning clouds as I, bag in hand, wondered if I were doing the right thing. Faded paint and doors that opened from the front identified the weathered old Ford. The worn seat covers revealed soiled batting, long since bereft of resilience. Sixteen-inch lengths of firewood had been stacked in the back seat and kindling laid on top.

Memories of the past few months faded as I dozed in the passenger's seat; also, I realized that thoughts of friends and relatives back home occurred less frequently.

The squeaking leather cup atop the fireman's artificial leg woke me before the trainman arrived.

My new friend, weary from the day's work, glanced into the rear seat, managed an appreciative smile, then explained, "The old bullcook here at the lower camp cuts this wood and puts it in my car during the day. I see he added some quick-start this time. Mama will like that."

The fireman maneuvered the overloaded old Ford along the narrow road and finally pulled up before a slab shack. Taking a few minutes to unload and stack the wood under a lean-to, we then picked our way around mud puddles toward the humble dwelling. On the small porch, the trainman politely moved aside and offered the one powder box, so I could sit while removing my muddy boots.

"Mama!" the fireman bellowed. "We got company. He's going to stay the night with us. Put on some extra grub, and fetch that tangle-foot. Come on out and say hello."

"Glad to meet you," Mama said, opening the door and smiling as she wiped her hands on a clean checkered apron.

Mumbling a bashful greeting, I felt relieved by her cordiality.

"I hope you don't mind me staying tonight?" I asked, returning her smile.

"Not at all. We need someone different to talk with once in a while. Come on in, and I'll get you a pair of slippers for your feet."

"Watch this stuff," the fireman cautioned, as he handed me a brown quart bottle. "It'll singe the hair on your head, and you might walk on your tip-toes and look over your left shoulder for a week, but it does warm you up."

Putting the bottle to my lips, I almost gagged from the strong odor, but I placed my tongue against the opening and pretended to swallow. Even with that, tears formed and several coughs escaped as a few drops leaked into my mouth.

"Not bad, huh?" the fireman asked. "Made it myself. Best you can lay your hands on 'round these parts."

"You guys better get washed up and sit at the table," Mama interjected when she saw the tears streaming down my face. "We've got some nice venison, corn bread, potatoes and gravy, and some good fresh vegetables. Then if you're not full, I've baked some nice cinnamon rolls to eat with a hot cup of cocoa before we turn in."

"Yeah," the fireman began as we sat down, "times were rough in those days. It's still not the best but it's a lot better than a few years back. If you can top a tree and hang a little rigging, you'll have work in no time, but in order to hold a job, you'll need to know how to rig a high-lead tree from top to bottom. Learning this takes time, and it won't be easy. You may get canned once or twice. Try not to make any big mistakes, and above all, work fast.

There's nothing worse than having a slow climber in the tree with a full crew standing around. The company wants these guys producing, not watching you up in the spar tree. More than that, you need to know who you're working with and what you might run into in town on the weekends. Isn't that right, Mama?"

"Yes," she agreed, "we know all about that."

Chapter 13

Bygone Days

With the fireman, Mama, and I seated comfortably around the small table, I listened intently as they cautioned against misfits and scoundrels in the logging world.

"You see," the fireman explained, "Mama and I both worked in one of the bigger camps. She was a flunky in the camp dining hall, and I had hired out as a hook-tender on the high-lead side. I was bashful as all get out. I had my eye on Mama, but she didn't know it. This other guy, a quiet fellow and not a bad looker, liked Mama too. But he seemed a little odd—you know, off in the head."

"Papa never let on like he even knew me," Mama added as she placed hot food before us. "And I acted like it didn't bother me, but it did."

This was the first time Mama had referred to the fireman as Papa; I wondered if they had children. They seemed to be very fond of each other.

"One Friday, most everyone left camp to spend a wild time in town," Papa continued. "Mama went to get her hair fixed and I went to the tavern to have a few drinks with the crew. It wasn't long until a guy, already half drunk, ran into the barroom and told me Mama was down the street, hurt real bad.

"When I got down there, Mama was lying on the ground with blood running out her mouth and her left hand bent funny-like under her side," Papa explained. "She never came to for quite a while after we got her to the hospital."

"I guess I was a terrible looking sight," Mama added, "All I could think about was my new hair-do."

"I finally got out of her what had happened," Papa resumed bitterly. "That damn sleazy son-of-a-bitch had tried to get Mama to go to a hotel room with him and when she refused, he hit her in the mouth and broke two teeth."

"I wouldn't have gone to a dog fight with that lowly bastard!" Mama proclaimed.

Her vehement outburst surprised me, but it expressed a legitimate hatred.

"The doc was sure the teeth could be fixed, but he wasn't so sure about Mama's wrist," Papa added. "It seemed it had been twisted and broken at the same time. When we got

Mama comfortable, I took off for town to even things."

"Boy, and how Papa evened things!"

"I caught up with him near an alley," the fireman said, "and I fixed him but good. He'll never do that to anyone again. After knocking him down, I put my cork boots to his head. When I left, I didn't know whether he was alive or dead, but I didn't give a damn. His teeth were all out in front, both top and bottom, and his damn face looked like he had smallpox; Jesus! Blood squirted out of him like a sprinkler. Those corks did their job."

As if on cue, we all fell silent until our plates had been emptied. Once or twice, the fireman offered me another drink from the quart bottle but remembering the first episode, I politely refused. However, I did accept an offer for seconds on the potatoes and cornbread. After warm cinnamon rolls and steaming chocolate, we pushed our chairs back from the table and the story continued.

"Papa stayed in town until I left the hospital three days later. Then we moved into a hotel for two weeks. When I felt like it, we went down to the nearest tavern that had a restaurant. When I wasn't feeling good, Papa brought my meals to me, and he put packs on my mouth and wrist. There wasn't much more they could do, and the doc said we could do it just as well out of the hospital. He saved us a lot of money."

"Didn't you have folks to stay with?" I asked innocently. Again the response surprised me. Wide-eyed, I listened, secretly comparing their life experiences with mine.

The story poured from the two as though it had been bottled up for years. Mama spoke first, reverting to the coquettish, teenage jargon of the deep South.

"Boy, my Daddy, him were real mean to us kids after my Mama died." Then, having made her point, Mama returned to her normal speech. "Three of my older brothers worked out. One was killed in the logging, and this made Daddy meaner than ever. He started drinking like a fish, and if he ever caught me out after dark, he'd take off his belt and tan my bottom until I was black and blue."

"Yeah," Papa interrupted, "down in that country, a girl is a virgin until she can no longer outrun her brothers."

A wet dish-cloth came out of nowhere and caught Papa smack in the mouth. Ducking as if he were about to be brutally attacked, the tough ex-hook-tender laughed and went on with the story.

"Mama ran away from home after her favorite brother got killed. Still in her teens, she had a hard time of it for several years. When I first met her, as I told you, she worked as a flunky at one of the camps. I didn't see her for a year, and boy, how she had changed! I couldn't keep my eyes off her, nor could that son-of-a-bitch who beat up on her."

Again, silence dominated the small room for a few moments, each satisfied with private thoughts. First to speak, I turned to the fireman and inquired, "Did you come from the same area?"

"No, my Pop and Mom were both from the coal mines. I never knew either of them very well. Pop died from the black lung, and Mom had to go to work in the city. She sent money home to the folks who took care of me, my twin brother, and two younger sisters. I worked doing odd jobs around the mines but got let out when the unions came in strong.

"Older people were hard on kids in those days. I can still feel the razor strap across my back when I got into trouble. It didn't hurt me none, though; if anything, it made me a better man. At least, I knew that life wasn't going to be all honey and cream.

"Working my way to the west coast, I took any job that happened to be open. For my first experience in logging," he said, repeating small bits of his conversation earlier that day, "I worked as a whistle-punk pulling a wire strung through the woods and attached to the steam-donkey whistle which, in turn, sent signals to the donkey-puncher running the yarder. Husky and fast on my feet, I got along quite well. Before long I hired out as a hook-tender, got fired a few times, but soon made a name for myself.

"After that, I had no problems until I lost my leg. Mama took care of me for over a year until I got my peg leg, and the company gave me the job as fireman. I sure miss the rigging, but I guess you can't have everything. At least Mama and I have each other. Next year, Mama can get her teeth fixed, and we'll have enough money to get into a better house."

Neat and attractive, the amiable housekeeper washed and dried the dishes while the fireman and I split wood and kindling for the next day. As we worked, he spoke with me as though I were a younger brother, warning of pitfalls and tutoring me regarding strategic moves to gain acceptance as a seasoned logger.

As darkness squeezed the final light from the sky, Mama called, "You guys better come in and get ready for bed. Papa, you know you've got to be at work by four-thirty."

"OK," came the weary reply from the trainman. Although his days were long and tiring, he never complained. This had become his lot in life, and he accepted it without apparent resentment.

Lying in the blankets on the wooden floor, I dreamed of remaining with this devoted, unmarried couple who had defeated the odds—that is, thus far.

Patting me gently on the shoulder, Mama whispered, "It's time to get up. I'll gather the blankets while you wash up. I let Papa sleep in as long as he can. Will you bring me some slivers and small pieces of wood from the porch?"

"Sure," I agreed. Because I had slept in my street clothes, privacy presented no problem. I threw back the covers, stepped into the slippers, and hurried outside into the crisp morning air, where several grouse scratched for a morning meal in Mama's tiny garden. Now fully awake, I returned with the wood and talked with the fireman's chosen partner.

"Thank you so much for letting me stay. It sure seems nice to have home-cooking for a change."

"We were glad to have you," she said. "Papa misses talking logging with rigging men. Working the locomotive gets to be a lonesome way of life; especially when the other man in the cab doesn't talk much. He's never worked on the rigging, so there isn't much to talk about."

I understood and added, "It must get lonesome for you sometimes. I'll be glad when you can get into your new house."

"There's time for that," Mama assured me but showed her appreciation with a pat on my arm.

Papa dressed and soon sat quietly at the table, content to let Mama and me lead the conversation. It wasn't long before the fireman and I left the slab shack with Mama waving good-bye from the small porch. Papa took me to the tie-hauler's slab shack, introduced us, and with a parting, "I'll see you. Take it easy," the ex-logger went on his way.

As we rambled down the rough road, the load weighed heavily on the durable old flat-bed truck. Brief exchanges let me know the tie-hauler had long since vowed bachelorhood. Deep in my own thoughts, I no longer pressed for conversation but soon came to a sudden realization. I didn't know the fireman's name.

"Have you known your neighbors long?" I asked the confirmed bachelor.

"Only a couple of years," he replied. "They came here in the middle of the winter and had no money nor a place to stay, so we all got together and threw up that old shack and they've been there ever since."

"Do you know their name?" I queried further.

"No," came the serious reply, "We just call him Peg because of his leg, and we call her Sis because she is so nice, just like a sister, and she's always doing something for one of us in the neighborhood. We don't need to know anything more about them. If they want us to know more, they'll tell us. So we leave it at that."

The tie-hauler whistled a simple tune as the old truck jostled us along the rough road toward the tie-docks in Chehalis. Before dropping me off near a local tavern where loggers gathered between jobs, he cautioned, "You'll get some good and some bad advice from the bartender and the guys that hang around this part of town. Be careful and sort it out before you jump at a job. But one thing you got to remember is that if you ever get locked into a naggin' old lady and a bunch of squallin' kids, there ain't no magic key that's goin' to get you out."

157

As the load rambled away, I noticed that, unlike most company trucks, no name adorned the tie-hauler's rig. Did this anonymity help to guarantee his cherished freedom from family responsibilities? Or was it just an inherent part of being a renegade logger? No one will ever know for sure. Perhaps, marriage and the life of a tramp logger are merely incompatible—nothing more, nothing less.

Chapter 14

Topper

The roaring tie-truck disappeared along the winding road as I moved unsteadily across the paved street, feet skidding this way and that. Walking on concrete while wearing calk boots reminded me of childhood attempts to ice-skate; the unknowing might have thought me intoxicated. Minutes later I arrived at the tavern where, traditionally, loggers met to drink, discuss past logging experiences, and exchange information regarding prospective employment.

Although the tavern had not yet opened its doors to the thirsty patrons, several men had stacked their bags outside, where the tavern keeper, who was also the owner, bartender, and swamper, had erected a small shelter for the patrons' sole possessions.

Adding my bag to the heap, I joined four unemployed men who formed a half-circle under the meager canopy. Angrily, they discussed the strike which had left them jobless. "What the hell are they striking for, anyhow?" one fellow questioned.

"No one seems to know for sure," an old-timer grumbled. "It's this way every time we go out. Those union officials are probably getting a cut."

"I'm going down along the Oregon coast as soon as I can get away," the third commented, "I hear there's good money to be made down there. Besides, the union isn't so strong in those smaller outfits. Strikes are OK if there's something to go out for. Besides, with the war and everything, these wildcat strikes are getting damn unpopular."

"There's a gyppo down the way that needs a second-loader who can do some climbing, but hell, I'm no climber," the oldest man lamented.

Pricking up my ears, I asked, "What's the outfit's name?"

"I don't remember," he replied. "But they don't have a camp so you're forced to live in town and sleep in crummy flophouses and eat in greasy-spoon cafes. It's sure nothing like grub in the camps, and there's no place to dry boots."

"Hanging around town at night gets damn tiresome after awhile. There's nothing to do but sop up beer and eat stale pretzels, beef jerky, pepperoni, and smoked salmon from those hundred year-old jars on the bar," a newcomer interjected, "but if you're interested in the climbing job, talk with the barmaid when we get inside. She knows more about what's going on than anyone else."

The regulars exchanged greetings with the portly bartender as he unlocked and swung open the dust-laden doors. Each loyal patron, eager to get on with the business at hand, perched himself on a worn bar stool and soon had a full mug of beer before him. Admiring smiles fell on the white head that capped the sparkling brew, and from that time on, no one spoke until each upper lip displayed a frothy half circle.

"What are you going to have?" the bartender inquired as I selected a stool.

"Nothing right now. It's too early for me," I replied apologetically.

"Keep it that way, and you'll be better off. Would you like a coke?"

An appreciative smile gave the bartender his answer. Sipping the soft drink, I listened to frustrations and accomplishments spouting from seasoned cohorts. As usual, modesty ranked lowest among their attributes. The more beer consumed, the greater the claims to fame.

A soft voice drew my attention from the braggarts. "That guy at the far end said you'd like the gyppo's name who needs a good man," she said, smiling warmly.

"Mmm, Yes. I mean I'm not an experienced climber but want to learn and I'm a good second-loader."

"Here's the name and phone number," she added, handing me a slip. "They're logging some State timber several miles down the Raymond highway. You can call the foreman at his home tonight after work. He's not the easiest man to work for, but if you try hard, you'll get along with him."

Now I recalled men talking of this unusual barmaid. After losing an intimate friend to a logging accident several years past, she tact-fully rejected advances made by other woodsmen, but seemed to enjoy the camaraderie in the tav-ern. Hearsay had it that this petite woman could tame the wildest drunk and knew when to set lim-its for overly amorous patrons. A tavern owner's dream, she had gained and held the respect of the rowdy customers, for she knew the logging game inside and out. "Take this other slip to this hotel, and tell them I sent you," she con-tinued. "The place is clean, and they don't tol-erate foolishness. Also, there's a nice cafe next door that serves breakfast and packs lunches. As for the evening meal, several restaurants claim the best food in town. Good luck."

Stuffing the instructions into a shirt pocket, I retrieved my bag and headed for the hotel, the barmaid's smile foremost in my mind. "She picks and chooses her friends carefully," the men acknowledged, especially if the speaker felt he ranked as one of the chosen few. Not bad, I thought. Wonder what she'd be like away from the tavern?

"Hey," a teenager squawked, "get out of my way. I almost ran over you with my bike. Why don't you listen for things coming from behind?"

Ignoring the brazen youngster, I continued along the street, where numerous cars parallel parked before the businesses. Cigarette butts, gum and candy wrappers, and empty potato chip bags littered the gutter outside the grocery store. A sudden cloudburst sent me dodging and weaving through laden shoppers rushing toward their cars.

Several minutes passed before I located the rooming house—not exactly a hotel, but freshly painted and well-constructed. A calico cat lounged in the window and ignored me; however, friendly barks brought the landlady to the door, where the barmaid's note gained me entrance to a small cubicle. She motioned me to a chair and turned to write my name in a small ledger. Now a wagging tail welcomed, then a wet nose nudged its way into my heart. I had neither seen nor petted a dog during the past months. Something about the soft fur and his chin resting on my knee, eyes looking straight into mine, affirmed immediate friendship, so I scratched behind his ears. Together, the dog and I followed the woman as she took my bag and led the way to a room overlooking a small city park where clamorous children, like yearling colts, romped on the grass, hung upside down on the horizontal bars, all the time shouting, giggling, squealing, or crying for an extra turn on the slide.

After unpacking, I descended the stairs to become acquainted with the owners.

"How's it going?" the man, asked, more as a greeting than a question.

"Fine, how about you?" I replied, adding a broad smile.

Obviously crippled, this man, no more than forty-five, remained seated, but looked toward the kitchen and nodded to his matronly wife. He directed me to a chair with another nod. Shortly, coffee and sweet rolls appeared.

"The residual from a logging injury limits my husband's activities to managing the books

164

and maintaining the building," the wife explained.

"Yeah," he interjected, "It keeps me out of trouble and gives me a chance to ogle the women in the Sears catalog and monthly magazines. But seriously, my only complaints are about occasional bouts with arthritis and the damn fools who come to town and raise hell after a stint in camp."

Cribbage, a longtime favorite among loggers, occupied otherwise dull evenings at the rooming house. Night after night, the landlady's husband and I sat at the kitchen table, dealt the cards, played our hands, and pegged our scores. The old dog slept nearby, one ear cocked for intruders or stray cats, but oblivious to our outbursts of satisfaction over a game won, or escape from a near death experience in the woods. Before his injury, the disabled logger had worked at almost every job in the camps, including climbing. What a break!

Two weeks into the job, and climbing hadn't been mentioned. Second-loading on a single-tong heel-boom proved easy, and I became bored with jumping on and off the loaded trucks to unhook the tongs. Early one morning in the third week, the side-rod caught up with me as we walked along the plank-road leading to the land-ing.

"We need a tree topped over the ridge. It isn't too large. Want to give it a whirl?"

Caught off guard, I faltered, then blurted out, "Sure!" "Belt, spurs, saw, and axe hang in the shack where the night-watchman stays. Pick them up and I'll be back to show you the spar."

Undisciplined enthusiasm challenged self-control, a dangerous condition, for as many men knew too well, rushing into unfamiliar territory had put friends six feet under. Realizing that, instructions, warnings and general advisories tumbled through my mind; others had shared valu-able information about climbing or, at least, topping trees.

The side-rod's return forced me to abandon euphoria and concentrate on the long-awaited op-portunity to prove myself. That I would be alone in the tree with no one looking over my shoulder giving encouraging advice or curt warnings failed to dissuade me. Momentarily I recalled teenage experiences climbing the forty-foot tow-ers to lubricate farm windmills. Would this be the same?

We headed across the ridge as I proudly carried the climbing equipment. At the crest, the foreman paused, glanced back to the landing, then led the way a short distance down the far side. He stopped in a clearing, waited for me to catch up, then pointed across the vale.

There it stood, with a huge "X" chopped in the bark to indicate the distinction of being selected as a spar. Straight and bare of limbs for two-thirds the way to the bushy top, it rose majestically above surrounding timber.

"I've got to go back and fill in until you've finished," the foreman said, showing no reservations about my ability to perform the task. He did, however, face me and say, "OK, climber, it's all yours. You're on your own; show your stuff." With that, he turned and disappeared back over the ridge.

Startled by the side-rod's final statements and abrupt departure, I stood alone in untamed wilderness, pondering the change in status. Today there had been no ifs, ands, or buts … no fatherly explanations as to why this or that had to be, just the expectation to fulfill my responsibility: top the tree.

First I had been a millhand, then a chokerman, a second-loader, a fire fighter, and a member of a rigup crew—all under the supervision of more experienced men. But now I had earned an opportunity to be a climber, in many ways responsible only to myself and the companies I worked for. Rigging trees and directing rigup crews would come later. Now I recalled what the old Swede hook-tender had said: "Few men make it." Well, I'd make it!

Still savoring the new position, I took time to admire the surroundings. Timbered knolls and ravines stretched into the distance. Nearby, a small creek, cutting its way through the velvety blanket of fir needles, bounced over jagged rocks and skirted large boulders to form quiet pools below. A resolute woodpecker searched vigorously for its morning meal in a distant snag. Shortly, a camp-robber, its metallic blue feathers glistening in the sun, perched itself gracefully on a nearby bush. Swaying in the gentle morning breeze, my new friend surveyed me with a one-eyed stare as though expecting an introduction. Could be, for myth had it that these bold jays were dead loggers returning to be among friends. I chuckled at the thought and turned to the business at hand.

Considerable time had passed since I last used the old Irishman's climbing gear to scramble up the small trees near the landings. Nevertheless, strapping on this belt and spurs transferred me into a new world, a world of venture, of precision, of prestige.

With the short topping saw tied to one side of the belt by sash-cord and the razor-

168

sharp double-bitted axe tied to the other side, I threw the twenty-eight-foot climbing rope around the tree, tied the cat's paw knot, ready to ascend the Douglas fir. Throwing wide loops in the rope and jabbing the sharp spurs into the thick bark one deliberate step at a time, I arrived at the first branch, my body saturated with sweat. Now, a short rest. Minutes later, the heavy axe severed limbs from the trunk with a single blow, freeing them to plummet downward. Several feet higher, the tree measured approximately thirty inches in diameter, the right size for a sturdy main-spar. Now the supreme test! To cut the top from the tree.

Again recalling words of wisdom from my advisors, I reviewed each step.

"Put your undercut one-third through the tree, then sidenotch through the sapwood so it won't split. When you're finishing the backcut, never cut the top completely off or it could twist and come down on you. Always leave at least one inch of wood completely across the tree. When the top starts to go, get directly behind the tree, and brace yourself for a wild ride."

First, I chopped the undercut and soon discovered that chopping and sawing became easier when I kept the belt low on my back. Also, having the rope lower decreased the possibility of accidentally cutting it. Although the rope encompassed a small steel cable core, under certain circumstances, a sharp axe could sever it. Each swing of the axe sent large chips flying into what seemed to be bottomless space. Even after beginning another swing, I could hear the results of the previous effort crash into the brush one hundred forty feet below.

A mild breeze wafted from the direction the top was supposed to fall, but I gave it little thought and moved around the tree to side-notch. One more phase completed. Now the back-cut.

Forcing the glistening teeth into the wood with all my strength, I moved the short topping saw back and forth through the cut. A pause to catch my breath, check the do's and don'ts, then I worked tirelessly until only a three inch strip of unsawed wood remained. A few more strokes and it should go. The wind, timber fallers' worst enemy, seemed to have increased, but again, I shrugged it off.

"What the devil!" I exclaimed. "What made the damn saw stop like that?" I looked up the tree as though expecting a mysterious force to be hovering nearby.

Then it came to me. The wind had blown the top back onto the saw, pinching it in the cut.

What to do? The spring breeze, dangerously unpredictable, controlled the situation.

With no wedge or hammer, should I wait for
the gust to relent? No. If I wait, it might get
even stronger and cause the trunk to split downward, squeezing me to death. Or, the top could
twist, permitting it to fall in any direction,
also dangerous.

Noting that the breeze had waned, I
grabbed the saw handle and jerked. The blade
moved slightly, but refused to slide back and
forth in the cut. Soon, another gust rocked the
top back on the saw, holding it like a vice.
Forget it, I thought. Can't rely on that.

I dared not chop out the backcut and allow
the top to fall with the wind, for the fouled
saw, once loosened from the cut, could be thrown
into me, its teeth ripping into my flesh. Besides, if the top fell into nearby trees, it
would surely kick back over the spar, crushing
me as it dropped off one side or the other.

Now the breeze whispered through the
boughs, its strength and authority expanding by
the minute, and I had nowhere to run.

"Slow down and think," I grumbled to myself, "there must be a way."

I could climb down the tree without finishing the task, but that also had its hazards.

To admit defeat meant squandering this valuable opportunity to prove my worth.

Frustrated and annoyed, I looked first at the fouled saw, then up into the branches, and finally designed a possible solution: loosen the rope, take a step or two up the trunk, and cut off the lowest limb to make a wedge.

Careful now, I thought, too much slack in the rope, one slip and over you'll go backward, then you'll hang there, upside down, until some-one comes to get you.

Up, up, one small step at a time, then a few inches of slack on the rope, I worried my way until the spurs were slightly more than two feet below the cut. Almost two-thirds of my body extended above the fouled saw, and the climbing rope remained only inches below the undercut on the far side. If the wind slacked or reversed direction, the top could fall while I stood in this vulnerable position.

Chapter 15

The Test: Brains, Guts, Or Luck?

Temporarily thwarted by the wind, I stood heavily on the spurs 140 feet above the ground, my rope perilously close to the cut that would free the spar top to plummet downward, possibly flinging me into space. From now on, the Irish climber's words, "There's no such thing as a brave man in the woods," must be the guiding principle. Topping a tree left no room for false courage or cowardice—only common sense.

Steady now, I thought, if the breeze dies, or the top moves, or the wood cracks, immediately free the spurs and drop down beside the spar.

With my arms and axe fully extended upward, I whacked off the lowest branch, leaving a short section attached to the trunk—a section just right for a sturdy wedge. Fortunately, the wind held steady while I flailed overhead until that short piece sagged and dangled by a few thin strands. One more swing would have sent it plunging to the ground; however, I cast aside the axe and grabbed the lower end, jerked it free, tucked it under my belt, and retreated to safety below the fouled saw. Now the tricky part.

To shape a wedge, I must position one end of the piece perpendicular against the tree, hold onto it with one hand, and wield the axe with the other, a true test of precision for even the most skilled axeman. The slightest error or deviation could result in a nicked or severed finger. Nevertheless, I shortened my grip on the axe handle and hacked gingerly until I held a rough-hewn three-inch by one-foot wedge. Now for an opportune moment between gusts.

My patience was soon rewarded, for the wind slacked just enough for me to insert the tapered end into the backcut and tap it in with the flat side of the axe.

Another flurry, but now I, rather than the wind, controlled the situation. One step around the tree placed me in position, and I went to work. Again using the flat side of the axe as a maul, I vented my frustrations on that small piece of limb. Careful, I thought, to strike a glancing blow could knock the wedge from the cut or sheer the axe into my rope—either could be disastrous.

Each blow drove the makeshift wedge deeper into the cut, and my legs and arms soon pleaded for relief, but the prospect of conquest forced me to push on. The fouled blade freed. Hot damn!

Mentally rejuvenated, I sawed with vengeance until only a narrow strip of wood remained between the undercut and the backcut. Now to pit human strength and endurance against the persistent wind.

Sweat rolled from under my hatband as I removed the saw and lowered it below my boots, momentarily watching it twirl in the breeze. Moving to the opposite side, I set the spurs and drove the wedge. Each swing forced the top into the wind, but also sank the spurs deeper into the spar. "Come on, fall! … fall!" I alternately begged then commanded.

Finally, the intimidating sound of breaking wood announced victory.

Again the instructions, "Get on the back side and brace yourself."

Viciously pulling and twisting, my tired legs failed to free the imbedded spurs; I remained helplessly anchored to the side, heart pounding, guts taut. Back, back the leaning top pushed the trunk. Momentarily, imagination exaggerated all movement "What the hell! What's happening? Won't this damn tree stop leaning? Maybe it'll fall over."

Eventually, the unsawed wood broke free, and the spar, like a retracted bow, flung the top into space with such violence that the spurs dislodged. Back and forth, around and around, one hundred fifty feet above the ground, the saw, the axe, and my body went separate ways.

At one time I glimpsed the twirling saw about shoulder high, but fortunately at a safe distance. The axe, like a snared animal, re-treated wildly to the end of its tether, then returned to slash at the spar just below my boots. With each reverse in direction, I slid several feet farther down the tree, skinning knees, chin, nose, and knuckles. It seemed hours passed before the thirty-second furor subsided. "Geezus!" I exclaimed, "In my wildest dreams, I wouldn't have expected that." Then, totally ex-hausted, I took in slack and rested, hanging limply alongside the spar. Although thirsty, bruised, and weary, I remained optimistic about my future as a climber.

The short rest found me anxious to examine my handiwork, so I returned to the top. "Man! What a ride! If my old friend, the Swede hook-tender, could have seen me, he'd have laughed for a week. I'd have never heard the end of it."

Still chuckling, I placed the rope near the top and pulled myself up to lie belly down across the newly cut surface, thoughts drifting back to the Irish climber. Lore had it that the old fellow, while still in his prime, had been known to stand upright atop a spar after he had topped it. No, to try that would be foolish, if not crazy.

Suddenly, an exciting surprise: things on the ground seemed vivid and graphic—things that had always been vague and sometimes distorted when viewed from ground level. Now I scanned the area. An old doe and her fawn, undaunted by the commotion, came to the creek for water. Even the felled spar top showed remarkably clear—maybe not perfectly clear, but much improved. Why?

From this height, I reasoned, it could be the absence of glare from the sky when looking down. Again peering along the horizon verified the theory. Yes, that's it! And that's why I could see the details on the old loader's face when I looked down on him when we had it out on the landing. What a revelation! All the more reason to become a climber.

Thrilled with the discovery, I carefully lowered my battered body to again stand on the spurs, paused for one last look, then realized that I might be the only person to view the world from this location—what a privilege. With that, tired and damaged legs took me to the ground, one painful step at a time.

Shedding the belt and spurs, I moved about unsteadily for a few moments, but soon regained control and headed for the creek, dropped to skinned knees, placed both hands into the cool mountain water, and drank greedily.

The bouncing stream muffled other sounds as I lowered my weary body to the cool moss, rolled onto my back, and looked up through the lush foliage, following vagabond clouds as they drifted across the pale blue sky. How beautiful and carefree, almost like the clouds on the prairie. Yet, how different.

The doe and fawn, undisturbed by my proximity, foraged in a nearby clearing. Camp-robbers again scolded neighbors while the wood-pecker continued his rat-a-tat-tat.

Darker clouds formed in the west as I gathered the tools and wound my way up the hill.

What a contrast, I thought, turning to snatch a final glance at the peaceful forest and its colorful wildlife. I then turned to the yarding and loading area where the men with their machines worked to earn a meager living while they marred the countryside.

Once, twice … five times, each doleful blast from the donkey-whistle echoed along the hillside, muffling any subsequent signals. Arriving with sirens wailing, the ambulance departed in silence, a silence that told the entire story—no need to hurry.

"A widow-maker got him," a bucker informed me. "Only two feet long and three inches thick, the damn limb broke loose from the top of the tree he was felling, crushing his skull. Blood ran from his ears so it looks like he's a goner."

"Well, that's two down and one to go," the whistle-punk predicted, then added, "They killed a slinger up-country last week, I heard. They always come in groups of three."

"What was the faller's name?" I inquired of a chokerman.

"I don't know. They called him Hungry, not for craving food, but for greed; he started working fifteen minutes before everyone else, took a ten minute lunch break, and worked longer than others at quitting time. It wasn't unusual for him to hold up the crew bus, so he could finish a cut."

By this time, others had already moved on to lighter subjects, but my interest spurred the man to continue.

"He was a single-jack, meaner than hell. No one else would work with him, so he went it alone.

"Everyone used to kid him about his lust for work," the informer recalled, "They accused him of having a bracket on his saw handle. When it came lunch time, the old single-jack, they said, placed a piece of hardtack in the bracket and took a bite each time he pulled the saw toward him. He ignored the ribbing and usually stayed to himself. Evidently he came over from Finland during his early teens and learned only the simplest words."

Obviously feeling the matter had been fully discussed, the informant turned to the man next to him and began planning for the weekend in town. I stared into space as the crew bus rambled along the plank road.

New belt, rope, and spurs hanging on one shoulder, I left the rooming house and entered the crew bus. The side-rod waited for me at the night watchman's shack. "There's a spar on the other road. You should top it today."

"OK," I replied, then asked, "Did you hear anything about the old single-jack?"

"No," came the emotionless reply. The side-rod offered nothing more, so I added a saw and axe to my equipment and hurried down the plank road.

A solitary six-foot old-growth fir stood in the clearing. High in the tree, fine scaly bark invaded my nose, mouth and eyes as I chopped the limbs. Bark slivers found their way into both shirt sleeves, and sweat trickled downward, saturating the woolen socks.

"What the hell!" I exclaimed, my inclination toward swearing increasing by the day, "Those damn small branches hid this huge limb."

An old-timer had warned, "Don't ever leave your rope below a sucker while you saw it off; it might tear a strip of wood downward along the trunk and pinch your rope. Some of them weigh tons and the weight will squeeze you to death. Always untie your rope and pass it above the big ones."

Jesus! I thought, do I really want to untie the knot and try to pull the loose end over that damn thing? I had one alternative, to climb down and admit defeat. No way!

Throwing the rope high on the trunk, I reached over the sucker, but missed. Again mustering strength, I threw the loop higher and caught it with my free hand. Even so, it was with reluctance that I held onto the rope with one hand over the limb and untied the cat's paw with the other, permitting the loose end to flutter in the breeze.

Now, one slip of the spurs could end everything. A cramp in a hand or arm could be equally disastrous. Inch by inch, now holding onto the rope with both hands, I pulled it over the sucker and retied the cat's-paw. Weary but relieved, I straddled the protruding limb and settled in for a welcome break.

This pause in the action brought back boyhood memories of climbing the tall pines in a relative's yard: so quiet, so removed from others, so in keeping with my dreams—romantic dreams of courage and conquest, fantasies, which had long since given way to matters of financial security and survival in one of our nation's most hazardous occupations.

Thoughtfully, I returned to the task at hand, mentally reviewing the ominous warning as I dug in the spurs for solid footing. With the saw in place and the climbing rope in the clear, I forced the blade into the gnarled outgrowth, sawing it from top to bottom. Sure enough, the huge limb tore loose from the tree and ripped a six inch strip of wood ten feet down the trunk—enough to have caught the climbing rope and rendered the fatal squeeze.

Thirty feet higher in the spar, another problem.

"Whoops, what's that?"

I had heard the sound before but recognition came slowly. Sure, wouldn't you know it, decayed wood inside a solid hull, like an over-ripe pumpkin—no ring when struck with the flat side of the axe. What to do now? No one had mentioned hidden rot.

Common sense dictated caution. A small notch chopped into the tree revealed a six inch outer shell of solid wood. Several feet down, no sign of rot. If I topped it there, the spar would be too short.

Now cursing under my breath, I returned to the ground, frustrated and disappointed, but I knew this matter must be discussed with the side-rod. After drinking my fill from a nearby creek, then a brief rest, I located him and, contrary to my expectations, he explained what to do, registering appreciation for my alertness.

"If it's rotten where you chopped into it, but solid several feet down, you'll have to shoot it out," he explained. "If you try to top it where the wood is rotten, it could split and squeeze you to death." Six inches of solid wood at the very top will hold everything the passline can lift, but it won't stand dragging tons of timber uphill and around stumps. "We've got to pull logs over that ridge so we'll need every foot of lift we can get."

Seeing the perplexed look on my face, he elaborated. "I'll help you and we'll cut a piece of fire hose about the length needed to go around the spar at the top, fill it with dynamite, then place a detonator cap and a fifteen-foot fuse into the charge.

"Tie one end of this small 300-foot rope to your belt, climb the spar, cut a notch around the rotten part, leaving about two inches of solid wood. Then, put the small rope over a limb above and pass it down to me. With you pulling up on the rope and me pulling down, we'll raise the hose to the top, then you'll place it in the notch, secure it, light the fuse, then climb down to beat hell.

"Don't let out too much slack in your rope. You might flip over backward and there's nothing I can do for you if that happens."

The boss and I, seasoned woodsman and young aspirant, prepared the charge while he spoke words of logging wisdom.

"There's one good thing about working for gyppos; you learn to do everything. One or two years with the small outfits, then a man can hold a job anywhere—that is, if he doesn't get killed by worn-out lines and bum equipment."

With matches in an Alka-Seltzer bottle to keep them dry, I climbed back up the spar, cut the notch, placed the passrope over a limb above me and let the loose end down on the far side.

Up, up, with me lifting from the top and the side-rod pulling down from the ground, the fire hose, loaded with dynamite, detonator cap, and fuse, ascended through the warm afternoon air. Cautiously, I tied the fire hose into the notch, lit the fuse, then descended full tilt.

"What the devil?" I gasped. "Why won't that damn climbing rope drop on the back side. That fuse is sure burning fast!"

Throwing and jerking the defiant rope would not free it. One frantic thrust threw me sideways and I noticed the rope moved a short distance around the spar; it just wouldn't go up or down.

Working my way around the tree, I found the rope wedged behind a splinter left by the severed sucker.

"Wouldn't you know it? The only place on the whole damn tree that could foul my equipment."

Angrily I freed the climbing rope, then descended ten to twelve feet each time I kicked the spurs loose. Twenty feet from the ground, another stop to let out slack. Careful, not too much, I thought.

One last glance upward to determine if the fuse was burning near the detonator—I couldn't see from that distance. Two more long steps and my feet touched the ground. Belt and spurs discarded, I followed close on the side-rod's heels as he instinctively headed for a large fir in the standing timber, the best protection from flying debris.

The side-rod's pocket-watch grudgingly doled out minutes, seconds at a time. We had forgotten to check the timepiece when I lit the fifteen-minute fuse. Each minute expanded into a proverbial lifetime as we watched and waited. Now I guessed at time elapsed and counted from there. Fourteen minutes. Why didn't it go? Fifteen minutes. I felt weak. What had I done wrong? The fuse had been burning when I started down. Maybe a flawed detonator cap. Sixteen minutes—still nothing.

A brilliant flash, followed by a deafening boom and billowing smoke, allayed my fears. The huge top rose straight into the air several inches, settled back to its original position, then toppled slowly, gaining speed as it plummeted to the ground. We glanced at each other, smiled and, without another word, headed for the landing where the crew bus waited.

I heard the side-rod comment to the hooktender, "He's going to be OK. It may take a while before he gets good at hanging rigging, but that'll come in time."

I had never heard sweeter words. That night my dreams reflected deafening booms, falling tree tops, glorious conquests, and complimenting words—a proven tree-topper nearing my twenty-second birthday. One more step, high-rigger, and I'll be a full-fledged high-climber.

Carroll Going Up

Carroll Topping a Tree

Carroll Topping a Tree

Chapter 16

High Rigger

"Hey, climber," the matronly hotel operator shouted up the stairs, "they called and said there wouldn't be any work today. You can call to find out what it's all about. Sounds like it has something to do with money. I've got the phone number."

Moments later, now dressed in my street clothes, I descended the stairs two steps at a time. How could this be? Nothing had been said to us after work the day before. Maybe I had been fired, or perhaps one of the punchers called in sick. No, the side-rod could operate the machines.

I paused at the bottom to get the number, then rushed down the hall to the wall-mounted phone.

"We haven't been paid for our last shipment of logs," the bookkeeper announced. "We'll try to get your wages to you in a week or so. Looks like we won't be doing anything for awhile, but keep in touch. We want you back when things get straightened out."

"It happens to those gyppos a lot," the barmaid informed me. "I didn't think this outfit had money problems but you never know. They don't let on till it's over."

My thoughts returned to the old single-jack faller called Hungry, the man who had been killed by a falling limb a few days before. He had departed this world just in time. To have been working for an outfit when it went belly up would have been too much, especially if his pay had been jeopardized.

Besides, rumor had it that a Canadian firm was experimenting with a new contraption, a chain saw driven by a gasoline motor. Such tom-foolery would have been beyond his understanding and, to be realistic, would have out-performed the old-timer. For him, growing old would have been misery rather than triumph.

With that rationalized, I turned to the barmaid. "Do you know an outfit where I can work until I get a few bucks in my pocket?"

"There's a gyppo about thirty miles from here. The company leased the buildings at an old CCC camp near Doty, and they're logging about ten miles up in the hills. Word has it that the food is good, and the bullcook keeps the bunk-houses clean. They brought in a superintendent to straighten things out. Evidently the side-rod let the outfit go to pot, and this new guy has a good reputation. So far, the men have received their pay on time and, according to the guys who come in here, if you do your work, he'll meet you halfway."

"Think I'll try it," I said. "Do you have a phone number?"

As the barmaid reached into her apron pocket, and fumbled for paper and pencil, her face took on a rosy glow and she stood lost in thought for a few seconds. Finally, returning from her reverie, the attractive woman, perhaps three or four years older than I, scribbled a number on the pad, tore off the top sheet and handed it to me. Fingers touched, then hands. Finally, eyes met and held.

Momentarily electrified by the intensity of what seemed to be a mutual attraction, my entire body responded with a surge of emotional yearning. Then, almost as quickly as I had revealed my feelings, past experience warned me to question my interpretation of the situation. My confused mind searched for an answer. Why doesn't she look away? What is she trying to tell me? Don't spoil a nice friendship by assuming too much.

A roar of laughter interrupted our trance. Perhaps thinking the men might have noticed her attraction to me, the barmaid fought to regain her composure while I, bewildered and frustrated, crammed the phone number into a shirt pocket. We turned to find with relief that the laughter wasn't directed toward us, so we joined in, pretending we had heard the shady story told by one of the jobless men. The chug-a-luggers received refills before the barmaid returned.

Moving close, she suggested, "If you go to work at the camp, please stop in and see me when you come this way."

"OK," I beamed, putting aside previous reservations. "But it will probably be a week or so before I get a paycheck."

"Don't worry, we can go to a movie. I haven't seen a good picture for a long time. Oh, yes, there's one more thing I should tell you. There's a small town several miles beyond the camp. It's called Pe Ell and it can be a rough place. Many of the townsfolk came directly from the old country, and over the years, they've remained clannish and hard-nosed. Although the older people speak with an accent, the majority are good, hard-working men and women; but, as with most logging towns, this one has a few bad apples. They won't go against each other, no matter what their neighbors do or say."

I arrived at the camp office to find the superintendent perched cheerfully on a powder box unlacing rain-soaked boots. Although I had filled out to 175 pounds, I felt dwarfed by the 250-pound giant. Twinkling pale blue eyes, deep-set in the oval face, accented a broad smile.

"You can pick up shirt, overalls, and gloves at the office. The bookkeeper will take it off your first paycheck," the supe informed me. "We start work at seven-thirty, eat lunch at eleven-thirty, and quit at four o'clock. This leaves one-half hour for lunch. I may as well tell you that we've had some problems with the locals who want to abuse these schedules. We go to work by the whistle and quit by the whistle. I had to fire two men last week because they poked around after the starting whistle blew. I hope you understand that this is the only way this outfit can survive."

"That's what I heard," I admitted and continued, "I have no problems with that. Thanks for staking me for the clothes. The last place I worked, they seemed to have the same problems you're talking about. It will be nice to get a good meal again."

"You'll be taking the job of the last guy I fired, but I don't think there'll be problems with the other workers. If there are, let me know."

Gathering climbing gear and personal items, I hurried to the bunkhouse, removed my boots, dropped onto a lower bunk, and dozed until the dinner bell rang.

The balding cook mopped his brow as he banged the clapper around each side of the metal triangle. First in line, the younger men joked about their last trip into town and threatened revenge on the cops who had broken up a hell of a good party. It made no difference that they had practically destroyed one of the local taverns for no explainable reason.

No one attempted to hurry the overweight cook as he waddled to the doors, stood for a minute to torment the impatient, then flung the barriers wide to admit the ravenous group. I mixed in as we made an orderly entrance into the dining hall and sat on wooden benches. Contrary to what might have been expected, old and young alike chatted quietly with neighbors. Rowdies had suppressed their arrogance.

With everyone seated, several young flunkies delivered the freshly cooked food to the tables. Each woman carried two laden platters on one arm and the third in the other hand as she delivered assorted mounds of steaming meats, vegetables, and rolls. The bountiful meal, topped off with generous portions of pies, cakes, and other pastries, was supplemented with a snack to munch on later that evening.

Bunkhouses in this camp contained metal single-width beds with an upper and a lower berth, a small upright locker by each bunk, and a few empty powder-boxes for extra storage and seating. Noting that the top beds had no blankets, I inquired of a neighbor, "Why doesn't anyone sleep up there?"

"You can thank the union for that. Initially, the Wobblies (Industrial Workers of the World) forced their way into camps and cut the upper bunks off with hack saws. If you've never bedded up there you can't imagine the foul odors. The mixture of shoe grease, sweaty clothes, and the heat from the stove all rise to the ceiling, making it impossible to breathe, let alone sleep. Even if these haven't been cut off, no one is expected to use the upper bunk.

"I tell you," my neighbor continued, "some of those union radicals want to break the companies but they sure do some good, too. It's the damn union officials that I don't like. They usually strike us right at the time we need to work, and they don't care if we're broke since their pay goes on. Besides, we still have to pay our union dues. Also, one of those buggers made off with our strike funds during the last shut-down."

With that, he reached into an empty pow-der-box, pulled out a can of snuff, carefully separated the metal lid from the container and indulged in a huge pinch. He then located his coffee can and explained, "I guess they're a necessary evil. For some reason, we can't get along without the unions, but I sure think we could be more careful who we elect. I've be-longed since they organized, and I've managed to stay out of trouble. Those officials are in hot water with the companies and the non-union mem-bers most of the time. Some outfits hire goon squads to break strikes and go after the radi-cals. I had a partner who got hell beat out of him just because he wouldn't walk across a picket line when management ordered him back to work."

Now he went to his calk boots standing near the potbellied stove and removed the crum-pled newspapers which had been inserted before supper. Finding the paper damp, he rumpled dry pages and restuffed the heavy footwear.

Successfully spitting into the coffee can at five feet, my neighbor resumed his onslaught. "The unions are trying to get in here, but too many of the locals don't want it. Last week, a guy got fired and the union wanted to do something about it, but, for the most part, it has died down. Do you belong?"

Trying to think of a reason for not joining, I finally answered, "I haven't been working in this area long. Farther inland, the union seems different. Maybe they don't need it as bad as they do closer to the coast. I hear they're getting stronger up there now, besides, they're AFL (American Federation of Labor)."

"You're better off not to be in that damn AFL. They're nothing but a bunch of company men who work in the logging when they're not tending their goldurn ranches. When there's a strike, they do nothing to help. They either go to work somewhere else or sit at home by the fire while we're freezing our butts on the picket line. They're sure glad to hold their hands out for the pay raises we get for them, though. Let me tell you, the CIO (Congress of Industrial Organizations) is the only way to go. Actually I'm in the IWA (International Woodworkers of America), but it's a branch of the CIO.

"The labor movement has cooled since that hanging under the bridge up-country and the murder of that union official's wife down on the harbor. The Wobblies got the movement started, and they had to be rough to survive. Labeled 'Commies' by the companies, those first union organizers soon found it almost impossible to get and hold a job. Yeah, they did some good but their time is over.

"All we need to strike for these days is more money and fringe benefits. Things are pretty good around the camps now. But you should join up as soon as you get money for your dues. Things will go a lot better if you do."

His sermon finished, the fellow rolled over and snored the evening away. Beyond a doubt, this man had mixed feelings regarding the current status of his beloved CIO.

A soft mist dampened the ground and plank walkways as the morning call rang out through the quiet camp. This morning we waited in the bunkhouses until the dining hall doors had been opened by the robust cook. Boisterous joking and laughter came only after all bellies had been filled.

Certain that the seasonal rains could burst from the heavens at any time during the day, we dressed appropriately, adding black woolen underwear for warmth. "No matter how cold and wet you get, you're always warm and dry when you wear the long johns," old-timers claimed. This time of the year, our bodies and clothing usually became soaked a few minutes after we began work, but few complained.

"We're getting ready to move," the supe announced as he emerged from the cramped office. "Can you notch stumps?" he asked.

"I've notched a few, but I'm not the best yet. If you have a good axe and a file, I'll make a notch that will work," I offered.

"OK, but we're going to raise a tree. The faller I fired last week felled the only suitable spar. I don't know what the hell he was thinking about. He knew better than to cut a tree that had an "X" chopped in the bark. The "X" was over two feet high and four feet off the ground. He didn't seem to give a damn, so I ran him off."

"If I notch the stumps, I'll have you look at them before we get started up with the tree. OK?"

"Sure," the supe acknowledged with a smile of appreciation.

I knew that if the notch was not just right and the guyline came out as the tree was being raised, not only could men be killed but the entire effort would be lost and all the preparatory work would have to be repeated. Thousands of dollars could be lost just because of one sloppy notch.

Stumps notched and approved, I made myself available to assist in preparation for the miraculous event. Each time a different task came up, the supe made sure I became involved.

"Let's go back to the old landing and get ready to unrig and move," suggested the supe. "Then you can come back here and top the dummy tree while I use the crew to move the yarding donkey and rigging. We'll go back for the loading donkey after the tree is rigged."

"OK," I replied. "How high should I make it?"

"It's only about two feet at the stump. We don't want it too limber. Say about seventy feet."

The spar at the old landing, now unrigged, stood naked and alone. It had served its purpose and would soon be forgotten. By quitting time, I had topped the dummy and the supe had moved the yarder into place, ready to raise the mainspar at the new landing.

During the evening meal, the supe and I sat side by side planning for the next day. Totally absorbed in our conversation, we were last to leave the dining hall. Minutes later, we continued in the supe's office.

After completing our plans, the supe changed the subject. "I've got a son in the Marines. He's a little older than you and a lot like me—never worries about much of anything.

haven't heard from him for some time but something tells me he's OK." Then, anticipating the inevitable question, he added, "His mother had a bad time of it when she went through the change. She's up-country in a sanatorium. I used to visit, but she didn't even recognize me the last few times. It's hard to see her go downhill so fast. They say she'll never get better, and I should make a life for myself without her. Doesn't seem right, but I guess they know best. I still call in hopes she'll come out of it.

"Life's like that sometimes, but I never dreamed it would happen to us. She loved the woods and was my constant companion when I surveyed tracts of timber. I sometimes helped with the housework to free up the day for her. Of course none of that was possible when I worked in the upper camps. Maybe that was part of her problem, but no one will ever know for sure. Haven't told our son. They were very close, but you know how kids are, he drifted away and seemed to want his independence. Occasionally, He returned for a few days, and that pleased her, but I don't think she'd remember him if he showed up today."

"Do you have brothers and sisters?" I asked.

"Yeah," the supe continued. "My older sister raised my brother and me. We had a little business in the late twenties and early thirties but the Feds put a stop to that," he added with a mischievous smile, then said, "We better hit the hay. Morning comes early."

Chapter 17

Titles

Bright rays of sunlight streamed through the dusty bunkhouse windows as the get-up bell awakened the camp. It's going to be a great day, I thought. Snuff-users placed an extra can of Copenhagen into shirt pockets while they joined in the joking remarks about fictional occurrences during their last trip into town.

Time and again, I had pondered this beastly existence. All we talk about is logging, drinking, fighting, and the women in the houses. During my younger years on the prairie, the talk was of cows, horses, crops, religion, and the weather—two extremes. Would I ever get used to this limited and crude way of life? Why not? It's exciting, earns good money, and the woods present intricate problems and novel experiences that consume the waking hours of many honest hardworking men. Once entrapped, few leave. Besides, I had no alternative at this time, and my reputation improved with each passing day.

Stuffed to the gills with a hearty breakfast, everyone selected a lunch bag as we filed from the dining hall.

This morning the mood seemed exceptionally jovial as we anticipated a change of pace. Discharging the faller who had accidentally felled the spar, negative as it had seemed, created a day or two of respite from the routines of daily production. Spar tree raising always meant a demanding and unpredictable day.

While three other crewmen and I hung and tightened the three dummy guylines, the supe and other workers used the cat to drag in the mainspar and prepare for the raising.

The regular hook-tender had not arrived for work that morning, and it was rigup time. Concerned, I questioned the supe. "What will we do without the hook-tender? Everywhere I have worked before, he managed the crew."

"You and I did the planning last night, so we'll manage the crew today. If we keep our wits about us, there's nothing to worry about. Besides," he added, wiping the sweat from his brow, "if we can't do it, there's no use for amateurs to try." The matter settled, I dug in to assist my optimistic friend.

Working as though everyone on the crew were an experienced rigup man, the old supe patiently directed and encouraged us without signs of irritation or discouragement. Eye contact always drew a smile and an inquiry from our leader. "How you doing?" or, "Think we'll get her up this afternoon?" We responded by matching his smile, adding an affirmative nod.

By lunchtime, I had hung the blocks in the dummy, one on each side of the small tree. The supe and other men had prepared the mainspar. With the butt end placed in the center of a log mat, then tied in place with cable, we strung guys around the notched stumps and back to the new spar lying on the ground. Soon, a sturdy block and the raising guys had been attached to the tree—most of the planning and organizing lay behind us.

Only a few details remained before we, the untried crew, could view the results of our efforts. The passblock, with the passline threaded, had been placed at the top of the spar. Next, we threaded the yarder mainline up through one block in the top of the dummy, through the block on the mainspar, back up through the block on the opposite side of the dummy, then back to the ground, where we attached it to an anchoring stump.

Now, the two quarter-guys and the mainline divided the area into thirds—just right to steady the tree from side to side as the top end rose. These same guylines would also hold the spar upright after it was perpendicular to the ground. With the cat attached to the loose end of one quarter-guy and the yarder haulback to the loose end of the other, the supe called us together for final instructions.

"Take a big slug of water for you won't have another chance for about two hours. OK," he continued, "we're all going to have a new experience today. Don't worry, we'll do fine. Now, how about it? Let's give it a try."

Unseasoned, half frightened, and anxious to avoid mistakes, several men gathered railroad spikes and sledges, then hurried to an assigned guy stump. I was left standing with nothing to do but watch.

Assured everyone was in place, the supe helped himself to a large pinch of snuff, then turned to me.

"It has been some years since I've raised a tree. Always interesting, it will be more so today, working with a bunch of rookies."

Now the supe motioned me to join him among the network of cables, machines and the two spars, the smaller dummy tree standing ready for duty and the mainspar lying on the ground, waiting to be given new life as the key figure in the historic high-lead logging of the Pacific Northwest.

Eyes sparkling like a child with a new toy, the confident supe nodded to the yarder-puncher, raised his right arm, and the donkey emitted puffs of steam as it slowly rolled the drum. Restraining cables cinched into the spar's base with a groan while, high above, the mainline snapped and cracked before settling into a steady hum, moved a few inches at a time, then lifted the resistant tree.

Realizing the old-timer needed no questions or suggestions at this time, and not sure what needed doing, I walked a short distance one way and then the other, looking first to the dummy I had rigged and then to the stumps I had notched—no problems.

Up, up, the 140-foot spar rose. Eyes darting from one area to another, the supe signaled for slack on the guys as needed.

The magnificent tree, now looking awkward and helpless, like a person who had lost his balance and found it difficult to stay upright, yet enough in control to keep from falling, eased its way upward. Serious faced, the supe suddenly held both arms out straight with his palms down, and everything stopped.

In the ominous silence even the birds and winds seemed hushed. What an awesome sight, this towering Douglas fir held motionless at a seventy-degree angle. A bystander might think it had paused to determine whether to continue upward or return to its resting place on the ground.

With everything in order once more, the signal to roll in the mainline and slack the guys started the spar upward again. Inch by inch, it moved to a vertical position.

"Now we got it where we want it," the supe chuckled. "Let's spike her down." Then, lined face sobering as he scanned the area, the aging woodsman inquired, "Where's the woodcutter?"

"I think he went to check the intake up where we've got the water pipe in the pond," the puncher replied.

The third guyline, which had been hanging loose during the raising, was pulled around a notched anchoring stump and tightened. Spar now secured, it awaited the topguys, blocks and loading-boom. Puncher, skinner, supe, six chokermen, and I collected at the mainspar to celebrate with a sandwich or an extra large pinch of snuff, then a trip to the creek for a cool drink.

Gentle odors of felled fir, cedar and hemlock permeated the air around the giant spar that had, only a few hours past, stood among other living evergreens. Within weeks, this man-raised tree, fully rigged, would account for thousands of felled trees to be shipped and processed in nearby lumber mills, leaving nothing but stumps from which the trees had been cut, unsightly ditches along which the logs had been pulled, and pulverized undergrowth which would take years to rejuvenate.

Somehow, this mass destruction of the forests seemed immoral; even so, homes, schools, and other buildings were desperately needed and the industry provided jobs for thousands of able-bodied men who, by their general makeup, thrived on this hazardous and taxing occupation.

When I returned from the creek, the crew had disappeared—probably back to the old landing to gather small tools. Again, I stared in reverence at the raised tree, daydreaming that someday I would be directing rigging crews. These fantasies vanished as I caught a glimpse of the supe slowly trudging along the pipeline that ran from the pond to the steam yarder. Yes, he seemed to be showing his age. The concern that had shown on the weathered face earlier, now even more pronounced, conveyed an uncharacteristic hint of sorrow.

"Where's the crew?" I asked.

"I sent one of the chokermen to help the woodcutter but when he got to the pond, he found the old fellow lying face down in the water. By the time the chokerman had dragged him to the bank, he was already dead. We still don't know whether or not he drowned, fell and struck his head on a rock, or just died. I helped the others get him into the crew bus, then sent them home for the day. They'll leave him at the morgue."

"Didn't you want to go in with them?"

"No," the supe answered. "They'll see to it that he's taken care of. He's gone, and there's nothing I can do for him now."

"Did you know him long?"

"Well," he replied heavily, "you see, it was like this. He looked after us, my sister, my brother and me and he taught me most of what I know about logging. One of the best highball loggers on the coast, he was soon forgotten after an accident, the one that took away his fame.

"One day, some years ago, the mainline broke as he stood in the wrong place; the broken cable struck him on the head and crushed his skull. They didn't think he'd live, but he did and he eventually returned to work again. Even though they inserted a plate, it didn't help much. Usually, he seemed normal but couldn't think too well, and the only thing he remembered was what he knew before the accident.

"Since then, I've kept him with me. Steam yarders became his only interest, and he knew a lot about them. We've been together for years, but I guess it was his time to go. I could tell by his actions the past few days that he wasn't feeling well."

We sat silently for several minutes pondering the situation. I couldn't remember the supe having mentioned the woodcutter by name. What did this namelessness mean? It seemed customary—especially among tramp loggers. Perhaps, someday I would understand. Finally, the supe growled, more to himself and the world than to me, "I've got to do something. Let's splice a new eye in the mainline and haulback; they'll need it before long."

We completed the splicing and returned to the creek for a last-minute drink before the short trip back to camp. Kneeling, I paused, stared into the stream, reflecting on my brief life as a logger: Personal sacrifice and top performance are taken for granted. Names are not important—only titles.

After the evening meal, the supe took the wood-cutter's pay and drove into town. He purchased a simple coffin, a grave-plot, and a small marker. The remainder went to the orphanage that had raised the old-timer through his early teens.

Late that evening, as we sat silently on either side of the potbellied stove, the supe mumbled philosophically, "If he had to go, it's probably best he went now. He loved to work around the powerful and speedy steam yarders. This is the last setting for the one we used to raise the tree. Only a few remain in service, and with the new diesel engines becoming popular, those will soon be gone. We'll strip the lines and let her set right where she is. The brush and grass will grow up around her; just like around my old friend's grave—I never told him."

"Did you know his real name?" I inquired.

"Well, yes, I knew his name, but before the accident he always answered to nicknames, such as 'highball' or the title of the job he held at the time, such as 'hook-tender.' You see, many men working in the woods become proud of their jobs and prefer to be known by the work they perform, or they take on a name that fits them. For example, my old friend's last name happened to be 'Flowers,' which, for childish reasons became 'Posy' during his teens, but he soon fought and earned a more tolerable handle. More men than you might believe come out of the prisons to work in the woods; usually they're good workers, but they don't want their names known. Your guess is as good as anyone's why one man was called 'Diamond Jim' since his name wasn't even Jim. No one knew. Now 'Joe the Mule' received his name for obvious reasons.

"Then, there are hundreds of men with Scandinavian names, often difficult to pronounce, so you'll find many shortened or simplified names such as Nels, Lars, Ole, Jon, and on and on. Yes, it gets confusing, but everyone has learned to live with it even though sometimes it's damn ridiculous. One Swede bullbuck was called 'Big Ole,' and his helper, 'Little Ole,' but Little Ole stood a head taller and seemed twice as wide as Big Ole—the woods are filled with these contradictions, so it's easier to be called by the work performed. Besides, tramp loggers never stay around for more than a few days. By the time the crew remembers a name they're on the move, headed for the next camp. So you see, job handles limit or grant rank, privileges, and responsibilities—everyone knows where he stands."

Awakened to a foggy morning the following day, I felt relieved. The cold, damp haze usually burned off before noon and the day's work might end in warm sunlight. A new woodcutter had been hired and, fortunately, we started with a full crew.

Six one-and-one-half-inch top guylines, now strung around notched stumps, lay ready to be hung near the top of the raised spar. Last minute instructions and encouraging words, again offered by the supe, bolstered my confidence as I put on the belt and spurs. "These guylines are much heavier than you have hung before. The main thing is to use your head. You can't bull these babies. You'll do fine. Remember, this is the first time."

Passing the support guys on the way to the top, I felt uneasy about being in a raised tree, one with no roots. It was almost like passing into another world—a world in which all supports were man-made. Even my survival, now in the hands of other humans, brought doubts to my mind.

Finally putting the uneasiness aside, I tied onto the spar, lowered the passchain for the huge plates and then the first guyline, and the second, until all six dangled limply from the spar top. Having pulled and twisted the un-ruly cables for more than an hour, my body quiv-ered, exhausted and aching from head to foot as I again sat in the double pass chain and sig-naled to let me down.

"Hold it!" I shouted as I passed the sup-port guylines. Something looked strange. One guy had been improperly attached to the tree. The shackle (clevis) could have spread at any time, releasing the guy, permitting the spar to fall with me in it.

Damn, I thought, from now on, I'll personally supervise and double-check all preparation for tree raising.

"We're lucky," the supe muttered when I arrived back on the ground and told him what I had seen. "Before we tighten any of the others, we'll tighten the top guy that's closest to that support guy."

With all guylines secured, I strapped on the belt and spurs, ready to complete rigging my first high-lead spar. As the supe had recommended, brute strength proved to be no answer to hanging the three-inch diameter cable bullblock strap and the one-ton bullblock. Wearily, I finished rigging the tree and by mid-afternoon the logs began coming into the landing. Roaring trucks, loaded with forty-foot fir, hemlock, and cedar logs, headed toward the mills.

Stiff and sore, I looked back on my first two days as a high-rigger. I had successfully topped and rigged trees and, if necessary, I could supervise raising a spar. However, not all would be prestige and glory. I now shouldered the responsibility for the safety and production

of crewmen who worked under the rigging I had
hung.

Chapter 18

Settling An Old Score

The heavy rains held off and, again with a full crew, production improved. Everyone sensed the change: The cook whipped up extra-delicious desserts, the flunkies pampered the new men, the old bullcook built warmer fires.

"How about going into town tonight?" the supe asked. "We've been hitting it pretty hard."

"OK," I replied, adding, "it's been almost a month."

"I wonder if you'd mind working through until we finish this setting?" the supe continued. "It will probably take us about three weeks. Beyond that time, the heavy rains will have set in, then we'd have to put in plank roads for the trucks. By working weekends, we can finish earlier."

Remembering my commitment to the barmaid and feeling uneasy about such a rigorous work schedule, I hesitated, thought for a moment, then decided. I'd send an explanation to the barmaid within the next few days.

"Yeah, that's OK," I agreed. "About going into town, I'm not much of a drinker, but it might be interesting to see what's there."

"I'm no drinker, either," the supe admitted with a chuckle, "Only an occasional beer, no hard liquor."

Rays from the setting sun filtered through the saplings as the bunkhouse shadows slid toward the perimeter of the old CCC camp.

"Sooner or later, I've got some business to take care of, but we'll look around awhile before it's dark," the supe informed me as we drove along the winding gravel road.

"Do you know anyone in town?" I asked.

"Maybe, but I'm not sure," he replied without elaborating.

Dusk settled in as we rode up and down two of the five streets that divided the small community into rectangular blocks. Tire swings, broken wagons, and unoccupied kiddie cars cluttered many barren yards, but an occasional dwelling, surrounded by a manicured lawn, shrubs and a white picket fence, broke the monotony. Except for a few malnourished cats and dogs wandering in and out of the alleys, the streets were deserted.

His curiosity evidently satisfied, the supe drove through the other streets and then circled the small town. Passing a group of company-style houses, he slowed to examine one roadside mailbox. Then, resuming normal speed, he turned onto the main drag, and parked near one of the three local taverns.

"Let's go in and wet our whistles," he suggested. "You can't tell what you might find."

"OK," I agreed with some hesitation. "I'll try a glass of brew."

Rank odors and a dim shaft of light escaped into the night as we entered through the tavern doors. Three mill-workers, still dressed in work clothes, sat at a card table and guzzled beer while they pondered their cards. Precariously perched on a bar stool, a lone figure, also dressed in work clothes, sat motionless as he stared into the mirror behind the bar. We each selected a worn stool, leaving two empty seats between us and the mirror-gazer.

Eventually served by the aproned bartender, neither the supe nor I had finished a small glass of the frothy brew before the mirror-gazer slid across the empty stools to sit beside the supe.

"You got any kids in the war?" the sullen intruder asked.

"Maybe," the supe answered with a sigh of indifference, but added nothing more.

"What the hell!" the stranger roared. "Don't you even know if you've got any kids in the service?"

Turning his head from the indignant fellow, my friend mumbled a few incomprehensible words.

Another customer entered and sat beside me. Blurry-eyed and reeking from beer and snuff, the newcomer demanded an explanation for my presence. "Why the hell ain't you in the war? You sure as hell look fit to me. How did you escape the damned draft while other kids, far less capable than you, are off defending their country?"

I had been questioned on this matter before, so I hesitated, knowing what would happen if I answered honestly. To reveal my limited vision invariably led to an inquisition.

"Can you see my hand?" it would begin, or, "What are you doing working in the woods if you can't see?" Then the inevitable statement would gush from the intruder, "I'll be damned! You sure as hell could do something. There's hundreds of kids in there who don't see so well. My kid's in there and he wears glasses. Why the hell don't you get glasses and quit dodging the draft?"

No, I thought, I'll not fall into that trap again. I maintained my silence.

With the mirror-gazer next to the supe and the local drunk beside me, the situation intensified. Neither the supe nor I attempted to answer the onslaught of insolent questions. Suddenly, as though a dynamite cap had ignited his two-hundred and fifty pounds, the supe swept his obstinate neighbor off the stool with an outstretched arm. The unfortunate villager hit against the back wall, slumped to the wooden floor, and lay dazed until the other heckler rushed across the room and dragged the confused mirror-gazer to his feet.

A moment of drunken gibberish passed between the townsmen before they staggered toward the exit, keeping a wary eye on the supe. As they disappeared into the night, an angry warning came back through the half-open door. "You damn well better get out of town. You'll pay for this before the night's over."

"What do we do now?" I asked nervously.

"Nothing," answered my unruffled partner. "Let's go down the street for awhile."

"But what about your business?" I asked, now completely bewildered.

"That'll come later."

The tavern had fallen silent. No one spoke to us, but questioning eyes and heads followed as we passed into the darkness.

Down the street, the supe parked directly in front of the next tavern as though he wanted the hecklers to know our whereabouts.

He removed the pickup keys, an unusual act in these remote areas, and we entered the smoke-filled tavern. Loud laughter and bragging gushed from the mouths of the drunken locals. Either unnoticed or deliberately ignored by the patrons, we sat at the bar and ordered beer, drinking even more sparingly than before.

Minutes later, several rough-looking characters wandered in alone or in pairs. They spoke to those sitting close to them but seldom pursued extended conversations; they did, however, drink heavily.

"Well, what do you know?" the supe muttered half to himself, "He's here, and he took the bait."

"I didn't catch everything you said," I remarked.

"Oh, I was just thinking out loud, I guess. There's a guy I knew a long time ago. Haven't seen him in years. He just seemed to drop off the face of the earth."

"Are you going over to talk with him?"

"Well, not just now," he shrugged. "Maybe later on. I want to see if he recognizes me. Just sit tight, and don't look directly at him. He's the big fat one."

Without making it obvious, I finally stole a glance toward the man, who sat with several friends. A monster, perhaps an inch or two taller than the supe and much heavier, he dominated the group. Whether or not his bulk was fat or muscle could not be determined, for loose clothing hung on him like a sack and small pig-like eyes exaggerated the huge head. Another rowdy sat at the same table; they could pass for brothers except that this one, much smaller, had a sullen, stupid demeanor.

"There he goes," the supe spoke softly. "I'm going to get re-acquainted. You wait here. I'll be back in a few minutes."

He followed the man, working his way through the tables toward the rest room at the rear of the tavern—the place where customers drank moonshine, settled disputes, or both. Straight and angular, the supe walked like a man with purpose. Slouched and flabby, the stranger's appearance attested to a lifetime of carousing and dissipation.

"Is it always this busy on a week night?" I asked, turning to the barmaid.

"Well, not usually." The young woman swept a worried glance around the room. "Whenever this bunch gets together, there's usually trouble. That's all they do, just look for trouble. We're lucky if they don't tear down the place. They're never satisfied until someone gets hurt, bad."

With that, a loud crash came from the small rest room. The entire tavern immediately became a caldron of boisterous cursing, swinging fists, and violent threats. Another thunderous boom shook the building. Concerned for the supe, I pushed and dodged my way back to the rest room. As I opened the door, the hulk of the supe's acquaintance, blood streaming from his face, careened into me. Not sure what to do, I mustered all my strength, and shoved the brute, wobbly and spraddle-legged, back through the open doorway where the supe mercilessly pounded the bloody face.

At that moment, two men grabbed me from behind, pinning both arms to my sides. As I bent to break the hold, the sullen-faced companion of the supe's opponent stepped forward and landed a blow between my eyes, causing blood to spurt wildly from the bridge of my nose. I lurched and twisted, swung and butted until finally free, but could do little more than counterpunch, for the gushing blood further clouded my already poor vision.

Now the supe, certain his adversary had been completely subdued, turned to find me surrounded by glaring eyes, stubbled faces, and clenched fists, each villager hoping to get his chance at me. Even so, the supe, cagey veteran that he was, paused to scan the barroom, then charged recklessly through the milling bodies and moved to my side shouting, "Grab onto my hip pocket. There are too many of them!"

With me holding onto the pocket, swinging with my free arm, and the supe, slashing with both fists, we battled our way toward the front entrance. Those who ventured to block our departure either landed on the floor to be trampled by the crowd or spun out of the path cut by our savage onslaught. One bystander, eager for action, grabbed a chair and raised it high above his head. As it descended, my friend, now a raging giant, kicked it from the man's hands and it spun across the bar, smashing several wine bottles before it came to rest near the barmaid. Seconds later, we emerged into the cool evening air.

"Run for our pickup," the supe ordered, "but don't get in. When you reach the door, drop to your knees and crawl around to the far side. Then go for the railroad tracks, keeping the pickup between you and the tavern entrance. We'll get behind those loads of logs and watch."

Chapter 19

A Job Well Done

As the supe and I passed the pickup and disappeared into the darkness, drunken villagers, obviously feigning hot pursuit, ran to the tavern door and directed bloodthirsty threats into the night—the humiliation imposed on their leader would be avenged.

Meanwhile, night-blind and bleeding, I stumbled and bumped my way through trees until reaching the loaded logs. Now breathless and bruised, I listened for the supe. Nothing. Had my friend been waylaid? Or, did he mean what he had said, "behind the loaded logs"? After what seemed to be several minutes, actually less than thirty seconds, I heard his voice. "Down this way, we can see everything from here."

I hurried to his side and crouched, demanding, "What the hell is this all about? I thought that guy was an old friend."

"It's a long story and I'll tell you later. Right now we have to get you cleaned up so we can see whether or not you need something to stop that bleeding."

"It's almost stopped," I insisted. "It really doesn't hurt. My face just feels stiff from the dried blood. But if you really think it should be cleaned, one of the punchers who worked for an outfit that went broke somewhere down here. He has a funny name, and I'd recognize it if I heard it."

Watching from behind the loaded logs, the supe rubbing his bruised knuckles and I wiping dried blood from my face with my shirt tail, we watched three carloads of men drive up and down the main street, their eyes straining to see through the fogged-over windows. Two cars finally broke off and drove around the block several times, then disappeared.

"They're starting to sober up or get tired and sleepy," the supe theorized. "We'll wait a while longer and then see if we can find the puncher's house. I saw one car stop by our pickup and do something under the hood, so we can't plan on getting it started."

"If you can read the names on the mailboxes to me," I suggested, "I can probably recognize his name."

Back and forth the remaining car drove, then around the block and back to the main street. At one point, the drunken occupants stopped the dilapidated clunker a few blocks away from the pickup and turned the lights off.

Working our way down alleys, occasionally venturing between buildings to read the names on mailboxes, the supe and I located the house. Surprised to see me covered with blood, the puncher invited us in and his wife soon had the wound cleaned.

"Now, what's this all about?" the puncher demanded. "Who the hell clobbered you like that?"

"I'm not sure," I replied. "It happened at the tavern—the one farthest down the street. Two guys, one a great big man and the other not so big but looking like his brother. I'm not cer-tain who hit me, but I got in several good licks."

The puncher and his wife exchanged glances. Then the woman spoke.

"I hope someone beat up the biggest bully. He's my neighbor's cousin, and the other one is his brother. Well, I guess they're both her cousins, but it's the big one who has terrified many men around town.

"Ten or twelve years ago, he returned from the harbor, evidently evading the law, so a few of his relatives hid him. Each month, he became bolder and meaner. For a time, he and his worthless brother were content to get other men into trouble then sit back and watch them squirm. Later, they mercilessly dug up dirt on the locals and used it to control the entire town. Stealing from everyone they could con or threaten, those renegades caused many honest families to break up or go broke." Then she added, "I hope someone really beat him up good."

"You won't need to worry about seeing him on the streets for a few days," the supe interjected. "And as for the brother, I have a score to settle with him too. I got the climber involved in this without telling him what I was doing. That pip-squeak brother hit him between the eyes while two other guys held him."

"Yeah," the puncher added, "that brother brags about how his lodge-ring makes a dandy weapon during a fight. It has the horns and head of an animal for a set. The horns protrude more than a quarter of an inch from the head and are as sharp as razors. He has cut up the faces of several men here in town, always while someone else held them."

My face cleaned and a small patch on the gash, I thanked the woman as the supe and I walked toward the door, but her husband, now serious faced, insisted, "Just a minute and I'll get my coat and go down to your pickup with you."

"No," the supe answered firmly. "This is our doing, or rather my doing, and you have a wife and kids. You have to live in this town and we'll be gone from this area soon. Thank you, but we made our bed and we have to lie in it. But, thanks again. It was enough to let us in and for your wife to clean the climber's face."

Leaving through the back door, we walked to the alley, checked left and right, then, keeping in the shadows, returned to a point where we could observe the pickup. After half an hour, when no one appeared, we made a run for it. The supe raised the hood and noted that the ruffians had jerked the starter wires loose.

"We'll push her to get the motor running," he whispered, easing the hood down. "When it starts rolling, you keep pushing, and I'll jump in and put her in gear. When I let out on the clutch, keep pushing until she's going and then jump in."

Miraculously, the motor coughed, sputtered, and finally took off. Then we headed back to camp, I staring into the darkness, the supe flexing his swollen fist.

Suddenly, a huge buck loaped into our path, forcing a moment of wild maneuvering that took us into the ditch. To have stalled in the muck meant certain disaster, but the dependable old truck, accelerator to the floorboards, wheels spinning and skidding, fish-tailed its way along the slope and finally regained the road. Off we went, the supe humming, "The old grey mare, she ain't what she used to be," and I marveling at his ability to remain calm regardless of the situation.

Later, my partner turned to me and chuckled, "You're sure a pretty sight," adding, "I've waited for this for over twelve years. I never knew where that bastard disappeared to. But I knew that sooner or later he'd show up somewhere. The waiting has been worth it. This one chance was all I needed or wanted. Sorry I couldn't tell you what was going on. That guy is like a wild animal; his instincts would have detected anything that showed on our faces. When we get back to camp, I'll finish the story."

We again fell silent. Bright rays of moonlight reflected off the roadside ponds as we, the battle-worn trio, the pickup, the supe, and I, wove our way around the chuckholes.

Unaware of what they had missed, the logging crew remained asleep as the pickup pulled up to the office. Once inside, the supe kindled the fire and the small enclosure soon warmed. The reheated pot of coffee simmered on the pot-bellied stove. With mugs in hand, we each selected an empty dynamite box for a seat.

"Well," the supe began, "it was a long time ago. I was only a kid when I learned that everyone eventually has to make a living for himself, and usually for someone else. As I mentioned a few days ago, the old wood-cutter sort of looked after my sister, my brother and me after our parents were gone.

"My brother and I weren't old enough to work in the woods, so we did odd jobs around the cafes and card rooms for spending money and groceries. Then we took up with a guy a little older and he showed us how to get into the big stuff. He made moonshine and we delivered it for him. By the time I was—What the devil?" he exclaimed, "I heard a car outside."

Cautiously, he eased his way toward the window and stood to one side, saying nothing as he peered into the night.

I held my breath and listened. A car door slammed. Footsteps moved toward the building but stopped abruptly, and a backwoods twang pierced the air.

"Hey! You in there!" the drunken villager shouted. "Come out and fight like a man!"

The supe turned to me. "It's the guy I beat up and his brother. They're out there with a gun. The fat one's sitting in the driver's seat with the barrel pointed at our door. Don't get near that window and stay out of sight. I don't want them to know where you are. Let me do the talking."

A twelve-gauge shotgun stood in the corner, and I headed for it, determined to even the odds.

"No," the supe ordered, "we can't use that. We'd both have the law after us, and I've already had my fill of that. Just stay calm."

Unwilling to remain unarmed, I hurried to a small storeroom, returned with a huge, double-bitted axe, then stood near the door, ready for action.

Apparently understanding my concerns, the supe glanced at the lethal weapon but didn't object. His eyes gleaming like an animal's, the old woodsman slowly turned the knob then, without warning, threw the door wide open, simultaneously stepping backward several feet. The gunman had no time to react.

At the sight of their prey, weasel-face moved back a few steps. Speechless for several seconds, he finally collected himself and shouted with feigned bravery. "You yellow bastard! You beat up on my brother when he wasn't expecting it. Now, damn you, come out and fight me!"

With an odd smile on his face, the supe stared at the challenger. He made no move to go out or retreat; he just stood motionless and smiling.

Unnerved, the brother stepped back a few more feet, glanced at the car for reassurance and shouted, this time with less gusto.

"Are you coming out, or do I have to come in and get you?"

Without flinching, the supe invited, "Come in and get me."

"You lousy son-of-a-bitch," screamed the frustrated pugilist, "You come out here and I'll push your damn face into the mud."

A light went on in a nearby bunkhouse and a sleepy head emerged. "You drunken bastards knock it off; we got to work tomorrow. If anybody wants a little fun, wait a minute and I'll get dressed and accommodate you."

By this time, several underwear-clad men had emerged from the bunkhouses.

Outnumbered and without reinforcements, the unnerved combatant ran to the car. Almost blind from his earlier beating and with his brother only halfway into the car, the inebriated driver sped down the road, dragging his unfortunate kinsman. Several men ran from the bunkhouses to watch the renegades leave the premises.

"We better go back to our coffee," the supe suggested, then he laughed and added, "What a wonderful way to end a quiet evening."

Short two men the following day, the supe became the hook-tender, and I filled in as head-loader. After eight hours of trial-and-error loading, I felt the experience had been worth the torment. That evening, the supe met me at the cookhouse and suggested, "I lost my Stetson last night and I'm going in to get it. Want to go along?"

"You're going back after your hat?" I inquired in disbelief.

"Yeah," the supe insisted.

"OK, but what will we do if we run into that gang?"

"If we do, we'll at least get a sandwich while they're getting a meal. And besides, those guys were all drunk last night. They'll be hungover tonight. Generally speaking, they're a bunch of cowards, so I don't anticipate trouble."

We parked the pickup at one end of the main street and started toward the tavern at the other end. To my surprise, the streets were empty, reminiscent of a western movie. Neither

hurrying nor lagging, the old pro and I sauntered toward last night's arena.

Inside, the barmaid greeted us with a
smile, then reached under the bar to produce the
coveted hat.

"I'm sorry I didn't get it cleaned up for
you," she apologized. "We want to thank you for
what you did last night. They say his eyes are
swollen completely shut today. Evidently, one of
you also gave that louse of a brother a nice
shiner. Too bad he didn't get the same as the
big one."

"Can I pay you something for the broken
wine bottles and chair?" the supe inquired.

"No, you did enough," she reassured. No-
ticeably infatuated with my companion, she
placed her slender hand on his, lavishing additional words of praise. That he was old enough
to have been her father seemed irrelevant.

During our drive back to camp, the supe
finished the story that had been interrupted the
night before.

"Well, my brother and I finally came of
age and we started our own bootleg business. Before long, we delivered the liquor each morning
just like a milkman makes his rounds. Distilled
on the other side of the harbor, we brought it
across in small boats to an old shack on an is-

land near the shore. Each night, several gallons of moonshine were rafted to the mainland, where we loaded it into cars for delivery to businesses. For years no one bothered us, but one night all hell broke loose.

"This guy tried to horn in on our business. I think he was responsible for the Feds finding our cache and sending me to the 'big-house' for six months. Even though I feel the score has been settled, if I catch him away from his cowardly friends again, I'll do the same as I did this time. Just won't take the foolhardy chances. Still feel bad because I involved you, but chalk it up to experience."

"Have you ever been really afraid of anything?" I asked.

Amused, the old-timer replied lightheartedly, "Not knowing 'n fearing I might prevaricate, I hesitate to respond." A hearty laugh terminated the discussion.

Heavy clouds had formed above the mountain tops and deciduous tree leaves drifted to the ground. Noisy camp-robbers scolded as industrious squirrels spent hours cutting and hiding fir cones in preparation for winter. A few more days and the gentle old master-logger would be gone.

Loggers & Steam Donkey

Carroll may be the front left man.

Loggers & Steam Donkey

Chapter 20

So, What Else Is New?

Wet and tired, the faithful crew had worked seven-day weeks and ten-hour days to finish the setting. Heavy rains drenched the area as the last log truck plowed its way through the mud. The spar had been unrigged by quitting time and the old steam yarder stood alone as the boom, loading donkey and other rigging were loaded on trucks for the long trip back to the harbor.

Climbing rigging thrown over my shoulder, I walked to the crew bus before turning to watch the last steam escape from the leaky valves of the old donkey:

How many logs had she dragged to the landing?

How many saplings had she destroyed?

How many men had she maimed or killed?

No one knew. Her secrets would remain with her for she had now been relegated to the annals of logging history—her glory departed.

Memories of her power and speed would linger in the minds of loggers for years, but her sub-structure, rusting boiler, and drums would succumb to the groping tentacles of thorny blackberry vines. Without the old wood-cutter around to protect and pamper her, this favorite workhorse of the highball loggers would have to tolerate intrusion by forest animals and birds seeking refuge in her fire-box and towering stack.

The supe had been called away during the night—something regarding his son, the bullcook informed me. Putting aside my disappointment, I knew that logging friends often parted without a goodbye or handshake. Sooner or later, we'd meet again, either in town or in other camps, and it would be as though we had never been apart, no handshake, just a broad smile and the inevitable "How's it going?"

Now unemployed, I finished breakfast, packed meager belongings, shouldered climbing gear, and hitched a ride into town. Bypassing the loggers' hangouts, I deposited a sizeable paycheck in the bank and enjoyed a leisurely lunch at a local cafe.

For a time, I had been uneasy about returning to this infamous village where the supe and I fought our way through the tavern brawl. However, the daytime crowds remained amicable.

Late afternoon took me along the main street where I entered the fateful tavern, scanned the patrons and, seeing none of the previous adversaries, placed my climbing gear in a corner near the door. The sallow-faced owner stood with his back to the public as he checked the till. Noticing my reflection in the mirror, his eyes searched the glass. Evidently reassured that I had arrived alone, he resumed counting.

"Where's your partner?" the barmaid asked, registering disappointment.

"Called away for the day," I replied. "Might be in later, but I'm not sure."

"I understand you're finished with that setting," the owner interrupted. "Where are you going next?"

"The outfit's going back to the harbor, but I'm planning to stay around here if I can find a job."

"Yeah?" the owner questioned, then added, "They're starting a reload near town. I understand they'll need a climber to get rigged up, then work as a second-loader."

"Who should I see?" I asked.

"The fellow who's putting up the money will be in town tomorrow; better talk with him. There are rooms across the way," he indicated with a nod.

245

Torrential rain drenched me as I sloshed across the gravel street and entered through the unpainted doorway. Climbing the rickety stairs to the second floor reminded me of my earlier experience in Cheyenne, Wyoming. I chuckled, wondering how my two friends were doing back on the prairie.

During an economic slump, this building had been divided; the bottom became a logging supply store and the second floor a low-cost hotel for tramp loggers. What wild escapades must have taken place in this primitive structure!

The stench of mold, mingled with fumes from a neglected toilet, crept along the second story hall and tumbled down the stairwell. A few feet beyond the top step, a discolored bell sat on the dust-covered ledge below the penciled sign "Manager".

Several persistent rings brought the caretaker. A middle aged woman cracked the door and made a one-eyed observation, evidently to reassure herself that I was neither a local drunk nor the law. Methodically she removed the safety chain and scrutinized me from head to toe. Satisfied, the manager motioned to me with one arm, holding her faded robe closed with the free hand.

"Take the third room down the hall," she rasped. "It's cleaned up and it has heavy blankets. The toilet's next to the back stairs."

"Could you give me a shout in the morning, in case I oversleep?" I requested.

"Here's an alarm clock. Set it at whatever time you want. Just be sure you leave it in the room or, better yet, bring it to me here at my office. You can pay me now," she ordered, pushing the hair from her eyes.

Beyond a doubt, the ancient steam radiator had been broken for years. I gave the valve knob a vigorous twist, only to find the disintegrated part lying loose in my hand. Calk boots had splintered a once beautiful oak tongue-in-groove floor, and a cracked mirror hung above the pitted washbasin and a two gallon galvanized pail, half full of stale water.

More like a hammock than a mattress, the old feather-tick puffed up around my body as I dropped into it, sighing in resignation. Not ready for sleep and with the light still burning, I surveyed the cracked plaster ceiling, which supported dusty cobwebs. The unshaded light-bulb, dimmed by lint and insect droppings, hung over a straight-backed chair.

What the devil's that, I thought, watching a solitary blob, evidently dangling from the ceiling by an invisible strand? It seemed to be moving. Inch by inch, the thing extended its tether until it came between my gaze and the light-bulb. A damn spider. Refusing to pull my eyes from the loathsome critter, I watched its downward progress.

Suddenly, it dropped to the patch-work quilt and scampered on its way. The tiny legs tickled as the strange bed-fellow ran across my face. Flailing with both hands, I finally smashed the unfortunate intruder.

Feathers had penetrated the mattress cover for I could now feel small pricks from the spiny ends—or could I? No! Something was biting me! Leaping from the bed, I stood on the dilapidated chair near the light. A red spot verified my fears. Now teetering on the rickety perch, I stared down at the louse-impregnated bed.

Within minutes I had dressed and knocked on the manager's door. Silence. Another knock, louder this time. The shuffling bedroom slippers finally announced the landlady's approach.

She peeked from behind the partially open door and demanded with a toothless yawn, "What the hell do you want now?"

"Something's biting me! They're in the bed! I'm covered with bites!" I shouted, my voice escalating with each statement.

"You brought them with you. If I'd known you carried them, I'd never have rented you the room." Shoving a small bottle through the opening, she ordered, "Put this on, and you'll be fine. I don't see why you're so damn skittish. Sooner or later, everyone gets them."

Before returning to my quarters, I entered the raunchy toilet where repulsive odors, combined with thoughts of the infested room, and the derelict manager, soon forced me to the streets. The chilly night air seemed like paradise.

Walking resolved nothing, so I returned, undressed, and applied the mysterious potion. Solid in my conviction not to rejoin the voracious insects, I dressed and tried to make myself comfortable slouched on the unstable chair.

Why, I didn't know, but segments of past years darted in and out of my mind. The chaotic hodgepodge made no sense. I longed for comfort, orderliness and logic.

Awakened by a burning sensation spreading over my body, I rose from the chair and walked the floor. Again forced into the streets, this time to cool fiery skin, I went back to the familiar tavern and ferreted out the most likely patron to ask for a personal favor.

"Will you read what that small print says on this bottle? I got some in my eyes and they're watering," I lied.

"Ha! ha! Well, I'll be damned," the stranger guffawed, "Is this the first time you've had them? Who have you been sleeping with or where have you been staying?"

"Ah, mmm, well," I mumbled.

"That's OK," the new friend whispered. "I don't blame you for not wanting everyone to know your business. This stuff's called 'Git'em', a common cure for what you got. It says to apply and wash off in twenty minutes. It burns like hell if you don't. Wherever you're staying, you better get back there and get rid of the stuff. Take a bath with hot water and soap."

"Thanks a lot," I replied and hurried back into the night air. Another hour walking the streets failed to relieve the fierce burning. To my chagrin, a downpour forced me back to the room, where I undressed and bathed in the stale water. With only minimum relief, I again returned to the streets and walked until daylight. The severe discomfort had subsided and, even though it still bothered me to have my clothing rub against the irritated skin, I knew the worst had passed.

The initiation completed, I, now a full-fledged tramp logger and not entirely proud of the distinction, ate a hot breakfast in a small cafe, then left to find the man who financed the reload. He hired me on the spot.

Raising the spar had gone well and I soon learned that I worked with a superior crew. The head-loader had been brought in from the harbor and the puncher had operated steam-loading machines for years. Together, we had organized and rigged the tree in record time.

Unlike the larger steam yarders, the 9 X 10 duplex loading donkey was much smaller but highly efficient. The puncher, familiar with all aspects of the aging machine, patiently worked her over and with a few reconstructed parts, had her running like a top in a few days. Again faced with the decision to accept or reject a combination assignment, I negotiated an above-average wage, and settled in to wait for a full-time climbing job.

Installing a newly-designed single-tong heel-boom increased production and cut two positions. Our three-man crew soon earned the reputation for being the fastest loaders in the area. Only one problem concerned me: both the head-loader and the puncher drank heavily. As the reputation improved, the drinking increased.

Night after night the quitting whistle sent us racing to the tavern, where thirsty loggers downed one beer after another while one or two white-capped mugs waited. I usually gulped the first glass, then passed the time nursing a second while sharing small talk with the more moderate drinkers. No one, it seemed, gave consideration to loss of sleep or the hazards of working with a hangover.

Customary procedure was for the head-loader to place the tongs on a log lying on the landing, and I unhooked them after the engineer placed the log on the railway car.

One foggy morning, the puncher, his judgment and vision impaired from partying the night before, misplaced a small log at the top of a load, causing it to slip from the tongs. I had already sprang into action and looked upward only when my foot landed squarely on the bottom log. It was then that I faced stark reality. In my haste, I had committed myself without checking the situation and would now pay for the blunder.

The log turned, took several bobs up and down, twisted, and rolled toward me. Having little time to reverse direction, I instinctively whirled, leaped, and landed face down in the mud, the log missing me by inches.

Of course, I received a generous razzing, "Hey, buddy," a truck driver shouted from inside the cab of his parked rig, "are you afraid to die? That was a beautiful swan dive."

Nevertheless, the puncher absorbed a harsh tongue-lashing from both the loader and me, and the day's work continued. To display a hint of remorse, the puncher put aside the drinking for several days, but abstinence proved temporary—typical behavior for tramp loggers who worked within driving distance of local taverns. These nightly beer-drinking sessions, combined with weekends garnished with hard liquor, amiable women, and brutal fighting, sent many otherwise excellent loggers into early retirement, or into their graves.

By habit, we all gathered at a favorite hangout each Friday night for a ceremonious session of drinking, lying, bragging and raising hell in general. To have gone directly to a restaurant would have been an unpardonable sin, for filling our bellies with food always came last.

An hour or so into that particular evening, I left the gang and wandered back to the odorous rest room where the loader, by now more than a mere acquaintance, already stood before the urinal casually reading the graffiti on the dingy wall. By nature, he seemed a gentle soul, quick to smile, slow to anger, but abnormally secretive in personal matters.

Having fulfilled the call, he sighed in relief, grunted and read a statement for my benefit. "Kilroy was here." He added quizzically, "I wonder who that guy is? His name's in every can I've ever been in."

"Damned if I know," I replied. Then, for some ungodly reason, I asked, "Say loader, what's your first name?"

Casting a sidelong glance in my direction, he mumbled contemptuously, "Pete," his voice calculating and sinister.

"The hell it is," I retorted jocularly, only to make matters worse by adding, "When the bookkeeper handed you your paycheck, he said it, and it started with a 'P' all right, but ended with a 'y'."

Slowly, much too slowly, and knowing I had him dead to rights, he turned, bent and stuck a scowling face close to mine and threatened, "Now, you nosey bastard," he began, ending with, "if I tell you, and you spread it all over hell, I'll bash your damn head in." Before I could respond, he stepped back as though measuring for a solid punch, but unexpectedly croaked, "It's Percy."

Having forced the issue, I foolishly laughed and asked, "Who the hell gave you that handle?"

But he wasn't finished. "Now, damn you, what's yours?" he demanded.

Myself now caught in the proverbial bind, and knowing the man before me had sacrificed a lifetime secret, I recalled childhood fights over my own given name. Grudgingly I recipro-cated and awaited his reaction.

Up went his arms, extended toward the ceiling as though reaching for the stars, then down they came with a loud slap on stone-hard thighs, eyes watering in gleeful revenge. The muscular legs buckled slightly as he collapsed against the wall, giggling like a schoolgirl re-ceiving her first kiss. Momentarily a compas-sionate smile spread across the weathered face and he reclaimed his six foot two inches—friends forever.

"What the hell's going on in here?" a stranger asked, his bulk filling the doorway, "What's all the ruckus about?"

"None of your damn business!" the loader bellowed, ending the inquisition. With the matter settled, we all turned to read from the wall and further discuss Kilroy and his travels.

One night after a stint in the tavern, the puncher, drunker than a hoot owl, rolled the car over an incline, delivering us into a farmer's front yard. Within minutes, the night-shirted owner met us with a shotgun. Although we escaped serious injury, the car had been totaled, and the farmer threatened to call the sheriff; however, he listened to our ridiculous fabrications and relented.

Again, 'How many years?' crossed my mind—time to move on.

Chapter 21

A Tough Decision

Several months had passed since I sent word to the attractive barmaid, delaying our plans for a movie. She had helped me obtain employment on two occasions, perhaps she knew of others. Just thinking of her had increased my desire to see her again. Maybe she could put some logic into my life.

The bus arrived at the Chehalis station about noon, and I hurried across the street, anticipating a warm welcome from my friend.

"No," the bartender informed me, "she left a while back."

"Where did she go?" I asked, wondering what might have happened.

Turning his palms up, he shrugged and grumbled, "Don't know. Just up and left. Say, you're learning to climb aren't you?" Before I could reply, he continued, "Did you hear about that logger up-country who bought a small outfit and was doing well when he got killed? Even though he owned the company, high climbing had always excited him; he seldom turned down a chance to work in the spar.

"But one day, as they were un-rigging a raised tree, he went into the tree to lower the blocks. While he was still up there, a crazy rigging-slinger, trying to show his stuff, started knocking unimportant lines loose from the stumps. Then the goofy bastard made a mistake and knocked the wrong guyline loose—the one that held up the spar. The tree fell with the owner still in the top. Needless to say, his body, smashed so badly that they had to scoop him up with a shovel, was unrecognizable, like a blob of jelly. They couldn't even show him in the casket."

I thought that one over for a while, wondering how the man must have felt, knowing that his time had come and unable to do a darn thing about it. The entire incident must have lasted no more than five or six seconds from the time the spar began to fall and the time it struck the ground—not much time to dwell on it.

A few days later, I hired out to the largest firm in the area and set out to expand my knowledge of big-time outfits. The "slack-line", the ultimate in rough-ground logging, usually involved only the most experienced rigging men and required a tail tree as well as a head spar.

A regular high-lead tree required two sets of guylines, the top guys and the buckle guys, while the slack-line required three sets: the top, snap, and buckle guys and extra blocks in the tree.

Fortunately, the head-climber needed an assistant to help move the slack-line to another setting. A once-in-a-lifetime opportunity for me, I concentrated on each step of the procedure and learned from the seasoned high-rigger, who had an unmarred reputation throughout the industry.

One day at a time, we worked together in the tree; the old-timer sharing his knowledge, patiently guiding and correcting on matters of efficiency and safety. Together, we had the slack-line moved in a respectable time. Some of his reputation had rubbed off on me and I soon shared the distinction of being a top-rated high-rigger.

Monday morning. Hangover time for weekend topers. Several blasts from the donkey-whistle called me to swing the blocks on the tail tree.

Fifteen minutes later I arrived at the spar where the crew waited, the passline already hooked to the strawline drum. With my metal-handled rigging hammer tucked into the loop on the belt, I signaled with a nod, then steadied myself in the passchain. For the first time during my brief career, I continued up the spar to swing the massive blocks. Tied onto the tree one-hundred and thirty feet above the logs, I easily swung the haul-back block. To get above the bullblock, I needed to untie my rope and move higher in the tree.

"Take up the slack. Man on," I shouted.

"Man on," the hook-tender repeated to the puncher, indicating a loop going around his legs, and then holding up both hands to indicate easy.

"Hold it," I shouted and untied my rope. "Going up," I signaled.

Instead of going up slowly, I plummeted toward the ground, shouting at the top of my voice. The frightened hook-tender frantically flailed his arms, signaling the puncher as he screamed, "Hold it, damn it! What the hell are you doing? Hold it! Hold it! Hold it!"

Powerless to do anything but shout, I plummeted downward. Why the puncher finally placed his foot on the brake to stop my wild descent twenty feet above the logs, no one knew. Now the ashen-faced fellow gently lowered me to the ground, where other crewmen stood in awe at the close call.

"You're not going back up there, are you?" the hook-tender questioned, wide-eyed and disbelieving.

"Well," I replied, "just a minute and I'll let you know." Finally, as though defying the world, I ordered, "Get me an axe."

A chokerman, startled by the request, hurried to comply. Thrusting the handle into my outstretched hand, he immediately moved back a few steps to ensure that he would not be the victim.

I removed the belt and spurs, selected a vine maple bush near the yarder and, in full view of the puncher, cut a branch about three inches in diameter and four feet long. Next, I called two of the chokermen to me and gave explicit instructions.

"One of you men take this club and stand within three feet of the puncher. The other stand close enough so you can put your hand or foot on the brake if he doesn't stop when the hook-tender or I signal. Now, listen closely! If the puncher falls asleep again, you with the club, let him have it between the eyes and the other one get on the brake."

Somewhat unnerved by the situation, the hook-tender brought the passline to me and again pleaded, "Maybe you'd better wait until we can get another puncher."

"You may be right," I replied, "but if I don't go back up now, I may never go again. I can't afford that luxury—man on! Going up!"

Twenty minutes later I was back on the ground, both blocks swung. The yarder again working at full speed, I gathered my rigging and headed back across the canyon. Halfway up the far side I paused, turned and watched the logs come into the spar, two at a time. Chokers unhooked, the rigging returned to the log-covered hillside for another turn, and another, and another.

My thoughts wandered back to my young rigging-slinger friend, the old single-jack, the wood-cutter, the owner who loved to climb, and other unknowns. Who would be next to die? Dwelling on the subject had never been productive. Everyone accepted that accidents do happen. Considerations beyond this were seldom discussed. If a man is killed, another will take his place the following morning. Do I belong here? Am I truly one of them? Well, I suppose, it's yes and no. Why do I think and speak of them as apart from me one moment, then immediately consider myself a kinsman? Right now, I seem to be looking from the outside.

Even more puzzling, what makes these durable tramps wake up and optimistically go to work each day, knowing that they may not return to their bunks that evening? Are they as immature as the intoxicated sixteen-year old who, in his confused and boisterous state, is unable to evaluate the lethal capabilities of the powerful engine under the hood? Or are they more like the unsuspecting wild animal that has no concept of death?

For most loggers, there seems to be a compelling force that draws and holds each man until his time comes, whether it be debilitating injury, old age, or premature death. The need to pit one's body and mind against the myriad hazards seems uncontrollable. Regardless, life goes on. At the end of each day, those who survive can relax, knowing that there will be one more supper and breakfast.

The outfit, having lost a bid on a large tract of timber, cut back on its operations, leaving me again unemployed. Rather than hang around the twin cities, I purchased a bus ticket to Grays Harbor.

To my delight, an attractive young woman about my age removed her purse from the adjoining seat so I could sit beside her. She liked dancing and so did I; I got her phone number—lucky day!

Drenching rain and biting winds swirled around the bus as it crossed the Wishkah River drawbridge, gateway to Aberdeen-Hoquiam—a notorious bastion for loggers, mill-hands, fishermen, sailors, and longshoremen. An elderly woman leaned toward me and whispered, "You're now in Little Chicago. It's a rough area so watch your step."

My new acquaintance was met by an older couple, her mother and father, I guessed. Knowing nothing about the area except its reputation, I retrieved my small bag of clothing and climbing gear, selected a likely street and left the Aberdeen bus station.

Halfway down the first block I turned my back to the driving rain and patted my shirt pocket to reassure myself that the girl's telephone number remained dry. The first block comprised a furniture store, an obscure hotel and several other respectable-looking businesses. From that point on to the river bank, garish dance halls, odorous taverns, smoke-filled restaurants, and ancient flophouses dominated the scene. Turning away from the main street, I entered a tavern/cafe/cardroom combination, The Mint.

"There's not much going on around here right now. Everyone seems to be holding onto his job," a bar stool neighbor informed me. "What can you do?"

"Right now, I'll do almost anything. There's not much I haven't done."

"You'll have no trouble then," the other replied, immediately turning his back on me. I felt I had said something wrong, but what was it?

Chapter 22

The Harbor

Sitting alone in the loggers' favorite evening and weekend haunt, the Mint, I pondered my bar stool neighbor's sudden change. Why he so rudely turned his back went beyond me, but a broad-hipped young barmaid saved the day.

"If you're looking for a clean place to stay, there's the Wirta, some say it's the Virta. Nevertheless, go to the river and turn left two blocks; it's where most loggers stay." Then, she added with an encouraging smile, "I stay in the rooming house down the street."

Having made her point, the amiable woman again emphasized the virtues of the recommended hotel.

"It's owned by a family of Finnish people who have been here for years. If you're short, they'll stake you for room and board until you get a job. Besides, their cafe has good working-man's food. I sometimes eat there on my way home. And, there's a tavern close by where you can dance. Try it."

"Where do the loggers catch their rides to work each morning?" I asked, already plotting my strategy for getting a job.

"Most of them gather at the Up and Up, a cafe/tavern—the one just this side of the river bridge. It's about one block from the hotel. They make up good lunches and serve breakfast earlier than any other place in town. The cook's good even though he's drunk most of the time. Don't let that bother you; he's still the best."

On my way to the recommended hotel, I realized I hadn't eaten since early morning and it was now 2:30 P.M. The small restaurant looked inviting and clean. A young waitress, neat and smiling, took my order and disappeared into the kitchen. As the door swung open on the waitress's return, I could not believe my eyes. There in the kitchen stood a young woman who looked like the barmaid I remembered so affectionately, the one who had helped me get my first job. Could it really be her?

I had failed to return so we could attend the movies as planned. Had she left because I had broken a promise? Or was it, as the bartender had said, that "she just up and left"? A new dimension had now been added; the amiable girl on the bus seemed interested, the girl I had just met in the tavern wasn't bad, and now this. I wolfed the sandwich, drank the coffee, then departed to sign in at the hotel.

Noisy and filled with smoke, the daily departure point swarmed with rough, boisterous loggers. A pretty redhead served the long counter while a sallow-complexioned cook managed the grill. A young, black-haired bartender joked with the loggers as they waited for their breakfasts and sack-lunches. No one drank at the bar. That would come at day's end when these men, cold and hungry, returned for an evening of fun at the dance halls, in the taverns, or with the girls.

This morning, all outfits had a full crew, but I seemed to be a good prospect for one employer. "Stick around a few days," the owner of a small operation encouraged. "If you don't land anything before next week, I'll probably have something; that is, if you're willing to try anything that comes up."

With enough money to stay afloat for several weeks, I hung around until the men had departed for work, then chatted with the bartender, who was near my age, reasonably intelligent, and handsome. His dark eyes twinkled when I threw in a few Scandinavian profanities learned from friends. For sure, he understood but raised one eyebrow, looked down a sculpted nose and shrugged, "French descent." With that, he flashed a broad smile which revealed a gold-crowned front tooth, and turned his back to enjoy my reaction in the mirror.

For some reason, he seemed more like a banker's son than a man who willingly chose to shove beer and wine across the bar. Regardless, his age, devilish humor, and mutual interests made us immediate friends. I wondered why this healthy-looking young man had not been drafted, and perhaps he wondered the same about me, but neither of us broached the subject.

About 9 o'clock, winos and barflies wandered in and out of the place in quest of free drinks. The cook, bleary-eyed and shaky, retired to his upstairs quarters to rest or drink more before the noon lunch. A sulky, fat scoundrel took possession of the redhead and whisked her to who knows where.

Later I left the gathering point, leaving my new acquaintance, the bartender, to deal with the ne'er-do-wells. Deliberately, I avoided the small restaurant and the desirable barmaid, who now apparently cooked for a living.

Before stepping into the alley, I checked to assure myself that a speedster wasn't departing—nothing but a parked blue pickup. Strange, I thought, this truck seemed so familiar. Yes, the faded paint and the dent in the left rear fender set me straight. The supe! Could it be? Now brimming with excitement, I ran to the driver's side, opened the door, and slid into the seat. Sure enough, the faithful old truck! I'd wait. He couldn't be far.

Fifteen minutes, then one hour, but still no supe. With nothing more to do, I left and roamed the streets, hoping for a chance meeting with my friend. No luck. However, optimism forced a return trip to the alley. Gone! The truck had vanished. Cursing the bum luck, I re-traced my steps toward the hotel.

Cars, pickups, and logging trucks of various shapes, sizes, and colors moved methodically along the rain-drenched street. Suddenly, a blue streak darted from the far lane of traffic, completed an illegal and hair-raising U-turn, then pulled alongside. The supe, eyes twinkling, leaned over, opened the passenger door, and bellowed, "Well, I'll be damned! A man never knows what he might see when he's got no gun. Better get in here out of the rain."

As I climbed in beside my old friend, we exclaimed simultaneously, "How's it going?" No handshake, just two broad smiles indicating our pleasure in the reunion.

"What the hell are you doing down here?" he asked.

"Nothing yet. I just got in town yesterday. Staying at that hotel down by the river. It's supposed to be OK."

"We're not doing anything right now," he explained, "but if you can hold on a few weeks, we're going to do a little salvage work down the bay. It'll be just the two of us moving some equipment out of an old setting. When we finish, the same as when you worked for us before, we just let the steam donkeys set. The lines are worth considerable, so we'll go back and salvage them."

Darkness set in early as we rode along the streets, eventually arriving at my friend's favorite restaurant, where an engaging young waitress invited us to review the menu.

"I don't need this," the supe assured as he returned the folded page, "thank you anyway, I always eat the same thing—the fried clams." Then, turning to me, he explained, "The razor clams in here are the best in town, and they give the most, including potatoes and gravy and one other vegetable. Their pies are just like home-made."

"I'll have the same," I murmured, unable to divert my attention from the auburn-haired waitress.

"What would you like to drink?" she asked, looking directly at me.

"Milk," I replied, then hastily added, "please."

"And you, sir?" she asked, flashing a smile at my sidekick.

While waiting, the old-timer whispered, "She's new. Never seen her before."

Enthralled by her natural beauty and friendliness, we included her in our conversation, all the time admiring the waist-length pigtails, slender body, and flushed cheeks. To me, this girl, probably two years younger than I, had to be even more appealing than the woman who had given my friends and me the ride from North Platte, Nebraska, to Twin Falls, Idaho. Each time she returned to refill coffee cups, my emotions soared—what a gal!

Later, she placed the check on our table, resting one hand on my arm. "I hope you both come back," she encouraged. Her hand—I wanted to look down, but dared not. Her fingers, graceful and warm, squeezed ever so gently, then relaxed, remaining just long enough to assure me that the contact was more than an accident. She liked me!

Boyish ardor controlled the moment as I questioned, "What's your name?"

For no apparent reason, she paused, then replied defiantly, "My father sometimes called me 'Spit-fire,' my mother still calls me 'Sunshine,' and my brothers call me 'Pigtails'." With that, she gathered the dishes in silence and hurried to the kitchen.

Why didn't she want me to know her name? Had I misinterpreted her friendliness?

Bellies full, we paid the cashier and sauntered toward the door, reluctant to leave the warm building. Something didn't add up. Just one more look, I thought, then outside to face the winter storm.

Turning, I found my dream-girl sober faced, looking my way expectantly. She wanted me to apologize? For what? I had only asked her name. And then it hit me, I hadn't given her mine. Nor would I. We stood like statues, neither giving in. And then as if by magic, we both smiled.

An elderly couple approached the waitress and inquired about rest rooms while a local drunk noisily demanded a refill. Damn, I thought. Then, as though on cue, a flurry of late diners. Seeing no chance to regain that wonderful moment, I wheeled and dashed through the driving rain, where the supe waited patiently in the pickup.

With the heater turned on high, we rode in silence for a few blocks. I wondered if the waitress would have been so friendly if young men near her age were more abundant. Or, if she knew I had a vision problem? What then?

About names, I reasoned, they're only tags parents attach to kids long before the child is born. If, contrary to expectations, their desires are thwarted by nature, they frequently revise the original name to match the gender. Perhaps her parents had dreamed of a "Henry," so they saddled her with "Henrietta", or "Roberta" for "Robert", or "Josephine" for "Joseph". If something like this were true, it's no wonder she has kept it a secret. When we see each other again, if we ever do, I'll be more cautious about what I say, or the questions I ask; besides, she might insist on knowing mine. What a time the men would have with that.

This speculation is nonsense. Right now, it's a job that's needed.

The clean bed, the sink in the room and a closet to store my clothing and climbing gear—what luxury! Even though the bathroom and shower were across the hall, this room, very plain, was exactly what I needed. Hands and face washed, I sprawled on the bed and relived the past two days. My old friend, tasty restaurant food, attractive young women, the promise of a job, and a place to call home—the harbor, what a place!

Chapter 23

The Strike—New Romance—Old Friends

"The damn fools are talking strike again," my neighbor blurted as he slid onto the stool next to me.

"What is the longest strike you've been in?" I asked.

"Hell, if you want to know about strikes, ask Stubs, the old guy sitting on the other side of you. He's the talker."

I turned to find myself facing a broad smile and sparkling eyes peering from beneath unruly eyebrows. His right hand displayed four stub fingers, and he was ready for that which he enjoyed most—hashing old times.

"Well," he began, speaking with the propriety and verbosity of a lecturing professor. "It was in the mid-thirties, and times were tough. As I recall, the big one started small but soon exploded into an industry-wide shutdown. Increased violence and destruction filled the void left by the spreading strike; opposing factions closed ranks to defend their rights.

Day after day, pickets toted strike-supporting signs as they marched back and forth at strategically selected points. Lookouts, posted some distance from the main group, identified approaching traffic as scabs, goons, company bastards, or merely disinterested travelers. Hostile intruders received physical or mental abuse befitting the perceived degree of threat."

"Yeah," a bystander added, "us pickets stood in the rain for days on end with only a jelly sandwich and an occasional thermos of coffee to warm our insides."

Ignoring the interruption, Stubbs continued, "Theoretically, the union united workers around mutually beneficial principles, and although serious infighting often threatened the common front, most men remained faithful to the labor movement."

Another interruption: "Our strike funds were doled out a nickel or dime at a time, and I'm sure some was stolen."

"Yes," Stubbs acknowledged, "and for those indirectly affected by the strike, acquiring sufficient food and clothing became a serious problem. Many families earned a few dollars picking ferns for florists, while others raided squirrel caches and sold the fir cones to the Forest Service. First-time fishermen wound their way along rivers and streams, occasionally shouting latest strike reports to friends across the water. Youngsters, accompanied by mothers, spent hours searching beaches for the elusive razor clams. Generally, purchases of staples entered the merchant's ledger followed by a note that settlement would be made later."

Another old-timer summed it up. "Although sympathy strikes forced everyone to the bargaining table, final settlement brought on repetitive complaints; businesses declared they had lost vast sums which would take years to regain and we resented that the shutdown failed to accomplish what had been promised."

The girl I had met on the bus moved closer as we entered the alley leading to the back door of my hotel. I had called her twice since we parted at the bus station, but for an unstated reason, she refused to date me. My third call, to my delight, brought us together. We had attended a matinee, left early, then went to a tavern to dance and share a pitcher of beer. Now we hurried through the blinding rain to finish the afternoon at my lodging.

Somewhat unsure of myself, for this was my first experience at taking a girl to my room, I stopped halfway up the long staircase, placed one arm around her shoulders and blurted, "I'm so glad we met on that bus, and you gave me your phone number."

"Yes, I thought we'd never see each other again, but the wait has been worth it. I've had such a nice time today," she replied.

"This is my room, the one closest to the back stairs," I said, hoping she would approve.

Once inside, she looked around and whispered, "I thought these downtown hotels would be dingy and unkempt, but this is OK." Then, keeping her voice lowered, she asked, "Where's the bathroom?"

I faltered, uncertain whether she was only curious or wanted to use it, but motioned toward the door and mumbled, "Just across the hall, if you need it."

Evidently amused by my uneasiness, she smiled and patted my arm, then excused herself, returning moments later refreshed and even more attractive. Now, her face slightly flushed, she stopped a few feet from me and began, "I must tell you something before we go further. I'm more or less married, and I have a child. You see, we've been separated for a long time and I've been living with my parents. I hope this won't ruin things for you; I mean, ruin it for us."

"Not unless we want it to," I replied, closing the gap between us.

Affectionately, she placed her arms around my waist and pressed full length against me. A few minutes of intimacy and our instincts took over. We caressed, we loved, we slept—an unguarded sleep that, in some mysterious manner, put aside the past and realigned the future.

We woke to love again, my affection for her growing by the minute. Needless to say, our youth, unleashed from months of constraint, encouraged and demanded more. Fond exchanges suggested mutual satisfaction and an enticing future.

Drowsily she whispered, "It's so nice, I mean how well we get along." Then added, "It was so different with—I'm sorry!" she gasped, catching herself. "Oh, well, I guess I might as well tell you. My husband and I didn't have much in common. I mean, we weren't suited to each other. He has a serious drinking problem and besides, he showed no interest in me after the baby came. You know, other women. I've heard he's been drafted into the service."

"Now that that's out of the way," I assured, "we can get on to more pleasant things." For an unexplained reason, I felt no guilt about becoming intimate with this charming and forthright young mother.

Our conversation, partly serious, but generally lighthearted, came to an end when she glanced at my pocket-watch dangling from a shoestring looped over the bedpost. "I hate to go," she said apologetically, "but my mother is taking care of the baby. If you want, I'd like to do this again, but I can't stay too long. I'm not sure she knows I came to see you, but I think she does and just doesn't want me to know she knows. She nor my father liked my husband. Dad is home only on the weekends, so he doesn't know the half of it, and I'm not sure he would approve of me being here with you. It has been bad."

Arm in arm, ignoring the drizzle, we walked several blocks to her house, stopping a short distance away. Then, standing on tiptoes, she gave me a warm good-night kiss and vanished into the dark entrance.

Whistling "Star Dust" all the way back to the hotel, I felt that the world and I had finally come to terms.

A brisk rap on the door and the Finnish accent awakened me. "There's a note for you. The man asked me to deliver it early this morning."

"If you don't mind," I requested, "please read it to me. It won't be anything personal."

"It says that you should be ready for work this morning about 7 A.M. He'll pick you up in front of the hotel. It's signed … . I can't read the signature."

"OK, I'll get dressed and be right down. I think I know who it is. Will you ask the cafe to put up a lunch for me?"

I had almost finished breakfast when the familiar old pickup parked in front. Gulping the last few bites, I grabbed the lunch, paid the check and hurried toward the restaurant door. The driving rain reminded me of my raincoat. Turning, I scooped it off the floor, pushed my arms into the sleeves, then hurried through the downpour.

"We're ready to start that salvage project I told you about a few days ago," said the supe. "Are you still interested?"

"Yes, but what about that outfit that went on strike? We have to go along the road where they have pickets."

"They won't bother us, for we'll gather what we need today and then head out about four o'clock tomorrow morning. We'll quit early. I have a friend who'll get us through."

Perfect, I thought. If we get back in time, I can spend the late afternoons with my new girlfriend.

At the storage shed, we collected dynamite, detonator caps and fuse. Blasting away mud and rock slides was an inevitable part of opening an abandoned road. Saws, axes, wedges and sledgehammers, haphazardly loaded next to a small hand-winch, completed the load. Cutting and removing uprooted saplings which crossed the roadbed required minimum brainpower—just a #4 hat and a #44 collar.

Day after day, we sweated and strained as we moved miles of steel cable and small equipment from the logged-off area. As we fought the rain, muddy roads and the primitive tools, we hoped our salvage earnings would carry us through the winter.

One day the supe parked the pickup beside the harbor road. We walked a short distance along the water before the old bootlegger stopped and pointed to the small island where, years ago, he and his brother had cached their moonshine.

Deep in thought, the old-timer stared at the rotting boards that now marked the spot where their storage shed once stood. Then he turned to me, raised one pant leg and placed a huge finger on the small round scar. "The Feds gave this to me when I tried to escape through the back of the shed. Somehow the bullet missed the bone. I managed to get away that time, but as I mentioned before, I wasn't always so lucky." He pulled the worn cloth back down his leg and again turned to the water. Several minutes passed before he shook his head and smiled to himself.

Silently we turned and wound our way back to the pickup. Again on our way, the supe alternately hummed, then sang, "She's a pretty little girl who lives up town. Her daddy is a butcher, and his name is Brown."

Each time the telephone rang, the young mother, usually dressed and ready, hurried to meet me at our favorite haunt, the tavern/dance hall. In spite of the dark, rainy days, our lives again seemed worth living. Her mother had even agreed to care for the child once or twice each week. She knew and approved! What a break! But what about her father?

As the supe had predicted, the picket lines caused us no problem. However, we heard that one scab received a terrible beating when he tried to cross.

The shutdown, by increments, produced results; negotiations became serious and minor concessions grudgingly emerged from both bargaining committees. The supe and I completed the salvage job and banked a respectable nest egg which we split, then went our separate ways, parting with the familiar, "See you, take it easy."

I liked my new friend more than I had liked any other girl. I might even have loved her. I tried to make our dates special: picnics in the park, hikes along the river bank, searching for seashells along the beach. We danced to Miller, James, and Dorsey, or went to the movies, where I held her hand in the dark.

As time passed, we spent more and more time in the hotel room sharing small talk. "How will we know when we're growing old?" she would ask. Or, "Do you think there is really a God?" And, of course, there was the lovemaking.

Giant lettering announced the occasion: LOCAL STRIKE OVER. Store owners restocked shelves. Housewives cleaned lunch pails. "Houses" gussied-up the "girls" in preparation for the first Saturday night.

Several weeks had passed since I last checked the morning gathering place for logging employees. Peering through the steam-streaked windows, I noted that the cook, already half-drunk, wiped his brow as he methodically flipped the pancakes while keeping a watchful eye on the brew cup located within arm's reach. As usual, the young bartender chatted with customers and the redheaded waitress served breakfast as though the strike had been little more than a passing dream.

Smoke and boisterous laughter poured from the doorway as I entered. Good times reigned again; new faces blended with old and the camaraderie settled in.

"Hey, climber," the familiar voice called from across the crowded room. "Over here. Remember me?"

Baffled, I approached the big fellow. Sure enough, the loading-donkey puncher who had assisted the supe and me after the tavern brawl up-country.

"What the devil are you doing here?" I asked. Then, without waiting for a reply, I added, "How's it going?"

"I became involved in negotiations, and the company general manager made some wisecrack I didn't like, so I knocked him on his ass the

287

next time I caught him in the street. They blackballed me, so I'm here looking for work. I have a lead on a punching job near here. If they need someone, do you want me to let you know?"

"Sure!" I climbed onto the stool next to the puncher.

Two days later, I had another combination job, climbing and second-loading. Gathered around a large lunchtime fire, we speculated on where our first paycheck would be spent. Naturally, the houses and girls fared best, with drinks running a close second.

Then we spotted three men walking along the logging road leading to the landing. A choker-setter spotted them first. "Here they come to get their mitts on our money. It's that union business agent, the sheriff, and the lodge president. What the hell do you think they want now?"

"I'll be damned if I know," the hook-tender growled. "They better not ask me to support their strike fund again. I didn't get one red cent from them during this shutdown."

The observant chokerman slipped from the group and disappeared over the hill. I knew the sheriff had been looking for the fellow, but thought the cagey old veteran would never chance coming onto the job to make the arrest.

No one spoke as the men neared. "How's it going?" the union official asked.

"Not bad," the hook-tender finally replied, but added nothing more.

"The sheriff has something to tell you, and then the lodge president wants to give all of you some real good news," the business agent announced.

Stepping forward, the sheriff began his spiel. "You guys know the churches have been trying to close the houses. I'm going to run for sheriff again, and if I get re-elected, I'm here to tell you that they will NOT be closed! I've managed to keep them open so far, but the next guy may not be interested in helping you guys."

A few approving nods showed around the group. Then the lodge president spoke. "We've got a real good offer for you. Next Saturday, anyone who wants to join the lodge will get free drinks all day." Cheers went up and we softened. Bragging about guzzling, hollow legs, and hangovers rattled through the thirsty crowd. No one had earned enough to buy drinks for several months; now came the time to over-indulge at someone else's expense. What an enticement!

Chapter 24

The Union—The Lodge—The Law—The Religion

Radiantly beautiful and alluring, my friend twirled her body to model the pink flared skirt and flowered blouse. Dark brown hair danced around graceful shoulders as she paraded before me, displaying an aura of sophistication. The new pumps accentuated her shapely legs while the soft smile highlighted the drama.

We had been saving money for this occasion and the sky was to be the limit. Her mother had altered the hand-me-down skirt and blouse, but the pumps had been purchased under a layaway plan. One-half down payment had held them at the store; now they belonged to her—time for something special.

An attractive couple, we strolled, arm in arm, toward the exclusive restaurant. The menu, fastened to the window with bright red tape, caused her to beam with excitement. "It's so nice to get really dressed up and be with someone you like," she exclaimed, giving my arm a squeeze. "I hope it's a cozy place where we can have privacy and a delicious meal."

Flickering candlelight reflected in her sparkling eyes as she sipped the only wine we could afford. I ordered a bottle of imported beer. Warmed by the beverages and each other's company, we ordered fried clams and the trimmings. For a split second, the beautiful waitress, auburn hair done in pig-tails, flashed into my mind but vanished almost as suddenly as she had appeared. No, the girl across the table remained my choice.

Again on the street, we slowed our pace to examine new displays and bright lights beckoning window-shoppers. Reality disappeared as we romantically looked to the future, identifying items to buy when rich. Then, putting aside dreams and eager to be alone, we hurried toward the hotel. Drunken loggers and fishermen blocked the sidewalk, so we crossed the street, turned left at the familiar corner, and vanished down the alley leading to our one-room haven.

As she lay cradled in my arms, I noticed tears trickling down her face.

"What is it?" I asked, more out of politeness than innocence. I knew the answer, but we both had avoided discussing it. Several weeks after we had met, she told me that her estranged husband wanted to reconsider their marriage.

"It's just that I've been so happy with you, and I know what it will be when the war's over: the drinking, the nights alone, and our child asking unanswerable questions."

"Have you considered an alternative?" I asked, pulling her closer.

"No. There is no way out. I have to think of the baby. He didn't ask to be born into this situation. I was so young, so dumb. I've already taken one big step and don't feel like going back or taking another at this time. Maybe things will change, or I'll get enough gumption to do something other than complain, but I'm not there yet."

I offered nothing more. Was she waiting for me to suggest something? I again remembered the tie-hauler's warning. Would it be fair to her and the child? How long before I would be seriously injured or even killed? Again, does she know about the vision? What if it gets worse or even goes altogether? What would she have then? Nothing.

After carefully drying her tears with a corner of the sheet, I placed both arms lovingly around her and we lay silently for several minutes. Eventually, we put foreboding aside and enjoyed each other's love—the same gentle caressing and mutual concern for the final enjoyment that had so often thrilled us before.

The following day, she called and left word informing me that relatives had come to visit; she didn't know when she could see me again.

About ten o'clock the whistles blew, signaling a serious injury. I had been over the hill notching stumps for the next spar, so I dropped the axe and rushed toward the landing, but the ambulance crew had already placed the chokerman on a stretcher and loaded him through the rear door. According to other crew members, the mainline caught a small log and hurled it onto the unfortunate fellow.

"He had blood gushing from his ears," one observer noted. "He won't last long. It happened so damn fast. I didn't even realize it until I looked and he wasn't standing where I had seen him a second before."

Word came back that the chokerman had died on the way to the hospital. Because he had been hired off the street that morning, no one knew his name. Evidently, he had come up from Oregon after the strike. Another nameless tramp logger.

A chokerman muttered, "One down. Two to go. What a way to start after the long strike."

With the outfit shut down for the day, everyone climbed into the crew bus and sat staring into space. Within minutes, the loading-donkey puncher moved alongside me and asked, "Are you going to the union meeting this Saturday afternoon?"

"I hadn't given it much thought."

"We got to push all the harder for membership. Too many guys weren't signed up this time, so the company took us to the cleaners. We're shooting for a closed shop, then everyone will be forced into union membership before going to work. Have you joined yet?"

"No, but I suppose I should," I replied, annoyed by the pressure. Nevertheless, I understood the wisdom in having a closed shop.

Finally, the big event rolled around. Saturday had been designated for free drinks at the lodge, the same day scheduled for the special union meeting. Having nothing better to do, I arrived at the lodge about 1 P.M. to find mobs chug-a-lugging. Two hours later, the loudspeaker ordered everyone to the main meeting room.

"Now," the president announced, "let's all line up, and those who are new members raise your right hand and recite after me."

The indoctrination completed, old members as well as newcomers stood to have their pictures taken. With the free drink deadline approaching, each man gulped his favorite and ordered another, downing it as he moved toward the exit.

Once outside, drunken loggers, chirpy and boisterous, staggered their way toward the union hall. I joined the more sober or, if you will, the least drunk, and we followed along, enjoying the ridiculous antics of God's children.

With paid-up members present and the doors closed, union officials sat sullenly behind the long table, awaiting the onslaught from disgruntled men who had been unemployed for weeks. Within minutes, roaring voices boomed through the hall and the usual accusations and demands, accompanied by violent threats, echoed along the corridors.

Monday morning, the local headlines blazed, "LODGE MEMBERS SUPPORT INCUMBENT FOR SHERIFF." There we stood, lined up like birds on a telegraph wire, our foolish faces glowing with pride—or from the liquor. Suckers, all of us! We had been hoodwinked by the union officials, the law and the lodge. Or had we? Oddly enough, almost everyone took it as a joke and continued to patronize the lodge, attend union meetings, and support the sheriff for re-election.

A soft knock on the door awakened me from an unpleasant dream. "Yes. What is it?"

"Just a telephone number, nothing more," the maid's shrill voice echoed through the closed door. She read the number to me and departed.

I leaped from bed, dressed and hurried to the lobby telephone booth. For certain, I thought, my lovely girlfriend's relatives must have gone.

After several agonizing weeks, I had decided to reveal the full extent of my vision problem to her, suggesting that we could make things work if she wanted to leave her present situation. To continue seeing her without a commitment didn't seem right. The phone rang several times before an elderly woman's voice came on the line. "Yes?" she queried.

Startled, I delayed my reply. She repeated, "Yes, who is it?"

"Well, I'm … . I'm looking for someone," I stammered.

"I assume you are the fellow who has been seeing my daughter?" She waited.

"Well, mmm, I guess so. Is she all right?" I asked.

"I'm afraid I have bad news for you. We had relatives visiting and just before they left, my daughter's worthless husband arrived. Discharged! Imagine! My husband thinks he was booted out because of his problems, you know, the drinking and all."

Soft sniffles followed by several coughs came over the line, then a muffled apology before she continued, "He swore that the service had changed him and insisted my daughter should give him another chance. Eventually she agreed, so they packed and left for their home in Texas.

"My daughter insisted it was for the baby's sake, but I'm not sure that was everything. We had a few minutes to talk alone before they left. She told me of your dangerous work and poor eyesight. I'm certain these two things helped her make the decision. Beyond a doubt, the times you two spent together were the happiest of her life. I want to thank you for that, and I admire your courage, but it would be better if you didn't try to contact her." The phone went dead.

Strange voices from outside the telephone booth rumbled around in my head and my knees felt weak.

After two close calls on the combination job, climbing and second-loading, I collected my pay and moved to a camp several miles from town. Hiring out as a climber limited my work to topping and rigging trees, avoiding the hazardous work on the ground. The long evenings in the bunkhouse gave me time to reconsider my options.

Sunday evening, several weekend renegades, broke and hung over, returned on the early speeder. One man, a young cat skinner, came in reeling from the last-minute drinks he had consumed.

Staggering into the bunkhouse, he began his tirade. "You guys got to join up. You'll never regret it. I'm here to spread the word. He's waiting for you to come forth and be saved. Join me, brothers, in prayer. Come now, let's—"

"Knock it off, you mangy bastard!" the old faller roared. "Every time you go to town, you come back either converted by some tinkerbell, or you're moving in the opposite direction, the filth of the earth."

"The way you talk," the skinner admonished, "you'll never get there that way. Listen to me and I'll set you straight. Today, I became the messenger. I spread the truth. Please join me," he rambled.

"I said, knock off that bullshit. You don't believe a damn word of it. Do you remember how you ridiculed that street preacher not more than one month ago? You came in drunk and said, 'There he was with his plaster collar and tommyhawk hat, reading out of the old joke book, waiting for Jerusalem Slim to come along and carry him away to the promised land.' You got your damn nerve coming in here peddling that crap. And say, by the way, what are you going to do about that jailbait you got knocked up?"

"What the hell business is it of yours?" the skinner retorted. "You're too old to do anything, so you've got to stick your damn nose into other people's business. If you're not careful, someone's going to knock you on your can, old man."

Without warning, the faller leaped and landed a crushing blow to the skinner's chin. Reeling backward a few steps, the younger man finally regained his balance and flew at his adversary, cursing the old faller for having copped a Sunday on him. Back and forth they struggled—grunting, hitting, and kicking. The skinner tried to bite the faller's ear off.

Reluctant to have their beds overturned and powder-box seats destroyed, a bystander opened the door and several men shoved the combatants into the yard between the bunkhouses. Both men flailed with their fists and feet. Although the younger pugilist finally gained the upper hand, the old fellow held his ground.

"Hold it. What the hell's going on here?" the bullbuck roared as he rushed from his quarters. "Both of you get your gear and get to hell out of camp. You know there's to be no fighting here. Now, start counting ties. I don't want to see either of you around here again. They'll have your pay for you at the lower camp. Now get your hind-ends going."

Back in the bunkhouse, the card games resumed while the pugilists collected their belongings and started toward the lower camp, eighteen miles away. Strange as it might seem, the two fighters, after walking a few miles, probably laughed off the entire affair and later enjoyed time together in the taverns.

Chapter 25

Kit

Again searching for someone to fill the void in my life, I returned to the paved streets, odorous taverns, and garish dance halls. As the log truck crossed the bridge and pulled to the curb, my thoughts drifted to the barmaid/cook who had helped me locate my first job. I thanked the driver, crossed the street, and entered the small restaurant where she cooked.

Eyes sparkling, the amiable waitress served the midday customers with a smile, swapping flirtatious jokes with regulars. Her radiance, however, turned to scorn as she approached me, took my order, whirled, and entered the kitchen without a word. I strained to see beyond the indignant woman as she passed through the swinging door. No luck.

When the meal arrived, I inquired about the cook.

"Oh, she's not working here any more," came the roguish reply. Again cutting the conversation short, she turned to wait on another customer across the room.

Unwilling to accept the curt statement, I pursued the matter. "Where did she go? Is she working nearby?"

"Neither," she retorted. "She got married."

"Who to?" I blurted.

Then she dealt the final blow. "She married a police officer."

"She what?" I wailed, "A cop! How could she? When?"

"Oh, a while back. I think she got tired hanging around always waiting for you damn loggers to shine up to her. I bet she'll be real happy. I would."

Now even more conscious of my crumbling world, I finished the meal and left the restaurant. Once outside in the cool harbor air, I reasoned woefully: Although being the exalted climber made me top dog in the woods and taverns, it did nothing to assist in meeting suitable women.

Muddy log trucks, pickups, and cars rumbled by as I walked the streets searching for a familiar face. The supe, where had he gone? He hadn't contacted me for some time. We had eaten

together at … that's it! The auburn-haired waitress!

Had I not reacted impulsively to logging
camp isolation, life might have been different,
but a burning hunger for companionship overshad-
owed past disappointments. Just the thought of
her compelled me to race toward the restaurant,
fearful she no longer worked there or even remembered me.

Rising apprehension forced me to slow
down, walk by the uncurtained window and glance
in. Yes, there she stood, just as pretty as before, pigtails and all. To have rushed in revealing my joy with a hearty greeting could have
spoiled everything, so I entered quietly and selected a table away from other patrons.

When she turned to see who had entered,
our eyes met, igniting two cordial smiles—a
greeting that implied more than casual interest;
life was back on track!

"How are you?" she inquired, handing me
the menu. "I haven't seen you around lately."

"I've been working in camp, arrived back
today."

"I haven't seen your friend lately. Has he
been away also?"

"Not sure, but he said something about
rafting logs to a mill across the harbor."

Eyes and face brimming with curiosity and intelligence, she looked directly into my face and whispered with a voice soft as the spring winds, "I'm so glad you came back." With that, she left to turn in my order and wait on other customers while I searched for just the right words to use when she returned. Should I ask her to attend a movie? To dance in the taverns? To walk on the beaches?

Each time I looked up to find her glancing toward me, she blushed, and I gazed admiringly. Yes, I'll ask her. But what if she refuses? I have no one else. It's now or never.

"Would you like anything else?" she inquired, refilling my coffee cup.

"Yes, please. A piece of that chocolate pie," I replied, stalling for time.

Pie served, she questioned softly, "Do you ever go to the movies?"

Relieved beyond measure, I beamed, "I sure do! It gets me away from the logging for a while. How about you?"

"Yes, but I don't like to go alone."

On her days off we attended movies, and since she was still a minor, not quite twenty-one, we slipped into the dance halls through a side door and sat in the darkest corner. We drank coke and danced only when the floor was crowded. Her body, shapely and firm, felt like no other I had held.

Weather permitting, we jogged along the beaches or strolled, hand in hand, through the winding paths in the city parks. Although she had a car, gas rationing restricted its use.

"May I see your room sometime?" she requested one day as we neared my hotel. I had always dropped her off at the furniture store, where she could wait if I had to return to my room for something.

"Well, uh, yes, sometime, if you would like." Then I turned and looked directly into her eyes.

Now, another dilemma. The friend I had met on the bus had been married and experienced. Does this girl know what she has requested? Well, she had asked, and unless she changed her mind, I planned to someday comply.

Several days later she asked again. "Don't you want me to see your room? You said I could."

"OK," I replied with some reluctance.

She smiled and took my arm as we climbed the stairs.

"Oh, this is much different than I expected! Do you get this room every time you return from working somewhere else?"

"Well, yes. I hadn't thought much about it before but come to think of it, I do. It's handy for me right at the back stairs. I usually come that way. Also, the bathroom and shower are just across the hall."

"Do you eat in the restaurant downstairs?"

"Sometimes," I replied. "Shall we go?"

"Just a minute." She put her arms around my neck and kissed me tenderly.

Aroused, I encircled her waist and moved toward the bed.

"No. Please, not this time. I just wanted to see your room."

Uneasy about my impulsive move, I released her and stood awkwardly, arms to my side, wondering if this is what the men mean when they warn against jailbait?

Partly joking and partly serious, she said, "I don't think it's right to climb in with someone the first time you get near a bed. My brothers warned me about guys who insist when I've said no. I'm glad you didn't. I hope we can still be friends. Frankly, I'm pleased you are interested, and honestly, I am too."

Again encircling her waist, I swung her around and placed a peck on her cheek. "There's a brotherly kiss for you. Let's get out of here before one of us changes our mind."

No one went to work that day. The winds swirled around the old buildings, rattling business signs and wrenching doors from unsuspecting hands. Coastal storms, usually more violent and less predictable than inland, habitually drove otherwise brave men from the woods. The hazards of being in standing timber during a raging gale are unfathomable. Anything more than a strong breeze had always been a legitimate excuse for lying in.

After the crowd had cleared from the restaurant area, I mounted a bar stool and chatted with the black-haired bartender. As usual, our mutual interest, girls, guided the conversation. Eager to show off his new Chevy, the bartender insisted that I go out with him and two young women he knew.

Again, feast or famine, I thought. One minute no girlfriends and then an overabundance. Does everyone experience these disturbing fluctuations? Where is the continuity, the stability, or, is this just a life doled out by bits and spurts, so different from the rationally balanced existence I remembered on the prairie?

"Hello, climber." The soft feminine voice made me turn and stare in amazement. Wistfully searching my eyes, the barmaid/cook who had married the cop, purred her way back into my heart. "I haven't seen you for some time. Have you been away?"

"Well, yes and no," I stammered. "I left for a few weeks but I've been back for a while. How did you know I came down here?"

"Oh, I've seen you around ever since you arrived in town, but I didn't know whether or not you wanted to see me. I left the tavern in such a hurry, and I didn't let you know. Shall we leave and go where we can talk privately?" she suggested, tugging gently on my arm.

"Fine," I agreed, but remained curious why this cop's wife wanted to talk with me.

Without further discussion, we went directly to my room. The ensuing activity, actually no surprise to me, served more as a tension release than a romantic interlude.

"That was nice," she whispered, snuggling by my side. Then her story gushed forth like a small child having been deceived for the first time. "I became tired of hanging around the tavern, hoping that someday I would meet another decent man. It wasn't to be, so I came down here. I met this police officer; we dated for a time, then he proposed. I was flattered, and he looked so neat and clean in his blue uniform."

"And?" I encouraged.

"Well, too late, I learned that this town is no place for me. In a roundabout way I discovered that my husband is involved in a racket illegally taking money from others. I don't understand it all. Why can't he be satisfied with an honest job? He's nothing but a damn leech preying on innocent people."

She stopped, hesitated, then continued. "Please excuse my anger, but that's the way I feel about these things. The same person told me that he, along with others, protect cab drivers and those who peddle hard liquor to Indians and underaged boys and girls, charging them two to three times normal prices. And, worst of all, they provide protection for pimps who control street prostitutes, many of the girls being runaways from who knows what. I tell you, it's a rough town to live in."

Wondering if everything she had said were true, I did not encourage her to go further, but she continued without persuasion, never identifying the source of her information. "When I found out my husband was involved in all of this, I threatened to leave him unless he found other employment. Although he has never admitted any of it, I know he loves the money, the power, and the fact that he is untouchable. Someone told me that the police chief is unaware of his sidelines. I don't like it and as soon as the right time comes, I'm getting out.

"I've wanted to talk with you for some time. It's probably too late for us," she said sadly, "but if you ever return inland, I'll be around. Oh, by the way, do be careful. You know, your vision isn't the best. Logging is a serious and dangerous business. Is it so important to be a climber?"

"How did you know?" I blurted, almost pleading for the answer, yet afraid of what I might hear.

"When I wrote the phone number for the foreman when I helped with your first job, you couldn't read the note. In fact, the paper was upside down. Also, you sometimes failed to notice me when I approached from the side without speaking. And there are other things that many people may not notice or you explain away with some flimsy excuse, like having something in your eye."

Ambivalent about the disclosure, I watched from the bed as she dressed. Yes, she's beautiful, but could she still want me, knowing what she does?

At the door, she turned, with a departing smile. "You're a nice guy. Thanks for what you did for me today. It's been a long time. Take care and good luck."

For a moment, the silence rebuked my negligence. I had neither thanked her for her help, nor requested that she stay. The descending footsteps slowed, stopped, then continued downward. A part, yes, a very important part of my life disappeared into the moist harbor air.

Now my mind whirled. Could all I heard be true? Suddenly I thought of my new friend, the beautiful pig-tailed waitress. Could she be victimized by these scoundrels? How can I protect her? Even if I tried, would she listen? The young, black-haired bartender, could he be a part of the rotten bunch? And there's the red-headed waitress and that slovenly guy who whisks her away—could they be involved?

Cutting short a hot shower, I dressed and sprinted along crowded sidewalks, slowing only to pick my way through traffic at intersections. Finally, I arrived at the restaurant where she worked. Everything seemed OK, but to reassure myself, I visually measured her from head to foot. Perhaps the cop's wife had stretched the truth in anger.

When the pigtailed waitress delivered the menu, I asked, "Have you been all right?"

"Sure," she responded quizzically, "Why? Shouldn't I be?"

Feeling foolish, I masked my fears with a laugh, "Sure, you should be OK."

"But I've had something on my mind," she said slowly, "and I'd like to discuss it with you later. Can you wait until I'm off in about an hour?"

"Certainly," I assured.

With the counter and tables cleaned, we switched off the lights and locked the doors. Tonight the full moon shone through the trees, assisting the occasional post lamp to light the winding path. The park that separated the main street from her rooming house had become a favorite retreat. "Now what is it you want to discuss?" I inquired.

Breaking a handclasp, she took my arm and drew me nearer. "Can we wait a few minutes? I'm not sure I know how to phrase it, and I don't want to sound silly."

"Fine, we have all night. I don't think we'll go to work tomorrow; the wind is supposed to blow again."

"OK, I'm ready. I left home and didn't tell anyone I was leaving. My parents don't know where I am, and I don't want them to know. They had plans for me that I didn't like, and there was no way to change their minds. Please don't ask me a lot of questions I either can't or don't want to answer. Can we be friends without your knowing my name or where I lived?"

Why this overt plea for anonymity? Until now, she had tactfully avoided questions regarding her name or home; we had survived on pet names or nicknames. A momentary silence gave me time to think.

She had entered my life without questions. For the past few months, my future had been dangling on a string, just beyond reach, but something told me that my world was about to change. In spite of recent encounters with other women, I felt unfulfilled and alone when my pigtailed waitress and I were apart.

Again the dilemma—should I end the restless search and commit myself, or would marriage only tarnish a beautiful friendship? Nothing resolved, I continued without a direct answer to her question.

"Maybe someday you'll want to have a family. I sometimes feel as though I'm adrift with no one to be responsible for. I know that isn't the way normal people live. So far, the old supe has been more of a family to me than anyone I have known for years. But I don't even know where he is right now.

"I do have you, though, or at least I feel as though we're close and I like you a lot. Right now, I don't need to know any more about you than I do. So let's both let our past alone. I won't ask you prying questions, and you do the same for me, OK?"

Breathing a sigh of relief, she said, "I have one other question. Are you ready?"

"Sure, shoot," I replied, satisfied that the matter had been settled.

"My twenty-first birthday is next week," she said. "Can we take my car and go away for a day?"

Possessed with a nameless joy, I tried to remain calm and speak carefully. "If you'd like, I'd be pleased to help you celebrate your twenty-first birthday; that is, if you really want me to. But I don't have a driver's license, so you'll have to drive."

"Don't worry about that," she said joyfully. "We'll have a nice time!"

The memorable birthday finally arrived. Humming tunes from the top songs on the hit parade, we drove down the coast, dining in quaint restaurants and walking along the beaches. One small cafe packed us a lunch, inspiring a picnic alongside a sparkling stream in a roadside park. That evening we celebrated with candlelight and champagne. The friendship, strangely sealed by a promise of anonymity, blossomed into a wonderful romance.

"Isn't this nice?" she asked, leaning over the table to squeeze my hand. "I'm so thrilled. This is the most exciting thing I've ever done on my birthday."

Carefully choosing my words, I replied quietly, "It's very nice, and I'm so glad you asked me to share it with you. Just the two of us."

Back in the room, we spread a map across the table and checked our location. Even if we took a different route, the remaining gas would get us home the following day.

My lovely friend, her eyes evidently fixed on nothing particular, stood with her back to me as she continued to study the map. For a time, I sat patiently on the bed, admiring her trim figure, shapely head, and neatly braided pigtails. Then, without warning, my soaring emotions pulled me to her. I cradled her shoulders in my arms, and tenderly kissed the back of her neck.

No response. Baffled, I relaxed the embrace, hands dropping to my side.

Suddenly she whirled and threw her arms around my neck, tears streaming down flushed cheeks.

"What is it? Is something wrong?" I asked, certain I had in some way offended her.

"Not really," she insisted. "It's just that I'm so happy, and … well, I guess I feel … I mean, I don't know just what to do next. I don't want to seem … you know, like some of those women I've heard about."

Ever so tenderly, I dried the tears and pulled her closer, whispering, "Never!" That single word, charged with sincerity and assurance, said everything. It was right, and we knew it.

Free from apprehension and irresistibly feminine, she stood on tiptoes, kissed me fervently, and relaxed into my arms, soft eyes locked into mine. Months of youthful desire turned to mature love.

Wistfully she caressed my face and shoulders, then breathed, "Why don't we turn off the lights and get ready for bed?"

With my beautiful companion pillowed on one arm, I drew her closer with the other and wondered how one man could be so lucky. We had shared each other's pleasures without guilt or embarrassment. Occasional exchanges of admiration had intensified and consummated the ultimate joy. During those glorious moments, she had released her entire body and soul to me, affirming her affection with whispers of belonging. Never before had I felt so elevated and complete in my love for another person.

Late in the night, we awoke, and in keeping with her inquisitive nature, she began asking questions about my work.

"Tell me about logging. Do they really kill a lot of men? Is it dangerous being a high-climber? Would you like to do it the rest of your life?"

"Well, Kitten, I don't think—"

"What did you call me?" she demanded.

"Kitten," I replied innocently.

"Why that?" she queried, a mixture of anger and confusion in her voice.

"Mmm, it just seemed right, er, it just came out," I replied awkwardly, wondering what had caused her displeasure. "OK," I finally explained, now measuring each word, "it's the way you purr when we're—well, when we're intimate like that."

"Are you sure?" she demanded again.

"Absolutely, I'm sure. Don't you like it?" myself now confused and exasperated. "I have to have a name for you sometime and I thought it would be nice—just between you and me. I'll never tell anyone how I came to call you Kitten, but if you object, I'll think of something different."

Now she lay quietly pondering my explanation while I stared into the darkness. Moments later, she turned, laid her arm across my chest and whispered, "I love my new name, darling; please keep it just for me. You can call me Kit when we're in public."

Chapter 26

The Union Organizer

"There'll be no work this week," the side-rod proclaimed. "The yarder motor's completely shot, and we can't get a replacement until next Monday."

As the men filed out, disappointed at the thoughts of another week without a paycheck, the loading-donkey puncher caught my eye. "Let's get coffee and throw the bull for a while. I'm in no mood to go home and argue with the old lady again. She wasn't happy with me when I left this morning."

"Yeah," I sympathized, "I guess they can get that way once in a while."

"Did you get your membership card?" the puncher asked.

"Yes, but what happens if someone doesn't? I've heard it can be rough."

"Well," he mused aloud, "it's like this. It took years for us to get things where they are now, and we don't want a backslide."

"Was it hard to bring about the changes?" I asked. "What caused the problems?"

"To begin with," he continued, "the hiring-halls, the bus companies, and the side-rods had a little business going. Each prospective employee paid the hiring-hall a fee to send him out on a job. In essence, the hiring-halls, rather than the logging companies, selected the workers.

"Then, the bus company charged each man a fare to the camp, and unbeknown to the men, the side-rod received a kickback from the hiring-hall and the bus companies for any man fired after a few days on the job—just long enough to earn another fee for the hiring-hall, another bus fare, and another kickback.

"Each morning, the side-rod checked his records, scanned the workers, then pointed to an employee whose time was up and shouted, 'Hey, you! Get your nose-bag and start counting ties! You're not worth a damn. There are men in town living on a cracker a day that'll do better than you.' Then he'd turn and select another victim. 'You! He needs a partner. And you! You can go with them.'"

"Knowing he'd intimidated the remaining men," the puncher continued, "the side-rod drove the skeleton crew for full production, aware that replacements would arrive in camp either that afternoon or early the following morning.

Over the years, he built up a sizeable nest egg, all from the sweat of the working man."

Sipping our coffee below mid-point, we called for refills before the puncher continued.

"For years, the companies hired at the lowest level on the pay scale, and as a man took on a higher paying job, his pay remained at the lower level with little or no increase as his performance improved. Hook-tenders often received chokerman's pay, and it wasn't until the union organized and moved in on this, that anything changed.

"Your life wasn't worth a tinker's dam, and if a man had no kin, who knows what happened to his earnings after he had been killed. It was nothing unusual to have a rigging-slinger give the signal to go ahead before the chokermen were in the clear. Many good loggers have been killed each year from logs being dragged over them. In those days, men were a dime a dozen, and it wasn't until we stepped in that anything changed. Even so, we still have to keep at the bastards, or they'll put things right back where they were." His already dark eyes became almost black and his fists flexed as though he were experiencing old times.

Caught up in the puncher's rhetoric, I vaguely understood why this woodsman chanced knocking the general manager on his backside after an unfavorable negotiating session. By this time, curious restaurant and bar patrons gathered around the persuasive voice that daringly chastised the logging companies. Rather than showing embarrassment over the audience, the puncher launched into a display of statesmanship that would intimidate the most eloquent politician. An occasional shout, "Yeah," or "You damn well know it," indicated support for the orator. Few could be indifferent to his charisma.

After railing on for several minutes, the puncher calmed the group with a warm smile and the comment, "We've got things under control right now, but mind you, the time will come when we'll again have to exert our strength."

I changed the subject by asking about the houses. "I've heard that some madams handle the men's money. Is it true?"

The puncher's dark eyes twinkled as he grinned and answered, "Some girls have had a rough time of it. Yes, I've heard the madams do keep accounts for the guys, but I've never learned that anyone has been fleeced. The girls give the men pleasure and the houses do more good than harm, regardless what the churches say."

"Someone said that run-away girls are swept into prostitution by unscrupulous people," I said as I raised the cup and finished the coffee. Again, the grin. "Well, this may be so. The girls, as well as others, need to make a living. They're all working stiffs and, eventually, everyone finds his niche."

Obviously the puncher's sympathies rested only with the common man, primarily those who worked for wages. Companies and their management remained the enemy. As for the girls, they belonged to the working class. Consequently, how they made a living was not for him to judge.

The coffee, despite its strength, seemed to have a calming effect on the puncher, and he soon departed, ready to face his argumentative wife. As he passed through the door, a voice in the crowd announced, "That guy is nothing but a damn commie. He's always spouting off at the union meetings and can stir up a crowd so damn quick you don't even realize what's happening. That bunch he hangs around with is always involved in the major strikes and travel long distances to speak with groups that are organizing. Mind you, he's trouble from the word go."

Kit and I judiciously planned our weekends around her gas rations; we took short weekend trips to places we both enjoyed—one weekend to a local celebration and the next to the coastal villages. She enjoyed browsing in the wayside shops, and we occasionally attended a movie before returning home. Dancing became a major pastime, but our ultimate happiness came from returning to the hotel where we had spent our first night together.

We had neither seen nor heard from the supe, nor did we know his real name, his address, or his phone number. Aside from worry, our only alternative was to wait and hope.

On rare occasions Kit spent the night in my hotel room, but she preferred not to make it a habit. On days when my work had been extremely strenuous and otherwise demanding, I failed to walk her home after work, dropping off to sleep on the bed only to wake up long after she had left the restaurant.

Around midnight, a knock on the door forced me from bed. Groggily, I stumbled across the room, fumbled for the knob, then demanded to know who had so rudely awakened me. My friend, the black-haired bartender, identified himself and asked to be admitted.

"What is it?" I mumbled, cracking the door.

"I need a favor," he whispered, glancing uneasily along the hall. "I have a friend who has asked me to help him. We need a place for this girl to stay. Can she sleep here until morning? Then we may be able to work out something better."

The girl stood behind the bartender, not making a plea on her own behalf but evidently resigned to any arrangement. She appeared pregnant. The familiar face forced the decision. Where had I seen her before?

Angry with myself but still willing to go along with the request, I asked her if she had agreed to the plan. She affirmed with a nod and a wistful smile; I motioned the bartender away, and my ward entered.

For a moment, we stood gazing at each other, then I waived her to the chair, and I sat on the bed.

"How old are you?" I demanded.

"Nineteen," she blurted, adding, "or I will be soon. I've always looked older than I am, so I tell everyone that I'm going on twenty-one."

"And what are you doing here? Don't you have a family?"

"Well, I'm here to have my baby. And yes, I have parents, but if they knew that I'm going to have a kid, they'd kill me—maybe not really but they'd be mad as hell; and besides, they don't have much money."

"What's your name?"

"He calls me Sugar," the girl replied flippantly.

"And who the hell is 'he'?" I asked, annoyed with her apparent indifference.

"Oh, he's the one who got me this way; or, I think he's the one. He's a cop and a real nice guy."

"Now, damn it, why don't you quit acting cute and tell me what the hell's going on?"

"There's not much to tell. Like I said, my folks don't have much and I wanted more than just working around home picking ferns for the rest of my life, so I ran away before graduating from high school. Made beds at motels for a while, then another girl told me about this town. 'If you're good looking and know the right people,' she guaranteed, 'you can make some good money.' There aren't many boys around my age, so I started going out with older guys. The cop was one of them. He treated me nice and gave me spending money when I was short. You know, tips in a greasy-spoon cafe aren't much to live on."

Now I let her talk without interrupting. "Well, my friend, the cop, the one who got me this way, came to see me in my room tonight. Then some woman came to the door and really read the riot act to him. I'm not sure who she was, but when we wouldn't let her in, she got mad as hell. After almost five minutes shouting and cussing, the landlord made her leave. When it was all over, the manager came to the door and apologized. You see, my friend got me the room to begin with," she continued.

"We got dressed, and he took me to another guy's car, told him to keep his mouth shut, and find me a place to stay tonight. So, that's it."

"What are you going to do now?" I asked.

"I'm not going to do anything right now. I heard my friend tell the other man that I'd have to find another place to live, I guess that's what they're doing tonight," she said, showing little concern for her future. Apparently, she would receive protection from the angry woman, have spending money and free room and board. All of this just for being a companion to an amorous policeman.

"But what about the baby?" I persisted.

"Oh, we're not sure yet. We may decide to get rid of it, or go ahead and have it then adopt it out. One thing I know I can do is go away from here, have it, adopt it out, then re-turn and work in the houses. One guy told me he could fix it so I'd have my own customers, and I wouldn't have to take on every bum that came into the place. That's what I plan to do sometime."

At least, contrary to my initial suspicion, it seemed I had not been set up to be a scapegoat for hoodlums. But who was the meddlesome woman who had forced the two lovers to evacuate the girl's room? Could it possibly be the barmaid who had married the cop? Was this girl's friend, the cop, the barmaid's husband? What a mess. To hell with it.

"You better get to bed," I ordered and she responded without question. Now what to do? Tomorrow, I planned for a long hard day.

Her breathing became regular, what a relief. Still sitting on the bed bemoaning the situation, I stared absently into space, wondering what looked so familiar about this runaway youngster. Totally exhausted from the day's labor and the eventful evening, I stretched full length. Unrecognizable people floated in and out of my dreams as the girl's body turned and twitched.

"Yes, what is it?" I inquired drowsily.

"I can't pay you for letting me stay here tonight but I'd like to do something nice for you," the pregnant girl offered. Tired and dis-

330

gusted, I administered a stern lecture, then ordered her to forget it and go back to sleep. Reluctantly, she moved away and soon slumbered without sign of remorse, perhaps feeling that she had offered to pay her debt. If I refused to take advantage of her generosity, that became my problem.

For the second time that night, I became annoyed with myself for having agreed to the arrangement. Cursing under my breath, I gathered work clothes, hurried across the hall, showered, dressed, and descended the long stairs, finishing the night in the laundry room, sleeping on bags of dirty linen.

Chapter 27

The Landlady

The roaring motor, the huge tires brushing my sleeve, then the leap to safety—another close call.

"Hey, get the hell out of the way," the truck driver shouted. "What are you trying to do—commit suicide? Don't ever walk behind my truck again when I'm backing up. Thought I'd killed you." My side vision had deteriorated during the past months, and I had failed to notice the truck as it bore down on me.

Later that morning the mainline broke. Everyone on the landing scattered, diving, running, and crawling away from the spar, as the frayed end, hissing and snapping, searched for a victim.

A wayward loop whizzed just beyond my head and struck the ground with a sickening thud. Whirling for a hasty retreat, two more lethal coils crashed to the ground before me.

A few moments passed before the predatory mainline lay in lifeless coils on the ground. No one had been injured. However, the loops had pulverized foliage and destroyed the loading donkey roof. Miraculously, the puncher escaped unharmed, but justifiably angry. Over the years, he had resented and protested the use of worn cables—gyppo operators were notorious for this.

"You knew that mainline was bad," the puncher accused the side-rod. "It should have been changed a month ago."

Incensed by the puncher's accusations, the side-rod responded, "You're nothing but a damn troublemaker. I've heard about you. Go get your damn nose-bag and get out of here."

Minutes later, the eloquent puncher had assembled the crew and convinced us to shut down the outfit. However, the puncher's hasty action worked to the company's advantage. Days and even weeks might pass before a new mainline could be acquired. With our closing down the outfit, the company had no responsibility to conduct non-productive activities just to hold us.

Again unemployed, we entered the crew bus, not certain we totally agreed with the puncher's reasoning. Common sense warned us that this outfit might be shut down at unpredictable intervals due to faulty equipment or union aggressiveness.

I found an experienced falling-partner, bought a new power saw, and set out to work in the rain forest between Humptulips and Forks. A crooked contractor brought an end to this venture.

Although my partner and I eventually regained a portion of the pilfered income, the continuous rain, the long rides to and from work, and complete fatigue at the end of each day caused me to abandon this enterprise. With money in the bank, in spite of my expensive trial as an entrepreneur, I decided to remain unemployed. Within the month, torrential rains and howling winds invaded the coastal area.

Hand-in-hand, Kit and I strolled toward her rooming house. Heavy clouds had threatened all day, but tonight the moon and stars, released from bondage, came out and graciously lighted the pathways. After a tedious day in the restaurant, these walks triggered a flurry of questions from Kit.

"What's a radical?" she asked. "Why are they disliked so much?"

"Well," I replied, having become accustomed to her unusual questions. "He's usually arrogant, bullheaded, strong union, and easily provoked. Why do you ask?"

"Today, I heard three men talking in a booth. They said something about that damn radical always causing them to be laid off. How can one man be so powerful?"

"He and his cronies are always at odds with the bosses," I explained. "They claim to represent the interests of the working man, and in doing so, the leader gets labeled a radical or commie. The label travels with him from camp to camp. Strange as it might seem, these troublemakers are simultaneously hated, feared, and admired by many men in the woods. Off the job, they're just devilish renegades.

"To better understand, all you have to do is watch the ridiculous performances during on-the-job disputes, union meetings, negotiations, strikes, and weekends in town. It's unbelievable—the way they become involved in skirmishes over simple differences, then turn their backs on the world and enjoy themselves in the taverns and infamous houses. Have you ever known anyone like that?"

"Not really," she replied thoughtfully. "But remember, I do have two older brothers, but skip that. I have a surprise. Don't ask me what it is. You'll like it." She pulled my arm around her waist, and we walked along the path, sharing a lovers' silence.

At the front door, Kit turned, threw her arms around my neck, and stood close for a moment. How sweet and fresh her breath, how firm her body, how delightful her whispers. Then, the surprise.

"I want you to meet my landlady. She's always asking about you."

"Why," I blurted. "I thought you are not allowed to have guests in your room."

"Not in my room, silly. In the kitchen. Don't worry, I've already told her about us."

"Everything?" I asked.

"No, dear, just that we like each other, and I'd like her to meet you, but I think she knows."

With the introductions completed, the landlady invited us to share a snack with her. As we sipped the steaming chocolate and munched on homemade pastry, the matronly woman looked directly into my eyes and conducted a merciless interrogation.

The questions, dealt with one at a time, took form in her cheeks and gushed from the thin Scandinavian lips in quick succession.

"What brought you into the timber industry?" "How long have you been in the woods?"

"Aren't you afraid you'll get injured or killed?" "Do you plan to make a career of being a high-climber?" and on and on. Soon we felt comfortable with each other and, as I had remembered home life with aunts and uncles, the kitchen became warm and inviting.

When Kit suggested it was getting late, the landlady looked kindly at us and said, "If you two are going off this weekend, please let me put up a picnic lunch for you. It must be terrible living out of restaurants all the time."

Like a small child rewarding her mother for a grand concession, Kit hugged the elderly woman and gave her a peck on the cheek. "You're so nice to me. And I'm glad you approve of my friend."

"Oh," the landlady said understandingly, "I've had considerable experience, and I usually do a good job of sizing up situations. I raised a daughter all by myself, and it's no easy task, but I'm sure you have a good man, so the two of you enjoy life while you have it together. My husband was injured in a logging accident shortly after we married. He never walked again. It became almost unbearable for both us. He always said he married me because he wanted to provide and care for me, but it turned out to be the other way around. God help me, but it seemed a blessing when he finally died."

Out of the landlady's sight, Kit again threw her arms around my neck and gave me a lingering good-night kiss.

Walking on air, I returned to my barren room. Life had been good to me, I decided, in spite of some difficult times. I often wondered about the teenage prostitute who had spent the night in my bed. How had her life gone? Why had it bothered me when I returned to my room after sleeping in the laundry, only to find her gone and the bed neatly made up? No one, not even the bartender, had mentioned the incident or the girl. Now, it was the landlady. Had she tried to send a message when she talked about her dead husband, and her daughter whom she spoke of as being in the past?

When Kit had days off, we spent the time together, as the landlady had suggested. Weather permitting, we swam in a lake several miles from Aberdeen. Sport fishing, either for the magnificent Chinook salmon or multi-colored rainbow trout, excited Kit beyond my wildest hopes. But our favorite place remained the quaint lodging where our tender romance had first blossomed; we returned time after time to relive the joy of our first night together.

A short walk through the park, followed by hot cocoa and cookies, became a ritual. Our mutually appreciative trio, Kit, the sage landlady, and I, spent hours discussing nothing in particular. Kit and I patiently listened to the widow review her interesting but stressful years.

After she had completed a saga that had relevance to our lives, we questioned her regarding the romantic details, but she only smiled and repeated the same line. "Everyone has some private experiences and thoughts they don't feel free to share with others. Both of you must have your own. Save a few, they'll keep you going during sad times."

On days when Kit's work had been stressful, I stayed only a few minutes to greet the landlady. One evening as I passed a popular tavern on the main drag, a friend asked me to join him and several others whose favorite house had acquired two new girls. I should help them evaluate the additions.

The rowdy group climbed the stairs anticipating conquest, but I went along secretly hoping to learn more about the teenage prostitute who had disappeared so mysteriously.

Extra chairs for inquisitive patrons came from the back room, while hard liquor, served in randomly-shaped glasses, rewarded those expressing interest. I requested orange juice, for past experience had taught me to keep a clear head in these situations.

First, two new girls, scantily dressed, slithered from a room to strut among the spectators. Greedy eyes and lecherous minds, naturally, went to the youngest and least experienced. The oldest displayed herself with the ardor of a vixen and soon shared the attention. Minutes later, several women joined the others and all paraded among us, giving special attention to oglers. Men made a choice, then turned to a neighbor. "She's the best of the lot, and I got her first! How about that!"

I carefully scrutinized each girl, but the poor lighting revealed only profiles, heights and weights, no details. No, I finally determined, the teenager wasn't among them.

A light caught my attention as a side door opened, silhouetting a shapely figure. More refined than the others, she emerged, closed the door and descended the stairs.

"Who was that?" I inquired of the guy sitting next to me.

"They say she's been here for about two weeks. Looks great now but give her a few months and she'll look just like the others. The two they gave us a look at tonight were no great shakes. But that one, she looks pretty darn nice, don't you think?"

Yes, I thought, as the fellow had said, she looked nice, but why wasn't she marched out to be eyeballed and fondled? Maybe she's one of those who start out by having a priority on the rich and famous.

To have remained longer served no useful purpose, so I rose to go, took one last look, then threaded my way through the chairs. Near the stairs, the pretty one reappeared. At close range, the checkered black and white raincoat, with the hood thrown back, revealed a nicely shaped head with a modest but becoming hairstyle. She paused and addressed me with a crisp hello and walked around me, disappearing into the side room. I should learn more about her.

Several days later, I returned to the house, hoping to locate the teenager. No luck. Had she remained with the cop? Or, as she desired, did she now have her own customers, protecting her from the run-of-the-mill renegades?

Perhaps she gave up on selling her body to these indifferent nomads. Where had I seen her before?

The tides had been perfect. Weary from clam-digging, Kit and I returned to our favorite weekend retreat, turned the catch over to the restaurant cook and retired to our usual room. We dropped, side by side, on the bed without undressing. "Isn't it wonderful!" she exclaimed. "Just being together and having this nice room all to ourselves?"

"Yes, Kitten. If anyone had told me a few months ago that I'd someday have a room like this and a beautiful girl like you, I'd have told him he was crazy. But here we are, real and alive."

"Now that you mention it, I mean 'alive'," she commented. "Did you hear about the two men who were killed yesterday? It seems one man felled a large tree and it knocked down a sapling which came back and killed him. The other one had been standing beside a truck loaded with logs and something broke, a cheese-block chain, I think they said, and the logs rolled off the truck and smashed him." Then, with a shudder, she added, "What a terrible way to die!"

Without thinking, I mumbled, "Two down and one to go."

"What did you say?" she asked, adding a horrified look. "I'm sorry, Kit, I guess I'm getting to be just like the others. In the woods, most old-timers feel that accidents happen in three's. It becomes a habit to add as they occur. Like 'one down and two to go,' or 'two down and one to go,' and when three have occurred, the men feel it will be a time before another series of three comes along. It isn't rational but it sometimes seems to happen that way. Even so, I don't think any man believes he will be the first, second, or even the third man to die or be seriously injured."

She lifted my arm, pulled it under her neck, and snuggled to me with her head finally resting on my shoulder. We lay quietly, engrossed in our thoughts.

I finally broke the silence. "Did your landlady send lunch this time?"

"Men," she teased, "all they think about is their stomachs. Are you hungry, darling?"

"Not really; I just needed to say something, and couldn't think of anything else." I paused, then continued, "What do you think you'll be doing five years from now?"

"Oh, I don't know. Maybe something different from what I'm doing now. There's no future in being a waitress, but I'm really not sure.

Right now, I can't think anyway. Maybe someday I'd like to get married and have one or two children, but not right now."

Her final statement caused my body to tense, and she guessed that something wasn't right, "What is it? Did I say something wrong?"

"No, Kitten, I guess I just had a slight cramp in my leg. It'll be fine in a minute," I lied.

Pretending to be satisfied with my answer, she again teased, "You poor old man. You're almost twenty-four years old, and you're already falling apart."

After a brief discussion of President Franklin Roosevelt's recent death, plans for the future dropped from the conversation, and we changed for dinner. Candlelight, drinks, and the prized razor clams, always so tender and delicious, carried us into fantasy.

Now ignoring the possibility of future problems, we appreciated each other more and more. Our fairyland existence continued to excite us—I, with my practical approach to life, and Kit with her innocent quest for knowledge.

The drive home had been uneventful and after we parked the car, I helped Kit into the house with the bags.

"Did you have a nice time?" the landlady asked softly. "I miss you when you're gone but I'm so glad you can get out once in a while. They've had another commotion downtown. I'm not sure what it was all about, but the police sirens have been going for hours. It's quieted some during the past few minutes. In past years, goon squads have been known to come in and promote gang warfare."

"I suppose I'd better get back to my room. It's late, and you need sleep, Kit."

As we walked to the door, Kit held me tightly and whispered, "Please be careful, darling. Don't get involved in their darn fighting. You sometimes take chances that maybe you shouldn't."

She clung to me tightly until, finally, we both smiled and released our embrace. I grabbed her again, held her tight for a moment, then, kissing her tenderly, turned and left, controlling the urge to return and take her with me.

Chapter 28

The Dilemma—Resolution

The nightly walks home and the hot choco-late sessions continued even though World War II had ended and servicemen, many disfigured and emotionally battered, arrived home. Few returned to work in the woods. Using their GI benefits, old and young alike entered college or a trade school in search of a less hazardous and demand-ing way of life.

Kit and I decided on a Friday evening movie. We held hands and shared a bag of pop-corn, Kit enjoying the film and I pondering a personal matter.

Mixing with the others as we left our seats and converged in the lobby, a heavy down-pour forced us to wait for a break. I stared through the windowpanes as though counting the drops, inwardly debating my right to expect this girl to be my lifetime companion. Kit's question startled me from the trance. "Is something wrong? You seem miles away."

Turning with an embarrassed smile, I replied, "No, Kitten, it's just something I have to work out."

"What?—I mean, you've never called me that in public."

Anxious to end the discussion, I gathered her close with one arm, opened the theater door, and we dashed into the night. The torrential rain had subsided almost as quickly as it had begun and, like the muddy water rushing along the gutters, we ran to the hotel, splashing through ankle-deep puddles.

Wet shoes removed and placed next to the old steam-radiator, we stretched out on the bed, still in our damp clothes.

Kit lifted her head, pulled my arm under her neck and turned to me. A full day's beard, combined with a ridiculous incident in the movie, gave cause for lighthearted discussion. She rubbed the stubble as I expressed my deep affection by gently stroking her back, adding an occasional pat for good measure.

What I said next altered both our lives forever.

"Kitten, I have something I want to tell—I mean, I want to ask you—well, I guess we should discuss it."

Using an expression learned from me, she directed, "Shoot, let's have it."

"Well," I stammered, "it's not—it's something like this." Caught in a whirlwind of emotion, I faltered. Kit seemed to understand that something dramatic was about to alter our happiness. She waited patiently.

A torrent of words, thoughts, and regrets flashed through my mind. Go ahead and tell her, you cowardly bastard. Yes. How appropriate—bastard. Get on with it. You can't stop now; it's now or never. My blood chilled at the thought of revealing myself so completely. Never before had I been brutally direct with the person I admired, loved and trusted more than anyone else.

Continuing by fits and starts, I drew her closer. "It isn't easy and I sure as hell don't like it, but here it is. Kit, I think you've come from an educated family and maybe from a family that is well-to-do. I assume, for reasons known only to you, that you came to this hellish place to escape something, which at the time, seemed very difficult or even unbearable. We all go through something like this when we're in our late teens; I know I did.

"Now, I'm going to ask you to do something, and I'll explain later. For some reason, you decided to tie in with me, and I think more of you than any other person I've ever known. Please, for both our sakes, return to your family and, if things were so bad that you can't do that, please enroll in college and finish your education. I know you have the smarts to do it. I would be proud of you and it will insure you a living without being tied to some damn logger—or whatever."

"But I don't want to—," she tried to interrupt.

Tears streamed down her cheeks as I continued. "Now I must tell you why I am asking you to do this, and I hope you understand. A few weeks ago, you said you would someday like to marry and have children. To my dismay, you sensed my reaction. There is nothing I would like better than to have you for my wife, and we could have one or two kids, but it's this way.

"I have poor vision. That's the reason I don't drive. The eye condition can't be helped with surgery, medicine, or glasses. It's gradually getting worse, and someday, maybe a long time from now, I might lose it all. I've never discussed this with anyone before, and I'm sorry that I wasn't totally honest with you."

"Oh, darling," she said tearfully.

"The eye condition is hereditary," I continued doggedly, "and, more than likely, our kids would have the same thing. I can't wish that onto anyone else, let alone our own children."

Her tears continued as she listened in anguish.

"High-climbing is the one thing I can do without being subjected to all the hazards on the ground. When I'm in the tree, I'm never more than an arm's length from my work; besides, I'm the boss, and nothing happens unless I direct it, or if I have made a mistake of my own doing, I pay for it. It's no one else's fault but my own. So, as you can see, I should do nothing but climb. To continue working at jobs, such as loading or something else on the ground, will get me sooner or later. I'm not afraid to die, not that I want to, but I could never stand to be injured, and subsequently be a burden on someone for life; I could never do that to you. Remember how your landlady talks of caring for her crippled husband until he finally died."

"Yes, but—"

"So, my sweet Kitten, I must go back to the camps where I do nothing but climb. The small outfits, such as those near this damn city, cannot afford to hire a man who does nothing but climb. A life living away from each other for weeks is not for us. So I'm asking you to do what I suggested. I can't imagine you married to one of these renegade loggers or other men hanging around this city. Do you understand, Kit?"

By this time, she sobbed violently, her entire body wrenching. With an unintelligible "Uh huh" she drew herself closer, and managed to stop crying long enough to blurt out, "Oh, darling, I do understand, and I know you're right, but it will be so difficult. You're a part of me."

As we clung together she rubbed her face against mine until, totally fatigued, she dropped off to sleep. I lay for hours, still not sure I had done the right thing. How could I hurt her so? Was I actually asking her to leave for her own good? Or was I asking her to free me from domestic responsibilities? Had the pull toward freedom made me so self-serving and insensitive that I remained duty bound only to the lofty spars—top dog in my own small world? Nothing resolved, I finally dozed.

A knock on the door woke me. "Yes?" I answered. "Who is it?"

"Maid service," came the brusque reply from the new cleaning lady.

I looked around; Kit had gone.

"Come back later!" I shouted through the closed door. Leaping from bed, I rushed across the hall to the bathroom. Empty!

Angry with myself for having dozed, I slammed the door as I re-entered. There it was, printed with lipstick on the mirror above the sink. "I'll be yours forever," signed with the sketch of a small kitten. Unbelieving, I sat dolefully on the bed, immobilized by the message. Then, gripped by hysteria, I vented my frustrations on anything and everything within reach. The lone chair crumbled as I smashed it against the wall. A random kick at the bed brought blood to my shin. One fist suffered as it flailed without purpose.

Grabbing hat and coat, I dashed from the room, only to realize I was still in stocking feet. When I returned, searing reality hit home—the emptiness left by her missing shoes. What to do?

Finding myself entangled in a web of cultural differences, I fought to clear my head. Since childhood, I had yearned for stability. Even so, at unpredictable intervals, my entire body and soul demanded freedom—an innocent,

light-hearted freedom, devoid of boredom, responsibility and, most of all, oppressive insig-
nificant rituals. I had overcome my cowardice
but honesty and good intentions had left me the
loser—or had it? Yes, I had my freedom, but to
what end?

Fully dressed, I descended the stairs two
steps at a time. Running down the alley at top
speed, I failed to turn onto the sidewalk, and
found myself in the rain-drenched street. A cab
driver, careening onto the walk to avoid hitting
me, cursed at the top of his voice, regained
control of the cab and sped on. One block, then
another, and another, I ran until, breathless, I
arrived where she usually parked the car. Gone!

My persistent banging finally brought the
landlady. She cracked the door without removing
the safety chain, and peered into my distraught
face.

Obviously expecting me, she had placed the
cookies on the table, and soon prepared the traditional cocoa.

A private person by nature, I uncharacter-
istically exposed the full extent of my deep affection for Kit, omitting only the most intimate
details. Without pausing, I anxiously expressed
sorrow regarding our lost happiness, but soon

realized how the confession must sound, so I smiled ruefully and waited.

She encouraged me to drink the cocoa and try her new cookie recipe, then looked directly into my eyes and began.

"Now, young man," her words, with simplistic candor, went straight to the point. "I know how you must feel. And, I also know how Kit, as you called her, must feel at this time. She came to me early this morning, broken-hearted and confused. Her story was as tear-wrenching as yours, but there are a few things that both of you must learn about life, and I hope I can get them across to you, as I tried with her.

"Dozens of young girls come to this wretched city every year. Many are running from something, who knows what, while others come to make a living. A few, very few, become accustomed to the weather, the shortage of respectable men, and who knows what else. The innocent get used and later cast aside by violent loggers, drunken seamen, unfaithful husbands, and vile hoodwinkers—all mixed in with churchgoers who think they're here to control the lives of others.

"Then there's that other bunch—the ones you don't talk about in public. After they're elected, they create more problems than they solve. Each one hires his friends, people who'd steal the clothes right off their mothers' backs, and no one can remove them from their plush jobs.

"Every time I go to the store, prices have jumped and banks insist that mortgage payments be made on the dot. Yes, things are getting worse by the day; this is no place for young people, especially young women. Do you know what I mean?"

I nodded.

"Now, with all its faults, this area, known for its free spending, free love, and un-enforced laws, has become a magnet for those seeking excitement. Many girls become so entan-gled in the turmoil that they can't get out—even if they want to.

"Knowing full well that they may not live beyond tomorrow, the loggers, seamen and other unstable rogues throw their money to the winds, returning to work only when they need to replen-ish their funds, leaving the cravings of these adventuresome young women to be satisfied by the next wave of scalawags."

Without explanation or apology, the land-lady, eyes moist, turned, first to the mantle clock, then to the front door, as though someone had been long in coming. Finally, she rose and pushed several sticks of wood into the stove, wiped her hands thoughtfully on the checkered apron, and returned to the table.

"Now, I must tell you that I was one of those girls. After the fling, down and out, I married and soon found myself sentenced to care for an injured logger for the rest of my life. He would give anyone the shirt off his back, but refused to give up one moment of his compelling and exciting existence to be with me when I needed him most.

"I started this rooming house on borrowed money. It's far from being paid for. Nevertheless, I've made enough to keep us going over the years. Someday, I suppose, they'll take it from me if I get behind in my payments."

Again she paused, examined her once beautiful hands, then reached for the scorched dish towel draped over her shoulder. Pulling it onto the table, she laid it flat and gently smoothed the blemished area as she continued.

"Many of my renters are girls, just as I was when I first came to town. For a time, they come home to their rooms every night. After a few weeks, I see them only once or twice each month. Finally, they vanish without paying the rent or claiming their belongings. In my garage, I have boxes filled with girls' clothing and other incidentals—nothing of much value. I suppose I could sell their things to get the rent, but it doesn't seem right, just as it wouldn't have been right for me to abandon my injured husband. Sometimes, I wish I had. But it's too late now. It's all over."

With tears once again in her eyes, she continued. "My own daughter left home two years ago, and I haven't heard from her. We had a falling out, and her bitterness has burned in my heart ever since. Somehow it seemed different for you and Kit. Both of you have been just like the children I would have liked. You have filled an almost unbearable void during these past months.

"Life has passed me by, and I didn't want the same for Kit. I hope you understand, she might have stayed, but I encouraged her to go. Please forgive me. I didn't mean to hurt you, but I could read the handwriting on the wall."

There, I thought. She said it so clearly, so forcefully, and yet, so nicely. How could I contest her intuition?

Time to wise up.

Feeling several years more mature than one hour before, I placed one arm across her shoulders and said, "Don't worry, you probably know best."

Minutes later we walked toward the front entrance, her hand holding my arm as though she suspected this might be our last time together. A spontaneous embrace, a soft goodbye, and we parted. Walking slowly along the street, I envisioned the prudent landlady shuffling back along the hall, refueling the stove, then locating herself by the kitchen table, where she sat misty-eyed, glancing first to the mantle clock, then to the front door.

Chapter 29

Moving On

It was only 2:30 PM and they were already at it. "You damn radicals are nothing more than conniving Reds," came the angry cry from across the smoke-filled union hall.

"The hell you say! You lily-livered bastards are going to let the management cut our throats until we're begging in the streets like starving mongrels," thundered a grizzled old faller.

"Order!" the Union president shouted, frantically pounding his gavel on the oak table that separated him, the Business Agent, and the Secretary/Shop-steward from the agitated loggers.

The president's shouts, barely audible over the raging turmoil, fell on deaf ears. After the first blow, which sent one chokerman reeling across chairs and spittoons, every man leaped to his feet, muscular hands and arms ready for battle. Within seconds, most conscientious union members engaged themselves in ejecting the fighters or they joined the fracas. Either way, the combatants would soon take their anger to the streets, where the police and sheriff would be obligated, if not delighted, to intervene, leading to a full-blown public disturbance.

Lately these brawls had lost their appeal, so I watched for a moment, then left by the side door. Even the tavern camaraderie failed to entice me; I waved and flashed a smile to friends inside but continued along the street.

Spotting three uniformed officers, my first inclination was to turn and avoid them, but I changed my mind and walked in their direction; I had to deal with them sooner or later. Perhaps memories of last month's brawl had faded from their vindictive minds.

The fight had been a wild, exciting experience, and although I had been, more or less, an observer rather than a ringleader, I had been in the general area when the upheaval began. Unlike the village brawl involving the supe and me, this had been a full-blown riot.

Pro-union factions alleged that one logging company had hired goons and scabs to beat up on certain union members. The mobsters, unsuccessful in the effort, had gathered their wounded and fled, leaving the logging community to its irreverence and divisiveness.

Now, the tallest officer slowed and asked, "What's doing?"

Suspiciously, I worked my back to the nearest building and answered, "Don't know," but added nothing more.

Braced for action, I recalled the warnings offered by an old-timer who had chuckled as he stated, "If you don't let those cops get behind you, you'll at least get a sandwich while they're getting a meal."

"Any strangers down there today?" the short one asked, pointing his nightstick toward the union hall.

"Don't know," I replied. "Paid no attention."

"Hell!" the first officer exclaimed. "It's going to be another rough night. When nobody knows nothing, there's always hell to pay."

Now the third and youngest officer maneuvered himself between me and the others and said quietly, "We've got to get going. Take it easy."

Simple and direct, the words assured that they weren't after me, at least not that night.

Turning my back on the triumvirate, I continued along the street, pondering the unanswered question: Why had the youngest cop befriended me?

Several sparrows and multi-colored pigeons pecked ravenously at a half-empty popcorn bag. As I approached, the flock dispersed but returned immediately after I passed. The chirping and romantic cooing recalled memories of the birds that nested in the grain elevators where I had played during my first six years.

Along the street, unsightly pigeon droppings decorated the buildings from the lofty nests to the littered sidewalks, where cool breezes sent empty cigarette packages and gum wrappers skidding along the cracked concrete. Now and then, a watery sun warmed my back as the cloud-cover intermittently gave way to blue sky, an unusual occurrence during winter months.

Farther down the block, a traditional red bulb identified the house of ill repute. Its weathered street-level door stood open as though inviting customers, but my only desire was to displace Kit's lingering portrait. Her lovely figure, her refreshing questions, and her sincere devotion had dominated my days and nights, but now life must be renegotiated.

Forcing thoughts to the teenage prostitute, I questioned the importance of learning her whereabouts. After all, I was neither her brother nor her father. Even if I found her, what sound advice could I provide, or would she listen? Then I made peace with the questions by recalling the puncher's theory, "Eventually everyone finds his niche."

Nevertheless, I climbed to the second floor that had for years been the workplace and home for many unfortunate women. If I didn't find her today, I could leave with a clear conscience.

Vaulted ceilings, supported by huge cedar timbers, ironically transformed the empty reception room into a provincial hideaway, a place to cogitate. I flopped into the nearest sofa and contemplated the age-old pictures that hung haphazardly around the room. The stone fireplace, long past its prime, cradled three burning logs, each sending crackling sparks into the chasm as the flames licked at bubbling pitch seams.

By habit, I quietly hummed my favorite, "Stardust," until the shapely blond entered. One look told me that she wasn't the aspiring teenager, but her presence gave me someone to talk with. I stayed.

"What are you doing here this time of day?" the young woman inquired, adding, "Why aren't you at the meeting?"

"Those guys are nuts," I declared with a shrug. "All they do is argue and fight. No one knows what the hell they're talking about or fighting for. If they'd put their heads together, they could get a lot done. But not the way they're going at it."

"Would you like something to drink?" she asked.

"Just orange juice, if you have it." I had never considered how these gaudily-dressed and over-painted girls looked or acted when they weren't working. Actually, the print shift, the refined manner, and the hair in curlers, contrary to expectations, stirred emotions long dormant.

As she turned with the refreshment, an afternoon sun ray forced its way through the dusty window to light her face.

Soft blue eyes, clear and forthright, betrayed nothing of her profession. Yet, something about her seemed familiar. Yes, she's the one, the pretty blonde who wore the checkered raincoat with the hood. She had spoken to me as I walked toward the stairs the first night. Few, if any, knew her name, only the raincoat; however, many were interested, which caused rumors to travel at will.

Recalling bits of gossip among the loggers, I said, "What are you doing here anyway?"

"Just what all the other girls are here for. Making a living," she snapped, eyes turning to an impenetrable violet. "And what business is it of yours?"

Taken back by the curt response, I mumbled an apology, but continued, "I understand you have two children attending school in the East."

"Who the hell told you?" she blurted, apparently fighting to restrain anger and sorrow. "I guess I should have known someone would find out sooner or later."

Tentatively, she came to sit in a nearby chair. No explanations or apologies, just being together made us friends.

Minutes later the young woman regained her composure and inquired, "You never do anything with the girls when you come up here with the guys at night?" Before I could reply, she added, "You have a very dangerous job. How long can you do it without being killed?"

"I don't know. I guess it's the same for everyone who works in the woods; you try not to think about it. A few men do leave the logging, but right now I don't have that choice." I didn't elaborate, and she didn't pursue the matter.

"Please be careful. I know you have to move on. It's written all over your face. Don't stay too long before you get out. Maybe we'll meet again someday."

Then I blurted out, "I wish to hell you didn't have to be in this damn place. I've thought about you for some time, and you don't belong here. Some day, it may be possible for you to have your kids with you."

Suppressing tears, she murmured without conviction, "I hope so, but there doesn't seem to be a chance right now."

We stood and joined hands, two strangers sharing an uncharted moment—one seeking companionship, the other, understanding and respect.

Lifting her chin with my free hand, I reassured, "Listen, Gal, we both seem to be in the same boat, but we'll make it, one way or the other."

She raised her lovely eyes and we both smiled, this time with mutual admiration. A momentary silence, a quiet good-bye, the two hands relaxed, lingering until the fingertips finally parted. I turned and, without looking back, retraced my steps to the street.

Within the past hour, gale-force winds had moved into the area and now ripped at the ancient street-level door, making it swing back and forth as though bidding farewell to a friend.

An ominous darkness blanketed the nefarious city as the winter rains began their unrelenting deluge. The pigeons and sparrows had long since finished the popcorn and found refuge among the lofty eaves and gables. Passing the crowded taverns, I noted that the afternoon seemed to be going as usual. Hours later, when the brew halls closed their doors against the thirsty loggers, the drunken nomads would move to the "houses" to be with the waiting girls and convert from beer to hard liquor.

Torrential water rushed along the dark streets as the three officers, warmly ensconced in their patrol car, drove back and forth, guarding the interests of hardworking citizens. By now, the windblown rain, the black cloud cover, and dusk combined to hasten darkness, causing drivers to use their headlights.

Nearing the alley-way, where I always turned to enter my hotel by the rear door, I stepped into the gutter, soaking shoes and socks. "Damn, am I glad to be leaving this hell-hole." I continued swearing half aloud, picking my way down the alley where several men had gathered under the light. Still some distance from the group, I heard a sickening thud, like a rotten log being struck with a club. Then a loud groan echoed down the narrow alley. The men alternately chattered and cursed as they milled around. By the time I reached the group, two men carried a limp body into the hotel basement.

"What the hell happened to him?" I asked a by-stander.

"They've been at it since the union meeting. It just came to a head a few minutes ago. The big Swede caught him under the chin. What a blow! It lifted him completely off the ground and his head struck the corner as he fell. He may be dead. Christ! Look at all the damn blood. I bet he has a bitch of a headache tomorrow, that is, if he ain't dead."

"Here come the damn cops!" a lookout shouted. Turning their faces away from the probing spotlight, the rowdy crowd dispersed before the patrol car screeched to a halt just beyond the alley entrance.

Nightstick in hand, a lone officer, the one who had earlier befriended me, jumped from the car and landed on the run, arriving to find that only one person remained—me. He demanded, "What the hell's going on here? We got word that another brawl had started behind the hotel."

"Damned if I know. The fight was in full swing when I turned into the alley. By the time I arrived here it had ended. Two guys carried another one into the basement, knocked out, I guess. Then you guys pulled up."

After the cop ordered me to stay put, he jerked the hotel door open, entered the hallway, turned into the laundry room, and momentarily called back to me. "He's sprawled on bags of dirty sheets. Got a nasty gash on the head, but he's coming around." He returned and tugged on my sleeve, so we moved around the corner of the building. "You better get the hell away from here before it gets hairy. My partners are parking the car, and they'll arrive in a minute or so."

"I'm leaving for the flat lands tonight anyway," I replied. "Look, do me one favor. You know that blonde who works in the house beyond the union hall? Keep her out of trouble, if you can. She's OK and may need some help once in a while."

"I'll try, but damn it, get away from here right now," he urged, glancing uneasily around the corner. Evidently his partners were in no hurry, for he turned, grunted a sigh of relief, and said, "That's odd, just about the time we got this call, the pretty blonde from that house stopped and asked me to look after you, something about not seeing too well. She wasn't dressed for work, yeah, the one who wears the checkered raincoat."

"You may not know it," he continued, "but you did me a mighty fine favor a while back. I hope to repay you sometime. I'm going into the service soon. Square up when I get back. Now go!"

Moments later, I entered my room, threw meager belongings into a small pack, gathered climbing gear, and for the last time, descended the front stairs to the desk. After paying the clerk, I forced the street door open wide enough to squeeze through without letting in buckets of rain. Outside, the storm raged. Huge drops pounded the streets, and sporadic gusts swirled the downpour against windowpanes, creating the sound of gravel pouring from a dump truck. I looked for a cab.

My animosity toward the drivers had never changed. Despite church and other community group efforts to quell the indecent activities, they continued selling liquor to Indians and minors at double or triple normal prices. Even more disgusting, they served as pimps for streetwalkers, brutally filching the take from the defenseless women. But tonight, I relented and took a taxi to the bus station.

In the cab, moving slowly past the loggers' haunts, I gazed out the window at nothing in particular. Then I saw her, a lone woman wearing a checkered raincoat. She stepped from the curb, placed a suitcase in the trunk, then slid into the driver's seat.

"Stop the cab," I ordered and reached for the door handle. "What the hell! Where's the damn handle?"

"I had to take it off," the driver replied apologetically. "The damn drunks and cheapskates kept jumping out before I stopped, so I took the handles off."

By the time the driver parked the cab, got out, and walked around to open the passenger door, I could do nothing but watch the tail-lights merge with traffic, then disappear over the bridge toward the main highway. "Well, hell. It's probably better this way," I finally mumbled partly to myself, partly to the cabbie.

We arrived at the station as the bus driver admitted the last passenger and followed her through the open door. Fearful of the consequences if I missed the bus, the man slammed on the brakes, leaped from the cab, and ran toward the closing door. Luckily, the bus driver saw him in the mirror and waited. With the climbing gear and pack loaded into the luggage compartment, I paid the cab driver and hurried to the ticket window.

"How far do you want to go?" the scrawny agent inquired, looking skeptically at me.

"As far as the bus goes tonight," I announced with deliberate indifference.

Rain pelted onto the metal bus as it pulled from the covered station. No match for the deluge, the windshield wipers labored fruitlessly as the driver squinted into the night, barely missing a parked truck. Along the street, the battered old door to the house of ill repute had succumbed to the raging winds; the top hinge had given way and the twisted door lay cocked across the entrance. Union Hall lights cast an eerie glow through the steam-covered windows and the patrol car, as though plowing snow on a winter night, forged its way along the watery avenue. Down the dark alley behind my hotel, nothing. The city slept.

Thirty minutes from the harbor, the rain turned to a drizzle, then stopped. Twinkling stars revealed themselves and the driver hummed a spicy Irish tune while the two children behind him made funny faces in the rear-view mirror.

I removed wet shoes and socks, reached into the small bag and removed a worn sweatshirt, then wrapped it around my bare feet. Before drifting off to sleep, I took stock of the past years and wondered if they had been worth the effort. A tormenting decision had again been made. Safely away from town, the unforgettable blonde mother was surely on her way to join her children. I had successfully completed a self-imposed apprenticeship working with tramp loggers along the coast. More than that, I had survived living in the small area said to have been the most notorious of Northwest logging communities. Again, my mind and body needed and demanded a change and a full-time climbing job.

Huddled together for warmth, the two youngsters eventually dozed, periodically shifting their bodies to gain added comfort. The elderly lady sitting across the aisle stared into the night as the oncoming headlights flashed across her weary face. His eyes fixed on the road, the driver continued to hum the Irish ditty, perhaps anticipating a warm bed and a romantic evening away from home. I slept.

Beautiful, inquisitive, and naive, she floated in and out of my dream. Far in the distance, I heard her quiet voice. "I love my new name, darling. Please save it just for me. You can call me Kit when we're in public."

Chapter 30

Triumphant Return—State Rep—White Lie

1947

I retrieved my gear and bag from the impatient driver, then entered the Chehalis bus station restaurant. Except for the waitresses, nothing had changed: the old clock mounted high on the wall, a few winos hanging around, late-shift workers on their break, and a few sleeping travelers waiting for the next southbound bus. I placed my belongings in a corner and hurried to the rest room.

Somewhat refreshed, I re-entered the restaurant and to my surprise, heard a familiar voice coming from the counter. Yes, I thought, the Cajun drawl, I had worked with him in the upper camp—a chokerman, I think. Seeing me, he cut short what seemed to be a romantic discussion with the waitress and turned, his huge frame spilling over the edges of the counter swivel chair.

"Hey, climber. How's it going? You're getting up in the world," he said, beaming from ear
to ear. Perhaps his joy stemmed from meeting a
fellow logger or from his pleasure in executing
the accidental pun.

"Not bad, how about you?" I replied. "It's
been a while since I've been up this way. Been
down around the harbor. What's new at Kosmos?"

"Remember the old one-eyed loader who gave
us such a bad time? Well, he got his damn throat
cut. Seems he crashed a party at a neighbor's
home. He was so damn obnoxious the owner ordered
him to leave. With that, the loader threatened
to kill the man; they were all drunker than
hell. As they went to the yard to settle the
matter, the owner grabbed a butcher knife and
when the fight started, he cut the loader's
throat. Nothing came of it. I guess the courts
determined self-defense."

He went on, without waiting for a comment.
"The real tough one came when the skinner accidentally bumped his cat against a big log while
his friend, that big Norwegian hook-tender,
kneeled beside it digging a choker hole. The
bump by the cat, ever so slight, caused the huge
fir to roll onto him. What a hell of a death! He
screamed like a crazy man until they removed it—
everything went quiet, he lay there on the
ground, deader than a door nail. He and the

skinner were lifelong friends and they had worked together for years.

"The old hook-tender you first worked with shot himself; no one knows why. He retired and had money, but maybe he just couldn't stand life away from logging.

"That chokerman who took your place when you went to the landing got killed. He and another guy went to Alaska and he got it while they worked on a steep hillside—not sure what happened. The other one probably wishes he'd got the same. A broken branch sticking out on a sliding log caught him in the belly and ripped him wide open; he'll never work again even though they did save him. What a life! Maybe the so-called lucky aren't so lucky as believed. I'd rather not make it under similar circumstances. That's about it. I saw you get off the bus. Where are you heading?"

"Just looking for a job. How are they fixed up where you are?"

"The old Irish climber hasn't shown up for several days. No one's heard from him, so they may need a climber. Why don't you ride up with me tomorrow night? We're going to the movies in the afternoon," he said, nodding toward the blond waitress who had been listening. "Why don't you come with us?"

An attractive woman, probably a few years older than the chokerman, she had a nice figure and a winning smile. As I glanced her way, she blushed and agreed to the invitation.

"Hey, climber," the chokerman interrupted, "did you see that guy who just walked out? I wonder what the hell happened to him? His face looked like it had been run through a meat grinder, or even worse, like someone had jumped on his head with cork boots, then twisted while standing on him. His teeth are out, both top and bottom, and one eye is cocked. No one seems to know how it happened, but the word is that some-one found him almost dead in the alley several years back. He hangs around and lives on what he can beg. Bartenders claim he doesn't know who he is or where he came from. He'll drink anything, they say. Probably never was worth a damn to himself or anyone else. How'd you like to live like that?"

I made no reply, nor was one expected. We both knew that injured loggers often disappeared from the camps, never to be seen again. But this one, what did the chokerman say? "cork boots … teeth out, both top and bottom."

Now I had it! How well I remembered the locomotive fireman, Papa, the one who lost his leg in a logging accident, and his common-law wife, Mama. Could this battered wino be the one who Papa beat so brutally—the strange fellow who injured Mama when she refused to go to the hotel room with him? If so, he paid dearly for his lechery. But what about the fireman? What terrible deed demanded retribution so severe as losing a leg? Surely not for avenging Mama's two broken front teeth and mangled arm! If not, then what?

Warm and friendly, the morning fire woke me from a sound sleep; how great it felt to be back. Before I had finished a leisurely stretch, the wake-up bell rang out through the camp, rousing the few late sleepers. Once outside, crisp mountain air, aromas from the cookhouse, and rambunctious camaraderie quickened our strides toward the dining hall, where we ate with the gusto of a bitch wolf nursing a batch of pups.

Within the hour, the crews emerged from the bunkhouses, fully dressed and mentally prepared for the long ride and the day's work. I remained behind to talk with the camp boss.

New to the outfit, the general manager found me lacing calk boots. Our eyes met and flashed a greeting.

"The dispatcher told me you're looking for a job climbing," he began, adding, "Everyone seems to know you, and I guess you've been told of the problems we're having with our regular climber; he's off to town half the time. If that old Irish bastard doesn't show up today, the job's yours. He's getting too damn old to climb, anyway. Hang around the dispatch shack; we'll know this afternoon."

Late in the day, the call came. "Tell the new climber to catch the speeder and come to the high-lead side. We're ready to swing blocks."

At three-thirty, when the speeder dropped me at the tree, the hook-tender waited. "We've got the passline hooked onto the strawline drum. Can you swing them before quitting time?"

"I think so. Let's give it a whirl."

"What the hell?" a chokerman bellowed. "It's almost quitting time. We'll be here until midnight. Forget it."

With a questioning glance, the hook-tender looked to me for guidance. Paying no attention to either man, I casually unstrapped the spurs from the belt and restrapped one to each leg, buckled the belt around my waist, placed the double-passchain around my legs, and bobbed my head.

Now only twenty minutes before quitting time, I passed above the buckleguys and signaled to stop. Sitting in the passchain one hundred and ten feet above the ground, I grabbed the small haulback block, lifted with all my strength, kicked with one spur, and swung the block into place on the opposite side of the spar. Now to swing the bullblock. "Up a little."

Slowly, the puncher wound in the small passline, raising me higher in the tree. At just the right moment, I swung the climbing rope around the spar, released my grip on the passline, and caught the loose end with the free hand. Perfect!

Tied to the tree, I signaled for slack, placed the chain on the block and shouted, "Up a little." Good, halfway around. One more time and the block hung in place on the opposite side. How lucky, I thought. I had seen seasoned climbers struggle with block swinging for more than half an hour.

Now the safety strap. Finally, a trip down and back up to thread the blocks with strawline, then back to the ground. Belt unbuckled and spurs in place, I shot a glance toward the arrogant protestor who feared missing a bite from the evening meal.

The hook-tender took out his pocket watch, turned to the puncher, and smiled, asking, "What do you think of that?"

"Damn fast," the puncher replied.

The tired crew, soaked by the afternoon rain, had gathered by the speeder and watched in disbelief. Finally, one slight young man broke from the pack to assist me in securing the passline in the clear. Our task completed, the chokerman inquired, "Someday I want to be a climber. Will you teach me?"

Turning to the eighteen-year-old, I replied, "There's usually an extra set of spurs around somewhere—probably on the yarder. Every time you get a chance, take those spurs and climb a small tree near the landing. When you've done this a month or so, if you still want to be a climber, we'll do something about it." Just then the yarder whistle ended another productive eight hours without a serious accident or death.

The following morning ushered in a bright day with an invigorating chill in the air. The gaiety in reunion brought forth the best side of the men, the humorous side.

"Hey, climber, how's it going?" the skinner shouted, quickening his stride as he recognized me. "My new wife was looking through some old newspapers and found an article that read, 'Logger and man fight in the street. Logger whips man.'"

My old friend, the troubleshooter, drove by, stopped and looked back in disbelief, then reversed the pickup until he could look me in the eye. Slapping his forehead, he flashed a silly grin and lamented. "I've got a real problem. The past three mornings, I woke up and found my old lady camped on my shirttail. What should I do about that?" Before I could respond, the carefree troubleshooter had driven away, laughing his head off.

The plank-walk creaked from the huge powder-monkey's weight. Catching sight of me, the weathered giant broke into a jovial melody:

"Oh, the Dutch company is the best company

that ever came over from old Germany.

Now, the Dutch cows' bags, they are deep
    and wide,

instead of milk, they have beer inside."

"Remember the good old days?" he roared. "Them there days are gone forever. I picked me up a mop-squeezer to keep house and cook for me. Maybe we can get some guys together and slip out for a few hours some night, huh?"

Except for the main line between the lower and upper camp, the railroad tracks had been removed. Huge trucks with extended bunks, used only on private roads, had replaced the old locomotives and railroad flat-cars. Worn and unpainted, the cabooses, previously used to transport men, had been retired to the upper camps to serve as temporary housing for key employees and their families during summer months.

Logging camp life, so long dominated by the tramp logger, soon became limited to the remote areas. The Taft-Hartley Act, requiring a cooling-off period, would from now on, negate the effectiveness of the wildcat strike. Marriage, because the men could live at home and drive to and from work, became more and more inviting. Since the demands of domestication took their toll in various ways, previously venturesome men abandoned themselves to gluttony. In varying degrees, they discarded, at least publicly, their disdain for servitude.

The harshness of the woods, which had for decades attracted young, able-bodied men, was being whittled away by economic and humanitarian considerations—safety headed the list.

Married and lower-camp loggers, quick to accept that safety would from now on be an integral part of working in the woods, presented no problems. Not so for the arrogant tramps dominating the upper camps. Always going to the limits of daring, they saw safety regulations as restrictions on their inherent freedoms: each man should live by his own law.

When the winter snows drove us from the uplands, several buddies and I usually high-tailed it for Oregon or the Washington coast. New territory consistently drew us to rough country, new faces, and freedom to try unconventional logging techniques.

Although I dreaded trips into the land of poison oak in western Oregon, three weeks of hard scratching usually defeated the pesky skin rash. The rough country around Brookings, Powers, and Mapleton supported gyppos always looking for men willing to live in less-than-adequate quarters and pit their skills against downhill logging, box canyons, and postage-stamp landings—all fraught with trying and dangerous situations.

Only the hardiest remained more than a few weeks in or near Forks, Washington. One short stint sent me scurrying back to Kosmos, my wanderlust curbed by unreliable equipment, worn cables, weekend brawls, indigestible restaurant food, coastal winds and continuous rain. Time to stop running and deal with the irreconcilable conflicts within a futureless occupation. I arrived ready to work in the lower camps and support a company safety program.

"The state has sent its representative to talk with us tonight," the company personnel manager announced to the select group. "After he speaks, we can ask questions."

"Men," the state rep began, pausing briefly to quiet one rowdy with an icy stare. He continued, giving each word its full meaning. "I have a personal investment in developing this safety program. Over the years, I have lost no less than three dozen friends and four close relatives to logging accidents. Ninety percent were preventable. The program involves nothing more than common sense. There are, however, certain mandates that logging companies and their employees must follow."

Each man, holding his allegiance to freedom, questioned the state rep in accord with a perceived threat to his ability to remain a fierce competitor—competing against himself, over-zealous supervisors, faulty equipment, and nature.

Union supporters voiced concerns regarding the consequences of non-compliance by management or workers. Each violation needed to be dealt with as it occurred; to wait for an accident would be too late. The idea was to prevent injury or death, not necessarily punish, for everyone understood the demanding law of chance.

"Nevertheless," the rep continued, "logging companies will have their industrial insurance sizably increased for each time-loss accident, whether it be minor injury or death. The companies will determine the consequences for each employee who fails to follow regulations."

The state man knew his business; he knew the technical and colloquial jargon, and he knew how and when to use them. As he shifted his warped body from side to side, evidently to escape pain which remained his business, he received and answered questions with ease. Still, no one had asked the most pressing question, the hard hats.

"Does this mean we have to wear those damn piss-pots on our heads?" one skinner finally asked. "I'm under the cat roof all day," he contended.

Another man, a donkey-puncher, inquired from the floor, "I'm also under a roof. Why should I be required to wear a damn tin lid?"

With unusual patience, the rep read statistics to show how each employee category, including cat-skinners and donkey-punchers, had been injured or killed by blows to the head. Selling the safety program wouldn't be easy.

I sat near the back, waiting apprehensively. Would the next requirement be my undoing—the mandatory physical exam?

The meeting terminated with no reference to the dreaded subject. Even so, I mentally outlined alternatives. If the physical exam became compulsory, weeks and years preparing for a respectable vocation had gone for naught. I would be doomed to a lifetime forever unemployed, or at least relegated to gratuitous and menial tasks. Regardless, the program must be supported and, for sure, a few would suffer the consequences.

"Hey, climber, I hear you've been down on the harbor," an old-timer called to me. "Is there any chance you saw my daughter?"

"Don't know," I replied. "What's her name?"

"She's going by some other name now. But she was about sixteen when she left school. Worked in restaurants for a while but we haven't heard from her for some time. Hope she isn't in trouble. Didn't know much about the cities. We heard once that she had a boyfriend, a police officer, I think."

I couldn't believe my ears. The teenage prostitute. Now it came to me; she had been a high school cheerleader for a visiting basketball team. While watching a game, two young men sitting near me had commented on her attractive figure, ample breasts, and enticing eyes. Come to think of it, as she had said, she did look older than other girls her age.

"No," I lied. "I'd need to know what name she's going by and what she looks like."

Disappointed, the old-timer headed out the door with me close on his heels, wondering if I had done the right thing.

"Hey, climber," the personnel manager called, "come on up here and meet the state rep."

"Here it comes," I mumbled to myself. "They're going to ask me about my vision. This is it."

Carroll

Loggers—After Hard Hats Were Required

Chapter 31

The Bond—Another White Lie

After nodding a greeting, the rep began, "I understand you're a strong advocate for additional safety measures. I'd like to hear your ideas."

Greatly relieved, I accepted a chair and coffee, then sat facing the rep. We launched into a stimulating discussion, two like-minded men analyzing an industry-wide problem. Hours later we parted, each aware that the next few years would bring dramatic changes to the timber industry. I looked forward to meeting him again, though he presented a potential threat to my continued employment in the woods. What's the difference? I reasoned. One way or the other, my hard-earned independence and status must someday end. To think otherwise would be fool's play. But what then?

The meeting hall, reeking with smoke, snuff, and damp clothing, drove me into the cool night air, where I breathed deeply and strolled toward the bunkhouse. Shuffling footsteps came from behind—the old-timer again. Puffing, he approached and spoke, "Here's her picture. Forgot

I had it in my billfold." He shoved his daughter's photo into my hand and awaited a reply.

The single yard light seemed to dim as I strained to identify the person. Then, as though he had erred, the old-timer reached for the photo, took it in his fingers without removing it from my hand, and turned it end for end.

"I'm sorry," the anxious fellow apologized, "I didn't realize I'd given it to you wrong end to. Now, that should do it. I got a better picture at home, but that's out near Tacoma."

Backed into the proverbial corner, I stared absently at the faded treasure, wondering how I could explain without revealing that his daughter planned to be a prostitute in the harbor area. That's it! The black-haired bartender who brought her to my hotel room: he's the answer.

"Yes, I've seen your daughter, but only once. She was with a nice looking black-haired young man."

"Did he have on his uniform?" the father asked, his excitement increasing by the minute.

"No," I replied, "But that doesn't mean he didn't have one. He may have been off duty." Then I had it. "Or, on the other hand, he may not have been an officer. These youngsters go

394

from one thing to another with the flick of your finger. Many young couples have been moving to Alaska, where jobs are plentiful, and with both people working, they can lay away a nice nest egg. When they return, they're rich. I wouldn't worry if I were you. Who knows, your daughter may return someday and have a nice bouncy grandchild for you. How would you like that?"

His voice one octave higher, the man exclaimed, "Well, I'll be goldarned! Why didn't I think of that? Sure enough, that's what they've gone and done. They probably don't want anyone to know what they're up to until they've made it big." Carefully pocketing the returned picture, the jubilant woodsman rewarded me with a broad smile and a quiet, "Thanks a lot." Neither spoke for a moment, then my friend, with doubt in his voice, philosophically added, "Even if it isn't that way, I hope it is, and I feel better believing it is."

Nothing more was said, nor was more expected. We both understood and parted with a sincere "See you. Take it easy."

After several weeks with hard-hats having been seen floating down the river or found smashed by a caterpillar track, we came to accept the inhibiting and degrading head gear. The emphasis on safety, although not replacing the demand for maximum production, was promoted and drilled into all employees.

Periodically, the state rep returned for an on-the-job equipment inspection and an evening meeting. His quiet yet commanding voice guided and drove the conversation. Always direct, fair and honest, his recommendations and ideas gained additional respect, and the safety program finally caught on.

By this time steadfast friends, the state rep and I spent long hours after each meeting discussing the pros and cons of safety suggestions forwarded by the men, as well as our own ideas. We became a two-man safety committee.

The rep favored one leg and his left shoulder sagged, but he never complained. Over the months, I noticed that this sincere and capable man had become less vibrant and responsive. "You seem tired tonight." I finally inquired. "Is something wrong?"

"Well, yes and no," he replied. "Since the safety program is getting underway, the people in my department are being asked to work on labor disputes."

"Do you think one union will gain control of all industries?" I asked.

"Probably not. Loggers, especially the tramps, are too damn independent and resistant to regimentation. Their loyalty is confined to themselves; they feel no obligation to dogmas, morals, or the law."

Suddenly, rumbling growls quieted us. As the ferocious sounds neared the building, I heard an occasional grunt and recognized the camp scavenger, an aging black bear. The old fellow had been a nightly visitor to the camp garbage dump for several months and, so far, had harmed nothing. Now, it seemed, he had only wandered in for a look around the buildings.

The rep, evidently noting my ease with the situation, shrugged off the matter, so we took time to rise from our chairs and stretch until the bear had passed on its way.

Chuckling, I suggested, "If he decides to raid the kitchen, we'll have some fun."

"Yeah," the rep agreed, adding soberly, "the larger outfits are hiring professional bear hunters to kill them. When the sap is running, especially in the Douglas firs, the bears tear the bark from the trees to get at the softer fibers. Evidently this has nutritional value; however, it kills the trees. Many companies have sought and received permission to destroy bears entering their private timberlands."

I refueled the potbellied stove, closed the damper, then settled back in my chair with a warmed-over cup of coffee.

Again seated, the venerable rep paused, absentmindedly reached down to re-tie a loose shoelace, examined his efforts, then turned in his seat as the night watchman opened the door and poked his rain-drenched head in, exclaiming, "Don't you guys ever quit? It's getting late and the rain's coming down in buckets."

Understanding the watchman's concern, the rep smiled as he waved to the retired logger.

We fell silent, a quiet understood and accepted without question. Then raising our coffee mugs, we stared vacantly into the dark liquid, sipped, held the mug close to our lips, savored the aroma, sipped again, then mechanically replaced the stained receptacles back on the worn table. These moments, by osmosis or otherwise, cemented a friendship based on empathy and respect.

"You've come a long way for such a short time in the woods. Do you plan to make this your permanent vocation?" my new friend asked. Uncertain how to respond, I faltered, so he continued as though delivering a message, or so I thought. "I broke my back and shoulder at about your age, and I miss the work more than I can say. The only relaxation I seem to get anymore is when I get out on the job for inspections and during these evening meetings.

"It's nice to find someone like you who is also interested in developing safety throughout the logging industry. As you may have guessed by now, I may not be back for some time, if ever. There's talk that I might get transferred to another department. It will mean more money but eliminate opportunities to get out into the woods.

"Nevertheless, if you ever decide to leave logging, please look me up. I'm sure there will be a place for you in our department."

Stunned, I could do nothing but stare blankly into his eyes—the face, the voice, the eyes I had learned to know and trust. How should I reply? What could I say? Fruitlessly I groped for a logical answer. Should I tell him? I thought. No. It would mean immediate discharge if they know my vision is getting worse and, besides, I can't do the office work which requires reports and continuous reading.

Frustrated and disappointed, I finally replied, "Well, sometime I'll probably take you up on that offer, but right now I have another commitment; in a way, it's an obligation to myself which I don't feel free to discuss at this time.

Sorry, and I do appreciate your considering me. Maybe later, I hope."

The angry dark cloud lifted as the rep rose to get his coat. "I know how you feel. I was the same way. It's a hard tough life but there's something that makes us go to the woods and, even more compelling, is the force that holds us. Each morning when I roll from my soft bed, I wish I were putting on calk boots to head for the brush, rain or shine. Yes. The feeling never leaves. And, in a way, I hope it never does. I would hate to know that I had lived without it. Most city people would never under-stand, but I know you do, and it's been nice sharing it with you. Maybe we'll meet again. Take it easy."

Watching the rep pass through the door, I felt that part of my life had been lost, dropped into a void from which it could never be re-trieved.

Torrential rain drenched me as I ran to the bathrooms, then on to the bunkhouse. How could the rep have missed this so much? Then I chuckled to myself. "Some people just don't know when they're well off."

Gale-force winds had prevented us from working, and as usual, the single men headed for town. For me, city nightlife had lost its appeal. Many longtime friends had married and were busily building, planting and generally becoming domesticated. Handshakes had become a part of greeting and many men dropped their nicknames or titles in favor of given names.

Although the former renegades complained about the proverbial rings in their noses, most hesitated to break faith with their wives and go into town alone. Actually, I found, they seemed to enjoy the constant companionship with the women. To be sure, their complaints about the terrible confinement fell only on the ears of fellow workers, but never within earshot of the "slave-driving" females.

This particular Saturday night the camp was deserted, so I stretched out on my bunk and listened to the driving rain and a portable radio. The strange feeling returned; again, I must choose between stability and moving on.

Within days, the drive for stability claimed the victory, and although the decision gave me no solace, the time had come to commit myself to something besides being the head-climber.

Could I fit into the good life—the life of conspicuous consumption, of daily routines, of mortgages, of family? I pleaded ignorance on such matters, for they had never been a part of my life. Mine had been a time of adventure, and learning, and beating the odds; could I accommodate to less? Or more?

Now I considered the concept of destiny. How often I had heard fellow workers state that when a man's time comes, he'll die or he won't. It's not really man's place to outguess what has been predestined. How ridiculous, I thought, yet there seemed to be a bit of truth in the theory.

Then I rationalized, the same fractured logic should apply to other matters. Let it ride.

Chapter 32

Mixed Blessing

"Hey, climber," the bullbuck called. "We've cut up to that spar over the hill. If you want to check it out, I'll have the fallers move over the ridge today."

"OK," I replied.

"I know the new regulations say you're supposed to have someone nearby when you top a tree, but I don't have anyone today. Can you make it? The fallers can see the spar top from where they'll be working."

"Probably," I replied, more uneasy about the disregard for safety regulations than for my ability to safely top the tree. Over the years, I had topped dozens without anyone around. It might be true that fallers could see the top, but was it or was it not a rule that a climber should have someone on the ground near the spar when he was in the tree? The regulations, vague on this matter, left room for personal judgment.

After a thirty minute ride, the cutting crew gathered tools, then wound their way across the ravine and scattered to assigned territories. The radio had reported zero winds, above average temperature, and variable cloudiness. What a perfect morning, I thought, noting that the spar had only a few limbs. I walked up the knoll to assure myself that fallers worked within shouting distance, then returned to strap on the spurs and belt. To be sure, this would be the easiest spar I had topped in some time.

Within minutes, I reached the top, ready to chop the undercut, but paused to look down over the valley from my lofty vantage point. How beautiful! So vast! So unusually peaceful and unmolested! But not for long. Next year this hillside would be nothing more than a barren mound of brush, tree stumps, dirt and rock. The winter rains would carve deep gullies, digging channels for dislodged silt and seedlings to be washed into the river far below.

Regardless, each man working on this hillside, and on thousands just like this one, needed to make a living, but would the slaughter ever stop? When would all-out re-forestation begin? Would these men ever be ready to adopt alternative methods for earning a living? Probably not until the timberlands lay bare—sad, but true.

Christ! What's that? I thought. Yes, that's it. Men's voices near the spar. Who are they? What are they doing?

First the starter cord, then the noise generated by the two-man motorized chainsaw goaded me into action. No time for thought, I let out additional slack in the rope, kicked the spurs loose, and descended at breakneck speed, the whining motor muffling my curses.

"What the hell are you guys doing?" I bellowed, leaping downward ten or twelve feet at a time. Neither faller could hear me. Now they lifted the saw to the tree.

Forty feet to go.

Just as the saw teeth tore at the bark on the spar, the loose end of my rope and my topping saw dropped onto the chainsaw motor. Next came my axe, swinging haphazardly in circles.

As the faller holding the motor end tried to dodge my topping saw, the axe banged against his hard hat, causing him to duck and run for cover, leaving the chain saw idling in the cut.

"What the hell. Where did you come from?" he stammered, ashen-faced and trembling from head to foot.

Wild with anger, I roared, "Don't you idiots ever look at anything except the end of your damn noses? Can't you see that 'X' on the spar? What the hell do you think you're doing? Knitting in a damn sewing circle? You guys were told to move over the ridge and stay away from here until I finished topping this tree. What the devil are you doing here anyway?"

Gathering his thoughts, the second faller spoke. "No one told us anything this morning. Last week the bullbuck told us that when we finished down below, we should come up here to work. But honest, he didn't say anything to us this morning. Maybe he talked with those fallers working over the ridge."

"Didn't you see the 'X'?" I demanded again.

"No." The motorman finally came to his own defense as he walked around the tree, searching for the identifying 'X'. "Usually there's an 'X' on opposite sides of a spar, but there's only one on this tree and it was on the far side as we walked up. Besides, it's cut only into the bark, not through to the wood, and it looks like another tree has brushed it. You've got to look real close to see it."

"Didn't you see me up there?" I continued, my wrath gradually subsiding.

"The sun was in my eyes, and I just took a quick glance. It has a definite lean, and I didn't need to put a plumb on her." Then he repeated, "Yeah, she leans that way, and I just glanced up. Besides, it's difficult looking into the sun, you know. You could have been on the opposite side."

Fortunately, the cut had gone only a few inches through the bark, with no serious damage to the integrity of the giant fir. Most disturbing to me was the fact that I had consented to work without a watchman, and the erroneous information that had nearly ended my life. I had knowingly ignored safety regulations; no more tree topping without a watchman and an 'X' on opposite sides of the spar.

All three familiar with codes of the woods, we realized that each shared responsibility for the incident. By this time the morning had passed and, as might be expected, a few clouds drifted over, dropping just enough rain to warrant a lunch-time fire. We squatted around the crackling wood, silently toasting sandwiches and staring into the flames. For a time after lunch, the head-faller listened to raindrops sizzle in the dying coals before he spoke. "If you want to finish topping the tree, we'll stick around and make sure everything goes all right."

Relieved, I accepted the offer. Forty-five minutes later, the spar topped and I back on the ground, the head-faller again approached and presented an unusual problem.

"I'm sorry about this morning. You see, I sometimes have a little problem seeing clearly. Glasses help some but not always enough. Also, the goldarn lenses get covered with bark slivers and sawdust; then I can't see much of anything. They seem to be getting worse, and I don't see well enough to drive, especially after dark. Maybe I'll have to give up the woods, but it's the only thing I know, and I'm too old to change to something else. I'd rather be dead than go on welfare. If it weren't for my partner, I'd probably be there right now. He drives us both to work. I'm glad my kids are raised and gone."

"Could you be a watchman who fuels and greases the donkeys and cats after the men go home at night?" I asked, racking my brain for a logical solution to the old fellow's dilemma.

"I could probably do the work; but again, someone would have to drive me to and from the job. I've thought of several things I could do but they all have hitches." Then he added, leathery face anxious, "I hope you don't say anything about this morning. If they knew, they'd fire me, sure as all get out." With that, perhaps feeling that too much had been revealed, he turned and hurried toward the standing timber.

Yes, I thought, the old faller has it figured correctly. If they knew, they'd probably fire him—and me too. Someday soon I'll have to do something about it; but give it a little longer.

What was it he said about not being able to see in the dark? Could he have the same vision problem? I've never known anyone who has had it except a few of my relatives. What a time he must have had: unable to drive in the dark, eyes sensitive to light, always hiding his poor vision, and raising children all these years. It seems he might do better in a city, with bright lights and buses that go all over town. Maybe that would be better for him—and maybe for me, also. Yes, the city, and why not? Reluctantly, I forced the matter to a remote area in my mind, gathered climbing rigging, then wound my way over and around the logs toward the crew bus.

Within the year, my vision had deteriorated so drastically that performing many routine tasks, aside from my climbing, became almost impossible.

However, the addition of a young apprentice brought efficiency back to normal; life was back on track.

The company featured me in its magazine as a major contributor to the national logging industry's best safety record. Since the climbing took me no farther than an arm's length from my work, I continued to top and rig trees, still master in my small, lofty world.

A ground swell of innovations brought dramatic changes to the logging industry. Steel towers, raised by hydraulic lifts, despite their high cost, threatened to displace the wood spar trees. Self-contained loading machines eliminated the need for booms attached to spars; expert toppers and high-riggers were sometimes forced into combination jobs, with little of the venerated climbing. Short-distance radios provided better communications and thus, more efficiency and added safety—excluding the cherished whistle-punk. More and more, the loggers married, moved to larger towns, drove miles upon miles each day to and from work and became less interested in or devoted to the unions.

After months of soul-searching regarding my diminishing vision, I gave in to better judgment and went to my friend, the general manager. Each season we had spent several amiable and relaxing weekends fishing the upper lakes. As though it were taboo during these outings, neither introduced discussions regarding work; by mutual consent, unplanned periods of silence prevailed—each involved in his own thoughts.

But now it was different; away from the soft fresh breezes and blades of warm sunlight streaming through the trees, we were now confined to a stuffy room where I fought against the only cowardice I knew: my reluctance to reveal the extent of my visual problem. Even so, I had recently found myself pondering what life might be like away from the woods.

The rational time for disclosure had long passed and now I faced my employer ready to accept the consequences. Certainly, I disliked losing my job, my status among the men, and my high wages. But, most disturbing loomed the possibility of causing injury or death to a fellow worker due to my poor vision—this I could not tolerate.

For the second time during the past few years, I was about to voluntarily introduce the extent of my sight loss. Would I again pay a price for being honest and forthright?

"I need to discuss something with you," I began. "It isn't going to be easy but it had to come sooner or later."

"OK," the general manager replied, beckoning me to a chair. Usually insistent on getting

411

right to the point, my fishing buddy now stalled for time. "Let's have some coffee first."

Feeling weak and nauseated, I contained my thoughts while the boss took his time pouring the thick concoction. Revived by a wisp of cool damp air gusting through an open inch of window, I regained my composure. It would have been easier, I thought, to face a dozen hazardous situations in the woods or to pit my strength against several drunken pugilists in a bar. Nevertheless, here it was, the time to introduce the dreaded subject. Sweat, salty and warm, rolled off my forehead, into my eyes, and down my nose, coming to rest in the corners of my mouth. Then the silence, not the congenial fishing silence but a vacuum in which two men, each respectful of the other's position, knew that a long, successful career must end.

Mustering my courage, I spoke first. "I've got to leave the woods," I announced, my hollow voice ringing in the distance. Could this be my voice; the voice that just yesterday had felt so strong, so alive and healthy?

Without asking me why, the general manager spoke. "Yes, Carroll, I understand. I should tell you that we have been considering how long you should remain as a climber, but we wanted to give you the opportunity to make the decision. We planned to wait until the first of the year

and then tell you. It's better this way. We have
a position for you here in camp. The pay won't
be the greatest, but you have given us the best
years of your life and we want to do something
for you."

Hearing my given name, Carroll, so out of
keeping in the logging world, caused my ambiguous past to race through my mind. Throughout
life, I had been identified by nicknames, job
titles, and reputation. First a prairie town boy
without hopes for a future, then a millhand eating sawdust, next a logger, where I had worked
my way from the lowest paid job to the highest
wage earner, the high-climber, and finally back
to square one.

Now even more upset and ambivalent about
the outcome of my career, I put disappointment
aside and searched for a scapegoat, a logic, or
even a mystical answer to my plight. Inwardly,
anger and relief battled for control.

They had known all along. Then why the
hell hadn't they said something to me rather
than discussing it among themselves? Then I reasoned, it had been a two-way street, but I chose
not to participate; I could have gone to them
before.

Nevertheless, now that I'm a charity case:
they want to do something for me. Why didn't

they offer it to the old faller who has the sight problem? I should suggest it. No, they'd just fire him and he needs the work—let it stand. Besides, the job belongs to the company. It's their reward to me, to accept or reject; it's not mine to give to someone else.

Warm sunlight filtered through the dusty window onto my lap as I pondered the situation. I'll never give up the title even though I know it will eventually be stripped from me and given to the next man who fills the position. Furthermore, the job won't be around long, and being older would make it even more difficult to adjust to something different.

Looking back, I thought of the words spoken by a friend who had been relegated to a do-nothing position after a logging accident.

"Jobs manufactured to repay faithful employees seldom turn out well. In time, both management and the employee resent the generosity. Also, there's the matter of self-respect. If I offer an opinion on something, no one pays a damn bit of attention. It was never that way before. Rough and tumble friends either avoid me or handle me with kid gloves. I'm always looking and hoping for something, but I don't even know what it is."

Through the years, I'd gone to work each morning unsure whether or not I would return that night. This way, I could hold my tongue, and bide my time while searching for that elusive something.

Carroll Getting Ready to Climb

Carroll

Chapter 33

Marginal Man: Two Down, One To Go

The following weeks ripped at my emotions and challenged the optimism that had pulled me through many difficult situations. Partly from habit, partly from the need to be around cronies, I arrived at the splicing loft earlier than required—a mistake I would not repeat.

What a way to end up, I thought, making a few absentminded observations before returning to the open doorway to watch the crew buses pull out. One by one they headed toward the woods—the center of my life for the past twenty years, fifteen years as a high-climber.

In my mind, I could hear the men boasting or complaining about their weekend in town, the cruelty inflicted by the wives who overworked and underfed them, or how their favorite football team fared during the Sunday game.

The yard surrounding the dispatch office, bustling with trucks, crew buses and boisterous friends a few minutes ago, now stood bleak and empty, leaving only tire tracks and the discolored plank walk.

The blacksmith's hammer brought me to my senses. I cringed at the prospect of spending day after day as the one-man crew in the loft, a job usually reserved for faithful employees who no longer had the stamina to participate in the actual logging. Just thirty-seven and still in excellent physical condition, I turned, collected my thoughts and plunged into the work, trying to forget the past.

Splicing cable warranted no distinctive title such as climber or hook-tender. Overnight, I had become a marginal man, untitled, unfit for the woods but too young to retire—neither totally blind nor fully sighted.

In less than two hours, I had completed the entire day's work, so I wandered into the adjacent blacksmith shop. Ignoring the intrusion, the old Swede smith went about his business, occasionally pausing to mop his brow on a faded shirt sleeve, stoke the forge, then return to the hammer and anvil. Hours passed before the wiry old fellow broke the silence.

His words revealed an accent so thick and clumsy that I had difficulty understanding the sing-song gibberish. A stutter, like an old hen clucking to her chicks, further complicated his speech. Nevertheless, within a week we communicated, using gestures combined with one or two-word phrases. By silent agreement, complicated sentences were banned.

A month or so later, torrential rain beat on the tin-roofed blacksmith shop while the old Swede and I exchanged comments regarding a new labor-saving machine. Distracted by a wailing siren, we turned to watch as the ambulance, a retired hearse, swung around the dispatch office, screeched to a halt, then stood in ominous silence. Several minutes passed before a crew bus pulled into the lot. Six men, four wet and muddy and two garbed in immaculate whites, carefully removed a stretcher and its occupant from the crew bus. After transferring the body to the waiting conveyance, they exchanged a few words, then hurried to escape the blinding rain. No stranger to the camp, the ambulance driver slowly pulled away from the mud-covered yard.

Later, the dispatcher told me it was the old faller who squinted and wore glasses—yes, how well I remembered him and his sight problems. But that had not caused the accident. Halfway into the backcut a gust of wind had barber-chaired the tree and it kicked back onto him. Vividly, I recalled his statement. "I'd rather be dead than go on welfare." Well, he wouldn't need to worry. Although they had placed him on a stretcher and carefully carried him across logs, a small creek, and up out of the steep canyon, he died in the crew bus before they could get him back to camp.

What power caused this old-timer to continue working in the woods, knowing his chances for being killed or becoming permanently injured? Had he actually chosen his own demise, or had it been a fear; an unknown fear greater than death itself, devised and enforced by the logging culture, so erroneously brutal and unforgiving?

The heavy rains continued through the day while the smith and I, our work completed, warmed our backs before the forge. A foreboding silence pervaded the soot-laden blacksmith shop. "One down, two to go" flashed through my mind. How long it had been since I last heard the phrase. Had the old curse returned? If so, who would be next?

The roaring crowd awakened me as the football game ended; for a change, my chosen team had won. Then three or four commercials clogged the airways and finally the announcement: A new educational program invited persons with sight problems to contact the state agency.

It must be for younger people ready to enter the work-force, I convinced myself, but stored the information.

Uneventful days rolled by until one bleak morning a familiar voice called from behind as I entered the loft.

"Hey, climber, I thought you'd like to know, my daughter, the one you saw down at Grays Harbor, came home, and like we thought, she brought a bouncy baby. It's a girl though, but that's all right. Husband's in the Navy. They're living in San Diego." Then, as though he had suddenly realized where he stood, my old friend asked, "What are you doing in here?"

I thought that one over for a moment, but couldn't come up with a suitable answer, so I grinned and replied, "Not much." At least, I thought, that's one bit of good news. She evidently had given up the idea of remaining in a questionable vocation. Once in a while, something turns out right.

Again, the old-timer scanned the room, threw me a questioning glance, then turned and hurried through the open doorway to catch the crew bus.

Bit by bit, the company cut back on its operations. Automation eliminated jobs without reducing production. With my splicing ability improved, I finished a day's work before lunch, then spent the afternoons assisting the smith. Other than that, I often perched myself on a bag of forge coke and thought about nothing of consequence, mostly bygone days and trivia. The radio announcement increasingly interrupted my nostalgia.

One bright morning after the crew buses had departed for the woods, the superintendent pulled alongside the splicing shed and asked, "How'd you like to take a ride? I'm going up the hill where we finished logging last winter." Delighted at the opportunity to get back into the woods, I grabbed my lunch and jumped into the pickup.

With windows rolled down, we rode in silence for a time, the fresh, cool breezes drifting through the cab. A few miles out, my friend broke the silence. "As you may know, they're planning to close the camp. The cat and truck shops will be transferred away from here, and the valley will soon be under water. They're going to build a dam on the Cowlitz below here, somewhere down by the Mayfield bridge, later another near Mossyrock."

His words, clear and direct, diminished my enthusiasm for the outing. The splicing loft and blacksmith shop had not been mentioned. Was he telling me that I would soon be unemployed?

At the highest point on the ridge, he stopped, parked the pickup, and we walked to a protruding rock. What I could not see, my mind supplied—vivid memories of the past. There it lay, beautiful and green, the valley, with its winding river and scattered houses, guiding the White Pass highway through the tiny village of Kosmos, the quiet logging community where I had spent much of my adult life.

Several snow-capped peaks reflected bright sunlight into the surrounding ravines. Mysteriously alive and vibrant, over the years each timber-covered hill had taken on a separate character. Although it had to be my imagination playing tricks, I seemed to hear the dancing river, the river that had taken so many lives, bidding me farewell.

Then an obliging breeze, echoing the phantom ring of the axe, the hum of the saw, the shriek of the donkey-whistle, spread the wonderful aromas that intensified my fragmented recollections. For years, these sounds and odors had been the center of my world—the vitality of my existence.

"I bet you miss it." my companion stated, showing an unusual empathy. He seemed sincerely concerned about my feelings. Then it came to me; we had spent many years working together, and we now shared a strange remorse, knowing the valley would soon disappear. His company house, no more than one-quarter mile from the camp, would not be spared. We had partied together, danced in the same grange hall, helped raise the tall Christmas tree in the triangle where the main roads intersected. Like colts turned out to pasture, we had finished the Saturday soaking up beer with friends in the tavern.

Finally, I turned and smiled. "It's been a long time. I mean, since the first time we met," I said. "A lot of water has gone under the bridge, and perhaps there will be a lot more."

Laying a huge hand on my shoulder as though detecting doubt in my voice, he countered, "You'll do just fine. Mark my words."

Before returning to the pickup, we surveyed the panorama for several minutes. The valley, far below, brought back memories of both peace and turbulence; life had become a combination of victory and defeat. As though again wanting to reassure me, he cleared his throat, paused, but said no more. We turned away from our valley for the last time.

On the way back to camp, engrossed in my own thoughts, I alternately cursed, then questioned that irrational logic called fate; yet, I had no cause to complain, for I remained alive and well. Perhaps, I had been, as the old saying goes, the author of my own problems, my own worst enemy: I had refused to forfeit the only life I had known for the past twenty years. Fate could not be blamed for that. Regardless, to have abandoned my exciting nomadic ways to accept any alternatives open to me during these years would have approached self-destruction; a life without purpose, motivation, or challenge— no, thank you, I've made it this far and I'll do it again.

Parked by the loft, I opened the pickup door, placed one foot on the ground and turned, half in and half out.

There he sat, his huge body comically stuffed behind the steering wheel, a broad smile flashing a last good-bye. I would have been remiss had I not recounted the many times he had been helpful; always ensuring that I had the best men when rigging a tree, providing the strongest cables and safety equipment, placing my name and picture in the company magazine, never forgetting extra-hazardous duties I had performed. He must have known all along.

Our eyes held for a moment, then I returned the smile, got out and closed the door. Through the open window, I added, "Take it easy. I'll see you."

He replied in kind as I turned and headed for the blacksmith shop.

Somewhere in the dust-laden interior, I should have heard the old smith. The forge had died to embers, and tools lay randomly on the bench, anvil, and floor; he had always been a devil for keeping the work area meticulous.

"Yeah," the dispatcher informed me, "we found him doubled up by the forge—chest pains. They took him to the Morton hospital. By now, he's probably lying in the special unit at Tacoma General."

I placed the shop in order, closed the huge sliding doors and locked them from inside, exited through the smaller walk-through door and snapped the padlock. It took only minutes to do the same in the splicing loft. Next, I collected my pay and began an annual two-week vacation.

At this time, I was neither a man to be remembered, nor one who had been dispossessed, yet, common sense told me that my time in the timber industry had ended. What now?

Long ago, I learned, sometimes the hard way, that the pipe dreams of others might lead you to believe that the world is an easy and effortless place. Not so. But, an existence reduced to a formula would be worthless. How many men move through life without hardships or change? Very few.

Hours of deliberation found me no closer to a rational alternative. Logging had been everything. Although I was ignorant about options away from the woods, everyone knew that blind people often begged on the streets, sold brooms in the neighborhood, and sometimes became an object of pity or a burden to community agencies—all unacceptable alternatives.

Intuition warned that destiny could neither destroy nor save me. To exchange the rural life for paved streets and tall buildings could be no worse than what lay ahead if I remained here.

Carroll in Front of a Douglas Fir Log

Chapter 34

Ultimate Freedom

1959

Several days later, I left Kosmos, never to return. Despite many unknowns, I felt vibrant, had escaped unscathed, and remained healthy—not true for many friends. Now freed from back-breaking work, day after day toiling in the rain, and twenty years in our nation's most hazardous industry, my passion for adventure remained.

I hitched a ride to Chehalis, then hurried to the state branch office, where the vocational counselor, somewhat surprised by my high test scores, suggested college. Although I had only fifty dollars in my pocket, the same optimism that had guided me through years in the woods caused me to cast aside misgivings. Why not? I had no alternative.

Bits of logging humor flitted through my mind as the Greyhound bus rolled through the crowded streets of Seattle, its tall buildings reaching into the heavens, its trolleys speeding along the avenues, its shoppers protecting packages under broad umbrellas, and its overflowing gutters directing streams toward Puget Sound. To become a part of this hectic world simultaneously excited and confused me.

"Yessler Way," the driver announced.

Then a vague recollection, Archie McDougall's hiring hall. Could it still be there? I left the bus and walked the cluttered streets searching old loggers' haunts. Never before had I seen so many winos, beggars, and vagrants leaning against buildings or huddled in doorways—what a disappointment!

Penetrating farther into the ghetto, I tried a bar on First Avenue. Drunks and barflies laughed guttural, mirthless bellows. Back on the street, disfigured men, more dead than alive, pleaded for handouts. Where were the happy-go-lucky, healthy young men—the arrogant tramps, forever willing and able to deal with anything the world put before them?

Then it came to me: These men and many women were remnants of the highball logging days. Too old to work or injured in logging accidents, nothing remained for these people except gratuitous handouts on a nickel or dime basis. Just enough to keep alive—and barely so.

What a way to go! Hollow-eyed, toothless, and palsied, one or two approached, put forward a hand, then turned to look after me.

Yes, I had dropped into the chasm reserved for a vanishing breed, but I was not one to accept this miserable existence; nothing could drag me into that.

One mile from the University of Washington campus I located a suitable rooming-house on University Way. The tall, pinched-faced land-lady, after considerable negotiation, granted me kitchen and phone privileges. From here on in, my life remained uncharted.

No! The State Department of Rehabilitation flatly refused to finance re-education for a thirty-seven-year-old ex-logger. However, if I could provide my room, board, clothing and other incidentals, the University would waive tuition.

Yes, I sold brooms and other items made by the blind, but only for a few weeks.

Fortunately, the logging company for which I had worked operated a plywood mill near the Ballard bridge. The vice-president, remembering my contributions to production and safety, hired me with the understanding that I leave the company and apply myself to studies when classes began. He even permitted me to select the job; what a break!

Each eight-hour swing shift in the mill brought me closer to registration for fall classes. Hot and sweaty from pulling mahogany paneling from the kiln-dryer, I often thought back on the haughty loggers—kings in the lumbering industry. How often we had belittled the lowly sliver-pickers who could do nothing but stand beside a green-chain, methodically removing and stacking boards in the lumber mills day after day. Now I did penance. But not for long.

Registration day found me totally unprepared for the youthful faces with their ceaseless chatter, the age-old buildings guarding the crowded quadrangle, and the walkways leading to who knew where. Eventually I located the administration building, plowed through the mobs, and stood apprehensively in line at the information desk. A pert student/employee, curiosity in her voice, directed me to the center hallway. I should knock at the third door to the right and wait. A pleasant lady will answer—if invited, go in.

Responding to the soft voice, I entered the book-filled office. The advisor, my records in hand, rose to receive me. Her mere presence bolstered my confidence.

"Are you just a little nervous, entering the University at age thirty-seven?" she asked.

Her warm smile ruled out any ominous reason for the question, so I replied truthfully, "Well, yes, but I can do it. That is, I think I can."

"What do you plan to study?"

Caught off guard, I stammered, "Well, something I can do for the rest of my life."

"All right," she continued after scanning my records. "At this time social workers are getting the best jobs."

"Social worker!" I wailed contemptuously. "Is that all there is?"

Amused by my reaction, she explained, "If you go on to get a Master's Degree, your chances for continuous employment will be greatly enhanced."

"Do I have to make up my mind right now?" I inquired, hoping that some miraculous occurrence might save me from going into a profession historically dominated by women.

"No, why don't we register you for classes that will apply to several professions?"

Evidently interested in logging, my advisor turned to questions regarding a woodsman's career. To my surprise, she demonstrated familiarity with the industry. Then, for no apparent reason, she asked if I had worked around Grays

Harbor. Mixed emotions flooded my mind: the men, dead or injured, the violent storms, the girl I met on the bus, the barmaid/cook who married the cop, the teenage prostitute, the old supe, and always in my mind, Kit.

My thoughts drifted further into nostalgia as she continued.

"One of my students, now married with two lovely children, had studied rigorously for three years before deciding to take a vacation, and … why she selected the harbor area, I'll never know, but for several months, she seemed happy in … for an unstated reason, she returned rather suddenly and … on several occasions, she revisited that notorious place, but returned disappointed and restless. Seems … had a friend down there, but didn't even know his name. Strange, don't you think?"

Once more, her question caught me off guard. My vagrant thoughts had betrayed me, for I could recall only fragments of the monologue. Now, thoroughly confused, everything seemed vague and disorderly, so I replied with a smile and a shrug. Graciously, she accepted the absurd response, placed my file in a desk drawer, and terminated the introductory session.

Officially registered, I set out to gather information regarding the suggested pursuit. Students, young and old alike, passed as I searched for the campus cafeteria; most ignored me, but a few turned to watch me pass. How different I must have seemed to the youngsters—the overalls, the work shirt, the wide suspenders, and the street slippers, all designed specifically for woodsmen and mill workers. Now on a self-imposed budget, I wolfed a hamburger, then called a new acquaintance, a counselor to the blind, the one person in the agency I felt would understand my hesitation.

"What do social workers do?" I inquired guardedly.

Perhaps sensing my uneasiness, his reply both amused and surprised me. "Well, I've been told that a real social worker is a person, usually a woman, who has her shoulder to the wheel, her nose to the grindstone, her head in the clouds, and her breasts in the wringer three-fourths of the time."

Evidently pleased with his contrived definition, the counselor chuckled, then continued, "If you want a job, that's the way to go at this time, agencies are hiring social workers over others in the helping professions; besides, they perform work others refuse to do, more are needed, especially graduates with practical experience.

"Many men are entering the profession and doing well. I've even thought of switching, but I'd have to return to college for two years to get a Master of Social Work Degree. Better get it while you're already in school. It's not easy to return."

I enjoyed the crude description he had allotted social workers. Coming from this educated man, it seemed uncharacteristic. Yet, it served its purpose. Before losing his sight, he had been a union official; we spoke the same language. Immediately, I understood.

The University registration required that I submit a notarized statement regarding the date and place of birth, so I took the city bus down Third Avenue, disembarked at James, then walked down the hill to Smith Tower, reputedly the tallest building in the city.

With the business completed, I returned to Skid Row. The same bent and damaged bodies supported unkempt heads as they moved from place to place, begging and drinking as their booty dictated. Well practiced in their art, bloodshot eyes squinted as they scanned the sidewalks for prospective donors.

"Got a dime for coffee?" a hollow voice called to me from several feet away. The southern accent seemed familiar, yet I couldn't identify the owner. A large man, sloppily dressed, he stood as though one leg were shorter than the other. The stubbled face, the slumped shoulders, the faltering voice, all combined to portray a worthless bum, totally unlike anyone I would have known.

Then he continued, "I got my back broke, and my money was cut off by those damn social workers. Now I got to beg for a living. She said I could work at something and just because I can't walk well, and I don't read or write, doesn't mean I need to beg. I've tried for months but no one will hire me. So if you could spare a little, I'd sure appreciate it."

The voice, yes, somewhere I had heard the voice before. Annoyed at my lapse in memory, I dwelled on the lifestyle of these forgotten men and women: the come-on must be the same each debasing and monotonous day—the parasitic challenge to passersby, the long nights unable to sleep due to unsolicited pain or hunger. What an existence!

Early in life, these once heroic men and women had dedicated themselves to a futureless vocation. Was this their reward, or had they knowingly manufactured their own demise? Destiny

437

held its place in the philosophical debate; yet many claim the concept had been invented, misinterpreted, and perpetuated by ignorance and myth. If so, argued the advocates, who or what protected those who escaped being number one, number two, or number three in the mysterious and dreaded series of three? The belief, unquestioned in the logging world, applied to injuries and deaths, but how about life in general? Have certain men and women, for whatever reason, been predestined to solicit in the streets? But for wild dashes to escape rolling logs, sleepless nights planning spar tree raisings, last-minute decisions against topping spars in rising winds, or alerts to danger offered by fellow workers, I might have been their competition.

Now the beggar stood silently, as though having depleted his vocabulary. Partly from disgust, partly from embarrassment, and knowing I barely had enough cash to pay for my room, I turned to walk away when he again spoke.

"Thanks anyway, climber."

Stunned, I turned only to find that the man had disappeared into the crowd. Scanning faces, I called, "Hey, chokerman," but to no avail. Was or was he not the logger who had given me a ride back to my old logging camp when I returned from the harbor? Several minutes passed before I reluctantly abandoned the search and headed back up James to Third Avenue.

Halfway up the hill, I realized my indolent mind, confused by unfamiliar faces and street noises, had betrayed me; I just thought he had said climber. Or, perhaps I wanted him to say it. Either way, I realized how the past years had influenced my thinking. I needed to be at the top. Someday!

The number seven bus, overcrowded with students and shoppers, swung around the corner onto University Way and pulled into the first stop. Young and old patiently awaited their turn, then stepped to the sidewalk and went separate ways. How nice it felt to be a bus rider, no longer dependent on others to get from place to place. I hurried across campus, entered the building, and passed the vacant receptionist's desk.

A gentle knock on the advisor's half-open door again elicited the soft voice. "Yes, I'll be with you in a moment." Then returning to her phone conversation, she continued, "Yes, dear, I can't be sure but it certainly seems possible. I felt you would like to know. You have worried all these years. Give my love to the children. Take care." Placing the phone back into its cradle, she called toward the door, "Now, please come in."

Apologetically, I stood before her, collected my thoughts and stated, "I'd like to firm up that opportunity to be a social worker. Can we rush things a little?"

"I'm afraid that will be up to you. The more you apply yourself, the sooner you will finish. If things go well the first year, I suggest that you attend summer school. Class participation may or may not help, you'll have to evaluate that for yourself; instructors vary on how they score class involvement. Even so, you can think it over and make changes as you move along."

For this sophisticated lady, life could be taken for granted, to be used appropriately within professional guidelines. For me, life had been doled out one precious moment at a time, to do with as I pleased.

Now, abandoning her advisory function, this unusual woman sought my permission to go beyond regimented questions. Leading with phrases and disconnected words verified her uneasiness in this role; nevertheless, she continued.

"If you don't mind, I would like to know more about your personal life—I mean, the things you have done; they all seem so exciting and interesting. Do you remember many people you met, or rather, did you have any close friends? I hope you don't mind me being so personal?"

Yes, this otherwise forthright university employee, her voice even more mellow than before, sought information—to make a decision or answer a question regarding my registration? I couldn't guess.

Before I could respond, she asked, "What years were you in Grays Harbor?"

"Years ago," I replied, again curious why she expressed so much interest, "but I think it was about 1944, '45, or '46—parts of those years; I just don't remember exact dates."

Now she sat behind the oak desk, saying nothing. The silence tormented my basic optimism until, moments later, she began another question, faltered, attempted to rephrase, then abandoned the effort and sat tapping her pencil eraser on the desk.

Why the hell doesn't she finish? In the woods, we questioned or proclaimed at will, dealt with the consequences, then went about our business—not her. She wants to ask me something but seems afraid. What can it be?

Again the quiet ruffled my stability. No cool breezes nor rustling branches to clear the cobwebbed mind, no crude joke to offset the vexing vacuum—just two strangers quietly facing each other in a room filled with musty books. What to do? Succumbing to the unidentified force, I apologized for monopolizing her time and turned to leave.

She rose, walked to my side, took my arm, and together we moved a few steps toward the door before she turned, this time looking deep into my eyes.

"You're a brave man, and I admire your courage. Remember, tomorrow we'll list the books you'll need, then I'll introduce you to instructors. A retired businesswoman has established a volunteer reader service for visually impaired students; she will locate several people willing to read the textbooks onto tape for you. Now, Mr. Ault, do you have questions?"

I flushed at the sound of my last name with a "Mr." in front; what a lift! Do I have questions? I repeated to myself. Suddenly, it came to me. The student, yes, Kit. What a remote and unsettling possibility. Even so, my heartbeat quickened as happy times raced through my mind. But soon, much too soon, reality forced the issue. Married, two lovely children, fourteen years; put it to rest!

Yes, as with the beggar, I had mixed desire and hope in a last-ditch effort to reconnect with the past. Whether or not my interpretation of her fragmented statements and questions verified the conclusion became unimportant. Nothing would change, nor should it.

Now I understood what must be done. "To answer your previous question about my past acquaintances and friends around the Harbor," I said, "at that time in the logging world, given and family names were unimportant—just titles and nicknames. I knew few of my friends' actual names. This applies to men and women alike. Sorry, but I can't tell you more, simply because I don't know more."

Evidently satisfied with my reply, she again took my arm and we moved into the hall, where she turned and spoke with sincerity. "Now, sir you are on your way. Be proud of yourself. Through the years, it certainly hasn't been easy, and though your pursuits might seem difficult, you can expect a new experience each day. Remember, nine o'clock tomorrow. Good night, my friend."

Finally free to pursue a teenage dream, I set aside nostalgia for the wilderness and steeled myself for an academic career. Shoulders back, head high, I walked down the long hall, not forgetting the many yesterdays but always looking forward to the next tomorrow.

The soft metallic click of the door-latch echoed along the empty corridor.

Chapter 35

Beyond The Eagle's Nest

Now several decades away from the woods, I look back on my good fortune. The fall of 1959, I exchanged calk boots and hard hat for a Goodwill suit and dress shoes to resume an academic career.

For six years, words and numbers, concepts and theories, and a plethora of worldly experiences, nourished my insatiable quest for knowledge. At one point, the Dean's Honor Role included my name. What a surprise and source of pride.

Competent instructors, devoted readers, and friends encouraged, assisted, and supported me until my sweat-filled hours and sleepless nights earned a Master's Degree in Social Work from the University of Washington, Seattle. Although subsisting on my own cooking during triumphs and near failures, I remained healthy and ready for the ups and downs of a reclaimed life.

Over the years, cataracts had superimposed themselves onto the inherited eye condition, compounding my already diminished vision. Cataract surgery, coke-bottle lenses, a ten-power magnifier, and a large-print typewriter improved my chances for employment. I could again read caption-sized print.

So be it, most agencies, to my chagrin, required employees to have a valid driver's license. Personnel officers suggested employment with the Department of Rehabilitation for the Blind would serve me best. Nevertheless, I took Greyhound to California and immediately obtained a position with the Department of Mental Hygiene where, for almost three years, I worked in the San Francisco Bay area.

Sitting through meetings, typing reports and dealing with a myriad bureaucratic problems held my interest only until I could find something involving more action. A friend put me in contact with the Veterans Administration Rehabilitation Services for the Blind in Palo Alto, California, where many blinded service men and women awaited training and counseling to offset the shattering effects of their service in World War II, Korea, or Vietnam.

I joined a dedicated group of Veterans Administration employees. Aside from working directly with the blinded veterans and their families, supervising college graduate students during their internship proved to be an enjoyable and challenging responsibility.

I served on the board of directors for several private and local government agencies providing services for visually impaired individuals, a responsibility taken seriously, for I remembered well the problems faced during my early years and after.

With the advent of the Closed Circuit television reading system, which magnified print many times normal size, reading again became a cherished activity. Revising guidelines for working with the blind and partially sighted became an integral part of my work.

Eventually, those promised years ran out. The dreaded white cane, the mysterious Braille, the tape-recorder, and the Dictaphone became the tools of the day.

Unwittingly, I may have repaid my debt to those wonderful people who assisted and guided me through difficult times, for I represented the VA Medical Center, Palo Alto, as one of six nation-wide contenders for "Outstanding Handicapped Federal Employee of the Year" (1979).

Now retired and married to a thoughtful and understanding wife, I look back with fondness on my life in the notorious logging camps of the Pacific Northwest, thankful to have survived twenty years in one of our nation's most hazardous industries.

Legally blind since my teens, and now in my eighties and totally blind since age sixty, I continue to experience that nagging, tantalizing, irresistible urge to move on. Beyond a doubt, it will be with me for the rest of my days. To satisfy my wanderlust and need for diversity, my wife plans surprise adventures about which I know nothing until we arrive on the scene; her vivid imagination and tact have carried me through many trying times.

A companion of several years, my computer, equipped with a voice synthesizer, has made it possible to share my logging experiences. Although the machine and I had our ups and downs, the most vexing moments came when the Carmel River flood (Carmel, California—1995) took all our household belongings, including my computer, printer, etc. and most of this book.

By the time we became resettled and I returned to writing, the incursion of advanced software such as Windows, icons, and mouse clicks had further complicated procedures for the totally blind writer. Yet, the time and effort required to master dozens of (multi-key) key strokes and other recurring innovations was a small price to pay for the privilege of turning my thoughts into print.

I, along with others my age, have adjusted to advanced technology and other unsettling changes. Regardless, our nation, now in the era of the spotted owl, steel spars, pressboard, and recycling, is confronted with the task of protecting and reforesting the ravaged timberlands of the Pacific Northwest. Even so, I hold fond memories of my friends among the ruffian tramp loggers of a different era, and I am forever thankful to have shared one of the most exciting and demanding periods of Northwest history.

To those old-timers who are still around, I say, "Revel in your retirement. You earned every minute of it, and much more."

To those who were killed while logging, I say, "Rest in peace my friends. I hope you are among our kind."

Glossary

AFL—American Federation of Labor, organized according to craft.

Arch—tall arched metal frame mounted on tracks or wheels, trailed behind crawler-type tractors (cat), used to lift ends of logs from ground when being dragged to landing by cat.

Barber-chair—while being felled, the trunk of a tree splits upward, breaks free, and frequently kicks back over the stump—usually occurs when the center of the trunk is rotten, during strong winds, when the lean of a tree has been seriously miscalculated, or the undercut is too small.

Blocks—pulleys of various sizes.

Boom—two small logs separated by spacers, logs straddle tree at one end and are held about twenty feet off the ground with a heavy steel cable at the other end allowing tongs to be raised or lowered to load logs.

Bucker—saws fallen trees into log lengths.

Bullbuck—supervises cutting crew, fallers, buckers, and scalers.

Bullcook—handyman around logging camp.

Bullhook—large hook spliced into cat mainline, choker eyes are threaded onto bullhook when yarding logs.

Bunks—beds in bunkhouse or heavy metal channels mounted on railway cars and logging trucks to support logs (see cheese blocks).

Busheling—falling and bucking timber by the thousand board feet.

Butt rigging—huge barrel swivels used to connect mainline, haulback (see haulback), and chokers.

CCC Camp—Civilian Conservation Corps—Federal Government work project for young men during the great depression, camp buildings were later used by a few logging camps to house loggers.

Calk boots—also "cork" boots, high-topped leather boots with small spikes protruding from soles, prevents slipping.

Cat—crawler-type tractor.

Cat logging—using crawler-type tractors to drag logs to landing.

Cat's paw—knot used by high-climber to take up or let out slack in climbing rope (sheet bend).

Chain-gang—part of surveying crew.

Chaser—unhooks chokers from logs at landing.

Cheese-block chain—chain holds pyramid-shaped metal block in place, block used to hold logs on railway car or truck bunks.

Choker holes—removing dirt or debris from under log so chokers can be shoved under logs.

Choker—a length of cable placed around logs for yarding (see yarding).

Chokerman—places chokers around logs.

CIO—Congress of Industrial Organizations, organized according to industry.

Clear cut logging—logging everything within certain boundaries.

Cold deck—a pile of logs that have been yarded to a spar but not loaded on railway cars or trucks.

Corks—also cork boots, colloquial for calks or calk boots.

Counting ties—fired from a job.

Cruiser—evaluates amount and types of standing timber within a specified area.

Crummy—railway caboose used to transport men.

Dead-heading—traveling without a ticket, usually railway workers or airline employees returning to home base from a work assignment.

Donkey—a machine outfitted with an engine (steam, diesel, or gas powered) mounted on a sled made from logs, equipped with three drums for holding cable, mainline, haulback, and strawline.

Donkey-puncher—also puncher, operates yarding or loading machine.

Double-bitted axe—axe with sharp blade on both sides.

Dummy tree—small tree used to raise regular spar.

Eye—A small loop spliced into the end of a cable, example—choker eye, eye of a strap, eye of mainline or mainline eye.

Flunky—waitress in dining hall.

Foreman—also known as side-rod.

Green chain—conveyor chain, mesh, or belt taking newly sawed lumber from one point to another, usually from head-saw to other machines for final processing or stacking.

Guylines—stabilizing steel cables fastened around tree plates near top of spar, guys are then tightened and spiked to notched stumps which are a designated distance from the spar.

Gyppo loggers—small logging outfits.

Hammer—maul or sledge, usually eight pounds, used to drive railway spikes into stumps on either side of guylines to prevent slippage.

Haulback—line used to pull mainline, butt rigging, and chokers from spar out into the fallen timber where the chokers are placed around logs for yarding.

Head-cook—supervises kitchen and dining hall.

Head-faller—senior faller of a two man crew.

Head-loader—also loader, supervises loading of logs onto railway cars or logging trucks.

High-climber—also known as climber, high-rigger, or topper, tops and rigs spar trees.

High-lead logging—a method for yarding and loading logs using a spar.

Hoe-dig—hand held tool with axe bit on one side and hoe on the other side, usually used for digging fire trails to prevent fires from spreading into unburned areas.

Hook-tender—also hooker, supervises yarding crew and equipment on a side.

Horse logging—using only horses for logging.

Industrial blindness—later termed legal blindness, defined as 20/200 in better eye with best correction, or less than 20 degrees of remaining peripheral vision, i.e., seeing at 20 feet what the person with ordinary vision sees at 200 feet, or no more than 20 degrees of remaining central vision.

Injector—a valve designed to put water into a steam boiler.

Interchange—location where private railway stops and commercial railway begins.

IWA—International Woodworkers of America. Branch of CIO Union.

IWW—also Wobblies, Industrial Workers of the World.

Landing—flat area around spar tree where logs are placed to be loaded on railway cars or logging trucks.

Lead block—a block through which lines coming from donkey drums pass, block guides lines on and off the donkey drums.

Line—any length and diameter of steel cable.

Mainline—largest cable on donkey drum, used to pull logs from outlying areas to landing.

Passblock—small pulley hung at top of spar.

Passchain—short length of chain attached to loose end of passline, used for climber to sit in when ascending or descending a spar, also carries equipment up or down spar.

Passline—three-eighths inch steel cable used to raise and lower equipment and climber up or down spar.

Patch logging—logging an area but leaving standing timber surrounding the logged off area.

Plumb—a weight tied to a string, used to determine lean of a tree when held in air and sighted past.

Powder-monkey—works with explosives.

Railroad spikes—long square spikes with an elongated head.

Reload—place where logs are dumped from trucks, sorted, then reloaded onto railway cars ready for the interchange.

Rigging hammer—medium sized hammer with a metal handle. Used by high-climber while rigging a spar tree.

Rigging-slinger—also slinger, supervises choker-man.

Saw filer—employee who sharpens saws.

Scaler—measures felled and bucked trees to determine number of board feet in each log.

Second-faller—works with head-faller.

Second-loader—assists head-loader.

Selective logging—logging only specified trees.

Shackles—clevises of various sizes used to attach blocks or cables to spar or other logging equipment.

Side—a logging unit consisting of donkey(s), cats, spar, and all other equipment necessary to perform the logging process.

Side-rod—also foreman, supervises one side.

Skid road—a roadbed made from logs or a street in a logging town or city where loggers or derelicts hang out.

Slab burner—metal enclosed, cone-shaped burner for disposing of scraps of wood and bark not useable for anything else.

Slash—logged off area wherein the remains of the logging are not removed.

Sliver picker—millhand

Snag—dead tree, often free of limbs and the top broken off.

Spar tree—a tree topped and rigged for yarding and/or loading logs.

Speeder—railway conveyance used to transport men

Splice—two types of splices were most common.

1. Splicing an eye in the end of a cable, loose end of cable is bent back on itself and cable is unwound for a short distance making six individual strands, then the single strands are inserted back into the cable to form a loop, better known as an eye.

2. Long splice connects two cables together to form a continuous length of cable by

inserting the strands from one cable into the other.

Springboard—2" X 8" X 5' board with a cupped half-round steel plate attached to one end, placed in a notch cut into the side of a tree. It serves as a platform on which fallers can stand to chop or saw when falling timber on steep ground.

Steam donkey—a machine powered by steam, usually logging, railway, shipping, or construction machinery.

Strap—a length of steel cable with an eye spliced in each end, used for loading extra large logs, also heavier straps are used to hold blocks in spar.

Strawline—small cable used to move larger lines and blocks from place to place, also used to raise and lower climber and rigging up and down spar(see passline).

Stump—portion of tree remaining after tree is felled.

Stumpage—buying timber but not the land.

Sucker—a large abnormal limb or growth growing from the main trunk of a tree.

Supe—superintendent, supervises all logging.

Swamper—a woodsman who cuts small brush away from trees so fallers' axes or saw will not catch on the brush while the men are working, or a woodsman who cuts the limbs from trees after they have been felled, or a person who cleans areas such as taverns.

Taft-Hartley Act—legislation limiting strike activities of unions by requiring a cooling off period before striking. 1947.

The old man—general manager, supervises entire logging operation.

Tongs—huge self-closing apparatus used to load logs.

Topping saw—short saw, usually a nine-foot falling saw cut in half.

Tree plates—heavy metal plates spiked on trunk near top of spar. Plates are designed to strengthen the tree, as well as support the guylines and bullblock.

Turn—when pulling logs to landing from outlying areas, one trip out from the spar with empty chokers and back to the spar with logs in the chokers is one turn.

Undercut—a V shaped notch cut into one side of a tree that is to be fell or topped, notch guides the tree to fall in a specific direction as the back cut is completed.

Water glass—a gauge to monitor water in boiler of steam locomotive or steam donkey.

Whistle-punk—also punk, relays signals to yarder engineer.

Widow-maker—a loose branch or limb falling from a tree, most hazardous to timber fallers.

Wildcat strike—striking without giving notice to company.

Wood-cutter—cuts wood for steam donkey.

Yarder—donkey that pulls logs from outlying areas to landing.

Yarding—dragging logs to landing for loading.